THE REBOUNDERS

THE REBOUNDERS

A Division I Basketball Journey

AMANDA OTTAWAY

University of Nebraska Press | Lincoln and London

Library of Congress Cataloging-in-Publication Data
Names: Ottaway, Amanda, author.
Title: The rebounders: a Division I basketball journey / Amanda Ottaway.
Description: Lincoln: University of Nebraska Press, 2018. | Includes bibliograph-
ical references.
Identifiers: LCCN 2017033926
ISBN 9780803296848 (hardback: alk. paper)
ISBN 9781496205872 (epub)
ISBN 9781496205889 (mobi)
ISBN 9781496205896 (pdf)
Subjects: LCSH: Ottaway, Amanda. | Women basketball players—United States—
Biography. | Davidson College—Basketball. | Davidson Wildcats (Basketball team)
| Women college athletes—United States—Social conditions. | BISAC: BIOGRAPHY
& AUTOBIOGRAPHY / Sports. | SPORTS & RECREATION / Basketball. | BIOGRAPHY
& AUTOBIOGRAPHY / Women.
Classification: LCC GV884.088 A3 2018 | DDC 796.323092 [B]—dc23
LC record available at https://lccn.loc.gov/2017033926

Set in Chaparral by E. Cuddy.

For my two families:
the one I was born into,
and the one I was recruited into.
I love you all endlessly.

But mostly for my mama,
the strongest woman in the world.

CONTENTS

NOTE TO THE READER

This book is mostly memoir, though I have researched and fact-checked it and confirmed accounts with others whenever I could.

When accounts of the same event differed, or when a party declined to comment, I used my own recollections and notes to write the scene.

The names of all Davidson women's players and coaches, and a few others, have been changed.

THE REBOUNDERS

Prologue

I'm sitting in the stands of our home court, sprawled in Section 5, dressed in street clothes. My senior season in college is almost over. It's an odd place to be, in the bleachers looking down at the place that for four years held more of my life than anywhere else on this campus. From here, finally, I can see the court the way everybody else sees it. I see how well it's been loved. The rims and their faded orange paint beckon warmly. The nets have relaxed with the weight of thousands of made shots. The empty court is glossy, symmetrical, expectant. I'm seduced under the familiar glow of arena lights.

From here I am overwhelmed with an urge to squeeze a plump, smooth basketball between my fingers and shoot, to hear the satisfying *chnk-whrr* of a solid bank shot or the whisper of an exquisitely aimed free throw, a shot so perfect I barely feel it come off my hand, that addictive precision I chase by shooting thousands and thousands of them. I crave from some primal place inside the heart leap that accompanies a steal and fast break. I need the crush of flesh that comes with setting screens and taking charges, the dazzling clarity of a clean pass, the steady knowledge that the ball will always bounce back up into my hand.

If I walked downstairs to the locker room now to pull on my sports bra and compression shorts, my jersey and shorts, my knee wraps, ankle tape, socks, ankle braces, high-tops, and headband, and stepped onto the court, if I prepared to play the way I did five or six days a week for fifty weeks a year, things would get complicated. I would stand on the baseline and feel small and panic about how far away the other end was. The baskets would tower forebodingly. The ball would sit hard and cold and slippery in my hands. My creaky, aching body would shift and stiffen—my shoulders tense, tendons swollen, lungs empty, stomach heavy, eyes unfocused. The happy flush in my cheeks, the delicious view I have at this moment, would be shattered. I'd struggle to dig up shards of the old feelings. I would forget, almost entirely, the way it used to feel to play basketball, how simple it once was to be in love with it.

The easy joy the sport brought me in middle and high school came with me to college, where it was challenged, where it blistered and bled and peeled off, where it got lost for a while, where it grew tough and leathery, like the skin of my dad's old basketball in the garage of the house where I grew up, like a callus over an old wound.

1 The Bubble

My mother and my sixteen-year-old brother, Luke, and I were headed south, our blue minivan crammed so full of pillows, bedclothes, lamps, totes, and duffel bags that the rearview mirror was useless for anything except making sure Luke's scruffy blond head was still poking through the clutter. The late August sun beat down hard. Two and a half years earlier I'd learned how to drive in this van. Now I was riding in it to college.

We trundled down Interstate 77, and I gazed out the window at the smooth lake stretching from either side of the highway and the sweeping, many-windowed houses that bloomed regally from its banks. Mom eased us off the highway to the Davidson/Davidson College exit, Exit 30, chatting about the lake. She loved that lake. So many people loved Lake Norman, we heard, that traffic on the interstate sometimes backed up because people slowed down their cars just to gape at it.

"I wonder if the coaches will be there to help us move you in," my mom mused cheerfully.

The coaches. My coaches. Deborah Katz, the Davidson women's basketball head coach, and her three brand-new assistants, all of whom she'd just hired that summer after the three assistants who recruited me quit in the spring. They said they would help us win our conference championship and get a bid to the program's first-ever Division I National Collegiate Athletic Association (NCAA) basketball tournament, the "Big Dance," the deepest dream of thousands of teenage hoopsters around the country, including me. Coach Katz told me I would be a big part of the team's success. I couldn't wait to be a Davidson Wildcat.

I grew up the oldest of five children and the only girl. Our childhood was cozy and raucous and colorful. I once had two Barbies, and I tore their heads off in my bedroom closet. My brothers and I preferred Matchbox cars. Instead of using knives at the kitchen table, we cut our food—pancakes, chicken, spaghetti—with a pair of scissors because there were so many of us and it was quicker that way.

Luke and I, the oldest siblings, spent much of our childhood in the bleachers of the gym at Saint Francis University, a liberal-arts college in the mountains of west-central Pennsylvania where we grew up. Our father, who'd been a high school basketball star in his tiny hometown of Corry, Pennsylvania, was a communications professor at Saint Francis. Because it was a small Division I school and he loved the sport, he got to know the basketball players and coaches and brought our family to their games. Luke and I obsessed over the Red Flash. We adored Sotiris Aggelou, a three-point-shooting whiz from Greece on the men's team, and Jess Zinobile, a star on the women's team who jumped for rebounds like a mermaid erupting from the ocean.

I relished those evenings, tucked snugly in the old wooden bleachers with my parents and brothers and sometimes a friend or two. We had concession-stand nachos and root beer for dinner and soaked in the electricity of what felt like a huge, passionate crowd. We watched the strange Saint Francis mascot, a plush Franciscan friar with brown robes and a huge round mascot's head, doing his goofy friar-mascot dance.

There are thirty-two leagues, also called conferences, in Division I women's basketball. In small conferences like Saint Francis's Northeast Conference (NEC), nicknamed "one-bid leagues," usually only the team that wins the conference tournament championship earns a bid to the NCAA Tournament at the end of each season. This tournament was supposed to be a collection of the best sixty-four teams in the country that then played for a national title, so the more competitive conferences sent more teams.

When I was a kid the Saint Francis women's basketball team dominated their conference. In 1996, when I was six years old, they won their first NEC Tournament Championship and went to the NCAA Tournament. Over the next four seasons, they won four more NEC Championships. By the time I was fourteen and decided that I, too, wanted to be a Division I basketball player, they'd won eight. They never won a game in the Big Dance, but they went.

I loved basketball more than almost anything else in the world. I wanted to go to college on a full scholarship, which I could do if I played Division I, to help out my parents, who had a lot of kids to put through school. Most of all, I wanted to play in the NCAA Tournament. It was a dream—a trip on an airplane (I had never been on an airplane) to a faraway city, national television coverage, the chance to play as one of the best sixty-four teams in the country.

As my mom, Luke, and I rode through downtown Davidson, I couldn't wait to see Olivia and Taylor again. The three of us, all part of the same recruiting class, had been looking forward to this since we came on our official visits to Davidson at the same time, in September of the previous year.

Olivia and I had known each other even before that. We'd played on the same traveling AAU basketball team, based near Pittsburgh, the previous summer. It was because Davidson's coaches were recruiting Olivia that they saw me. A few months later, Taylor, Olivia, and I applied early decision to Davidson, our scholarship offers contingent on our admission to the school. In mid-November of our senior year of high school, two months after our visit, we signed National Letters of Intent to play basketball at Davidson College. The NLI is a contract between a future Division I or II student-athlete and the NCAA in which the athlete agrees that, upon admission to the school, she will stay there for one year. In turn the university agrees to give her some financial aid. Most athletic scholarships are year by year; the NLI is binding only for the first year.

The Davidson women's basketball team had at that point only once made it past the semifinals of the Southern Conference Tournament. (That was in 1999, when they lost to Appalachian State in the finals.) They had never made the Big Dance. I didn't commit there because the program had a tradition of excellence and championships—it didn't. It had a tradition of being near the top half of the middle of the pack. But I fell in love with the campus and its people, and I believed, deep in my heart, that we were an underdog on the prowl. Coach Katz had helped convince me that with this new freshman class, the team had all the talent we would need to surprise everyone—win the Southern Conference and go to the Big Dance. After all, the Davidson men's team had done it. Why couldn't we?

In March of our senior year of high school, after Taylor, Olivia, and I had signed our letters and been accepted, Elon University beat the Davidson women in the first round of the Southern Conference Tournament and eliminated them. Davidson finished its season with a record of 19-11. The Davidson men's basketball team was still playing.

That year the Davidson men won their third straight and tenth total Southern Conference Championship. Because the Southern Conference was weaker than many other Division I conferences, it was, like the NEC, known as a "one-bid league" for both men and women. Davidson headed to the Big Dance as the Southern Conference representative. As a ten seed in their bracket, the Davidson men were obvious underdogs. They faced seventh-seeded Gonzaga in their first-round game and won, a minor upset. Then they played second-seeded Georgetown, fell behind by seventeen points in the second half, and pulled off an incredible comeback victory to upset the Hoyas and advance to the round of the sixteen remaining teams, affectionately known as the Sweet Sixteen. This was such a big deal that Davidson College's trustees, in an extraordinary move that a bigger school couldn't have pulled off, personally paid for the buses, lodging, and tickets of several hundred Davidson students to watch the next game against Wisconsin in Detroit, 610 miles away from campus.

Olivia Lowery had just gotten off a plane in Pennsylvania one morning in March when she checked her phone and found a voice mail from Taylor Patton, who was driving to Detroit with her dad and a friend and wanted Olivia to come. Coach Roe, an assistant for the women's team, had gotten them tickets to the men's Sweet Sixteen game.

"You're going," Olivia's mom said.

They called me from the students' hotel in Detroit after Davidson's 73–56 trouncing of second-seeded national powerhouse Wisconsin. National Basketball Association (NBA) star LeBron James, wanting a better look at the Cinderella team of the season, had sat behind Davidson's bench that game. The Wildcats would stay in the city to play top-seeded Kansas in the quarterfinal round, the Elite Eight, two days later. Davidson basketball fans were in a state of gleeful shock.

"You have to get here for the Kansas game somehow!" Olivia yelled to me over the phone when I picked up. In the background I could hear loud, excited chatter and a thumping bass.

"Hi, Amanda!" a chorus of voices hollered. "Come to Detroit!"

I grinned into my flip phone. College kids wanted me to come hang out with them! The next day I rode my first Greyhound bus by myself, 286 miles northwest from Pittsburgh to Detroit.

Most of the players on the Davidson women's basketball team were there. They'd ridden the buses paid for by the trustees and brought their Davidson basketball practice jerseys to wear to the games, establishing their presence, announcing their existence to the world. They were almost celebrities, famous by association, these tall, powerful women who shared a basketball court with the Davidson men. I was in awe of them. I was somehow one of them.

At a restaurant near the arena before the regional final against Kansas, two middle-aged men spotted Olivia, Taylor, and me in our Davidson gear. "You ladies are tall," they said. All three of us were around six feet. "Are you basketball players, too?" When we proudly told them yes, we were high school seniors who would play for the

Davidson women's basketball team in the fall, they asked to get their picture taken with us.

Those two men in the restaurant were not the only strangers fascinated by Davidson. It was the only Division I school in the country that also consistently ranked in the top-ten liberal-arts colleges. Sports journalists and basketball fans across the country fell in love with the smart, hustling Wildcats. They were enamored of sophomore guard Stephen Curry, whose jersey hung loose from his slim shoulders like a shirt off a clothesline, who was a genuinely good kid, and who scored 103 points in the team's first three tournament games.

Ford Field, where the Detroit Lions usually played, had been converted into a basketball arena and rocked now with the tones of Neil Diamond's "Sweet Caroline," the team's unofficial anthem, the song Davidson's pep band always played during the second half. The *New York Times* ran a story on the team, quoting that song in the headline— "Good Times Never Seemed So Good." Davidson graduate and writer Michael Kruse gushed that Stephen Curry was "the kind of face America loves to love." The pep band played the school's fight song. The cheerleaders spelled out "C-A-T-S" with their pom-poms for the ESPN cameras.

Davidson's small sports information office was overwhelmed with media requests. In less than two days they had received 332 email requests for interviews with Coach Bob McKillop alone. The idea that a team from Davidson College—a tiny, bookish school that held its athletes accountable for their grades—could compete on the same court with a nationally ranked perennial power like Kansas was news. Davidson College players went to class, lived on campus, and ate in the cafeteria with everybody else in the student body of nearly 1,700, graduated at a rate of 100 percent for every senior who passed through McKillop's program, and followed the school's strict Honor Code: no lying, cheating, or stealing.

Davidson, the lakeside town of ten thousand people that had grown around the college since its founding in 1837, had long adored its men's basketball program. The team had a history of success. Dean Rusk played varsity basketball at Davidson in the late 1920s and later became U.S. secretary of state. Coaching legend Lefty Driesell guided the team through the 1960s—when the school had an all-male student body—to three conference championships, three trips to the NCAA Tournament. He coached two Davidson teams that nearly made the Final Four. The head coach now was McKillop, who, in his nineteenth season at Davidson, had been at the school longer than any other coach. He and his wife sent all three of their children to Davidson and lived across the street from campus, next door to a Harvard PhD named Cynthia Lewis, who taught in the English Department and would later become one of my favorite professors. The "townies," as Davidson students called the townspeople, knew the players on the men's basketball team personally. They saw them over sandwiches at the Soda Shop on Main Street. They met their parents at games. They taught them in class and chatted them up around campus and at church.

Some of the townies were professors, and others worked in Charlotte's booming finance industry, twenty-some miles south. They lived in bright, spacious houses; dressed in crisp, well-made clothes; and on weekends brought their babies out to breakfast at the homey, sunny restaurant near the Soda Shop. People talked with just a kiss of drawl and smiled and said, "Hey, how ya doin'?" when you walked past them. You could leave your laptop on the table outside the coffee shop and nobody would touch it, because nobody needed one. Davidson was a bubble full of good, comfortable, happy people, and in 2008 this bubble lit onto the men's basketball team with earnest enthusiasm. Their home, now being described by the national media as a picturesque and "sleepy little town" in the South, home of tiny Davidson's David in all his Goliath-trampling glory, was a hard place to describe to others. Now they could just point to the television. "This is Davidson," they could say. "These are our boys."

The people of Davidson, for the most part, adored the students of Davidson College, athletes or not—women's basketball players were greeted warmly on the street and in restaurants, too. The men were different, though. They represented their town to the nation.

The women's basketball team considered the men's players to be like their brothers. They shared a gym and a training room and hung out on school breaks when both teams were stuck on campus for practice. Players went to Taco Bell together at night and did karaoke together, and they had TV nights together when they were all too tired to do anything else.

In the students' hotel the night before the Kansas game, the mood was ebullient. A drunk Phi Delt wearing a blond mullet wig sprinted across the lobby and belly-flopped into the decorative fountain.

If Davidson lost to number-one-seed Kansas the next day, their season would be over. If they won, they would advance to the national semifinals, the Final Four, and be the first tenth seed ever to do it.

We had seats near the floor in the huge arena. "Davidson College . . . Google It," one student's sign read. "WHY NOT?" another asked. "I know where Davidson is, but where is Kansas?" a third wondered.

The game was close all the way through, and the crowd buzzed with a palpable energy. With under a minute left and Davidson down five, Stephen hit a quick long three on an out-of-bounds play to make the score 59–57. The place exploded again as Davidson played an entire shot clock's worth of defense and a Kansas shot clanged off the rim, out-of-bounds.

Davidson ball, 16.8 seconds left. Down two. Would Stephen take the last shot, even though all five Kansas players and all fifty-eight thousand fans expected that? Would it be a three-pointer for the win, or would he look to dish or drive inside for a layup and send the game to overtime? Next to Olivia and Taylor, I squinted at the court and adjusted my backward Davidson baseball cap nervously as Stephen trotted the ball up the floor.

He dribbled left off a Thomas Sander screen and got double-teamed at the top of the key. Thomas set him another screen, and Stephen turned off it into another double-team and got stuck on the right side of the court, in NBA three-point range, with three seconds left.

It was a shot Stephen had made before, but the Kansas players were all over him. He dished to point guard Jason Richards. With 1.5 seconds left in the game, Jason put up a long three from the top of the key.

Every Davidson fan leaned forward and gasped. I smacked both hands to my forehead. The ball soared up and up and up and bricked hard to the left of the rim. The buzzer sounded. Kansas 59, Davidson 57.

Jason fell backward to the floor. Stephen put his jersey in his mouth.

"For these very special days, TINY and SCRAPPY little Davidson was America's sweetheart," wrote assistant director of sports information Lauren Biggers in her blog on the Davidson Athletics website. "I couldn't go anywhere this week without people asking, 'Are the players really as nice as they seem?' 'Is the coaching staff really as accessible?' 'Is Davidson really that special?' The answer is yes, and then some, to all three."

All spring anytime someone asked me where I was going to college, I could finally say "Davidson," and they'd know what I was talking about. They wouldn't think I meant Denison or Dickinson. "Oh," they'd say. "Davidson! Steph Curry? Boy, they had quite a run this year." And I'd nod and smile proudly. That's us, the underdog everyone loves; that's Davidson basketball!

For nearly seventy years of the twentieth century, "Davidson basketball" could only mean "Davidson men's basketball." Davidson College didn't admit a full class of women as degree students until 1973, four years after Yale and Princeton went coed, ten years before Columbia did. Once Davidson decided to let women in, according to some of its first female students, the school wanted them to make many of their own decisions about what they wanted from it, reacting to feedback rather than prescribing an experience. Many colleges in the South at that time, for example, had house mothers who did not let men into women's dorm rooms. The Davidson women wanted open dorms, and so open dorms they received.

According to a May 6, 1972, *Charlotte Observer* article, some male students were eager for the chance to "get to know girls as just people"; others were mostly excited to have more convenient dating opportunities.

It didn't occur to girls born in the late 1980s and early 1990s, like my teammates and me, that we hadn't always been able to play sports, or, indeed, go to college, the way boys did. Title IX, a law passed in 1972, required all schools that accepted federal funding to provide equal-education opportunities to men and women. It was the single most important legal framework in advancing women's sports. But we saw it as a distant struggle, like women's right to vote. When the law passed, just one in twenty-seven high school girls played sports. By the time my teammates and I headed to college, that number was about two in five.

When we were kids basketball was the most popular sport for girls in the country; a full quarter of girl students who played a sport picked hoops. I played soccer, too. Title IX meant to us that we grew up with Sheryl Swoopes and Lisa Leslie winning the gold medal in basketball at the Olympics and Mia Hamm and Brandi Chastain winning the women's soccer World Cup. When Brandi Chastain was a kid, she had only a "handful" of role models in the world of women's sports—there was no Women's National Basketball Association (WNBA), no pro soccer league for women. When I was a kid, I had so many options that I didn't know whose jersey to ask my mom for first.

We didn't realize how much we owed the women who came before us. Title IX in the twenty-first century meant that each generation of female athletes inspired even more female athletes—that when I was a little girl, I watched big girls play sports at a high level and decided I wanted to do it, too.

Back in the early 1970s, things weren't so easy. The Davidson Athletic Department, following the example of the school in general, said it would provide whatever women's sports women on campus showed interest in. So first, the women had to demonstrate interest.

Laurie Dunn, a freshman in that first class of women in 1973, was sitting under a tree reading when a sophomore who worked for the student newspaper asked her if she'd played sports in high school. She told him she had.

"You know you can get credit here at Davidson if you lettered in a sport in high school," he informed her. They barreled into the basketball office.

"You played high school basketball?" the junior varsity (JV) men's basketball coach asked Laurie.

"Yeah," Laurie said.

"Do you want to play here?" she says he asked her. "For the men's team?"

It would be great for publicity to have girls on the men's team, he explained. But Laurie wanted to play with other women.

A group of female students, including Laurie Dunn—whose daughter, Molly, became a volleyball player and a friend of ours at Davidson a few decades later—held several meetings to see how many women Wildcats were interested in playing basketball. The school had a women's tennis team, but that season was wrapping up, and they needed a different sport to play next. The group approached college president Sam Spencer and asked to start its own women's basketball squad. He said yes.

"Don't be alarmed one of these days if the Davidson College sports information office distributes basketball rosters with players possessing statistics like 36-23-36," the *Davidson Update* declared in January 1974, under the headline "Girls Now Playing Basketball." "If that sounds suspiciously like a well-proportioned female, your suspicions are well-founded."

They called themselves the women's varsity basketball team. They found a volunteer coach—the wife of men's basketball coach Terry Holland. Although she didn't have coaching experience, Ann Holland was smart and scrappy and had leverage, and she understood principle: one condition was that the Athletic Department give her a budget for uniforms. Her team, Ann explained, would not be playing in pinnies, like so many other women's teams of the time.

A few female students organized a sign-up sheet and made posters advertising tryouts. Ann Holland had to find court time for her team in Johnston Gym, which later became the student union, between the men's varsity, junior varsity, and intramural basketball sessions.

A couple of male students joined the volunteer coaching staff. Ann Holland left at the end of the year when her husband took a job as the head men's basketball coach at the University of Virginia, and the

student coaches—Joe Duncan, Charlie Slagle, and Ken Schmader—
stayed on to run the Davidson women's team alone, as volunteers.
Duncan had played on the freshman and jv men's basketball teams
but couldn't play as a junior because of an Honor Code violation, and
his coach, Terry Holland, volunteered Duncan to assist Holland's wife,
Ann, with the women's team. The women quickly swept up Duncan in
their enthusiasm and their desire to be taken seriously.

"The women just wanted to play so bad you could not help but do
anything to make it happen," he wrote to me nearly four decades later.
"I give them a lot of credit. They did not get handed a lot of stuff. They
just wanted to play basketball. They made a team out of desire."

The Davidson women played eleven games that first season, winning
eight of them, including eight of their last nine. The women's team
went to men's games like everybody else and didn't seem to mind that
the men did not come to theirs. The men were a legacy. The Lefty Driesell days of the 1960s were still fresh in everyone's memory—Terry
Holland had himself played for Driesell at Davidson—and the women
were just a fledgling program. It wasn't intentional or malicious sex-
ism. It was simply the way things were.

These first Davidson women's basketball players felt like they had
made the big time. They got practice gear, uniforms, and warm-ups
with their last names pinned on the back. After practice they threw
their gear in a net bag, and someone else did their laundry for them.
They took vans, driven by the coaches, to away games. They loved eating meals together.

But the organization of their program remained relatively loose.
Many didn't tell their professors they played a sport. Becca Stimson,
who also played tennis and field hockey, had a bum ankle and learned
how to tape it herself. There was no curfew, no strict team alcohol policy. They shared the common locker room with other female students.

In 1975, coached by the three male students, the Davidson women's
basketball team upset Kay Yow's North Carolina State team. (In 1976
Davidson hired twenty-three-year-old Susan Roberts as a paid full-
time coach of the women's basketball and field hockey programs.) Over
the next few decades Yow became a women's basketball idol, guiding

her teams to more than seven hundred wins, making twenty NCAA Tournament appearances with NC State, and being inducted into the James Naismith Basketball Hall of Fame before succumbing to a long bout with breast cancer. From 1997 to 1999 Deborah Katz worked as an assistant on Yow's coaching staff. In 2001 Davidson College hired Katz as its head women's basketball coach, and a few years later she recruited Taylor, Olivia, and me to come play for her.

Coach Katz reminded me of a red-headed Dolly Parton in petite sneakers. Raised in rural Tennessee, she had grown up playing several sports, showing horses, and pitching in on her grandparents' farm. She spoke with a southern drawl thick as country gravy and used funny phrases like "quick as a hiccup" to describe a fast player and "grab and growl, 'Cats!" when it was mealtime and "we just might could do that" when talking about possibility. She had a head full of fluffy bright-red hair, which she teased into bouncy ponytails. She had played guard in college in the late 1970s. She wore matching tracksuits to practice, pantsuits and heels to games, and pale foundation and blue eyeliner to both. Her manicured eyebrows sat high on her forehead to give her a look of perpetual surprise.

We had spoken mostly with assistants while we were being recruited, but those assistants were not at Davidson anymore. Taylor, Olivia, and I weren't sure why they had left. I had had minimal contact with Coach Katz, and some of her players coming in saw her as someone like the Wizard of Oz—a loud, mysterious, powerful voice, hidden for now behind a curtain, untouchable until we earned her attention. Her time was precious. We could not waste it with trivialities. We wanted to impress her immediately.

The summer before my freshman year of college, I signed a scholarship letter for $40,814: the cost of tuition, fees, room, and board at Davidson that year. So did Olivia and Taylor. As I carefully inked my name on the paper, I tried to comprehend how much money $40,000 was. I couldn't.

The three of us spent four days that June in Belk Arena with Coach Katz and a bunch of our new teammates, corralling dozens of preteen and teenage girls in ponytails and T-shirts around the court at the Davidson women's basketball program's overnight summer camp. We worked from seven in the morning until midnight. We made sure the girls got out of bed in the morning and that they went to bed on time at night. We attended late-night camp staff meetings and ran warm-ups, shooting drills, dribbling and passing drills. We coached and refereed scrimmages. We played pickup and lifted weights when the campers had free time. We were exhausted. But Coach Katz had the energy of all those campers combined, and she riled them up, her enthusiasm rippling down their jumping-jack lines in the mornings, her extraordinary twang bouncing off the rafters. She was in her element. "Y'all ready to play some basketball today, gals?" she would ask brightly.

They shouted, "Yeah!" and they looked at us like heroes.

My mom, Luke, and I, in our brimming minivan, crawled down Griffith Street. We bumped slowly over the railroad tracks by the admissions office, and the van practically groaned.

We hung a left on Main Street and turned into the campus of Davidson College, all glittering green grass, wide brick sidewalks, and red-brick buildings that looked the same. We followed the signs down the campus's main road, winding past dormitories and fraternity houses and upperclassmen apartments. Students and their parents milled around everywhere.

A "Welcome, Freshman Families" sign told us to pull up onto the sidewalk, so we did, joining a line of similarly stuffed vehicles. People scurried around us, carrying TVs and crates of clothes and food and holding doors for each other. Two guys in T-shirts approached our driver's side window. One of them was holding a fake microphone, and the other had a camera.

"Hi, we're *The Davidson Show*," one said. I knew about *The Davidson Show*—which was a comedy webcast produced by students—because two of the guys on the men's basketball team, Stephen Curry and Bryant Barr, had guest-hosted it from their dorm room that spring. That episode made the rounds on the Internet when the team became famous.

"Could we ask you a few questions?" the guys asked.

One of the guys stuck the microphone in my mother's face. She looked so tiny at the steering wheel, dwarfed by my life packed into bright boxes behind her.

"Have you cried yet?" the guy wanted to know.

My mom smiled up at them. "Not yet," she said brightly. Mom was tough. She cried over little things when she was frustrated after a long day of work at the pharmacy, like when the dog peed on the floor or when one of us spilled something in the kitchen. But my mom didn't let us see her feeling the big things. If moving her oldest child into college nearly eight hours from home made her sad, she didn't let on.

"What are you gonna do with her room now that she's gone?" they asked.

"Ummmm," Mom deadpanned while I grinned goofily from the passenger seat, "I think we'll convert it to a bed-and-breakfast."

She pulled the car up a few feet and parked in the grass where a volunteer was pointing, and then it was time for us to start unloading, fast. Upperclassmen in matching white T-shirts that said "Orientation Team" swarmed the car, greeting us warmly, wanting to know where my room was.

"Base Belk," I told them. Then I saw a familiar face.

"Lyss!" I exclaimed, running toward her to bury her in a hug. Alyssa Petteys, a rising junior on the team, was walking toward us through the grass, dressed in a cut-off T-shirt, gym shorts, and sneakers. We'd hung out on my official visit and then again in Detroit. She was cheerful, talkative, and gentle.

Lyss hugged my mom and then Luke. "Welcome to Davidson!" she said brightly. "How are you guys doing? How was the drive? What can I do?"

My dormitory, the largest underclassmen dorm on campus, loomed over us in a U shape, four stories of classic redbrick and white columns. Lyss, my mom, Luke, the student staffers, and I all started carrying bags and boxes and lamps and a lime-green plush folding chair through the right-side door and down one flight of stairs to the basement.

My roommate, Brooke, had already moved in, because she ran cross-country and they had come a few weeks earlier for preseason training.

One thing I liked already about Davidson was that Coach Katz didn't make basketball players live with other basketball players. Instead we took a Myers-Briggs personality test like all the other freshmen to be matched with a random roommate. We would spend enough time with our teammates. We didn't need to live together, too.

Brooke's running sneakers, damp from that morning's workout, sat stinking in the window. She and I had chatted on Facebook over the summer. She was tall and sweet, a premed student from Long Island. We hugged hello, awkwardly.

That night we ate dinner on the patio of the tavern across the street from campus with Olivia, Taylor, Nicole Cooper, and their families. Nicole was an anxious, talkative freshman walk-on from the Boston suburbs. Her dad was a military man, and she had thought about going to West Point but decided on Davidson.

Nicole loved basketball. She kept an old book at home, what she called her "I Love Basketball" book when she was little. It was filled with inspirational quotes and plays she'd drawn up and an essay she wrote in fifth grade about hoops. When she decided to go to Davidson, she blitzed Coach Katz, sending game film and calling her and writing email after email, asking if she could walk on with the program—be a full member of the team without receiving any kind of scholarship in return. After much back-and-forth Coach Katz said yes and emailed the rest of us over the summer to let us know Nicole would be joining the team as the fourth freshman.

My first reaction when I read that was to bristle. I sent Nicole a friendly Facebook message right away, introducing myself, marking my territory. She was a guard. I had also been recruited as a guard. I didn't want to fight with her for playing time. Was she even any good? I looked her up. Her stats were decent. Coach Katz had said she hustled. *I* hustled.

Luke and my mom stayed on campus to attend the orientation activities for families. On Friday, after a good-bye luncheon, they hugged me and headed back to Pennsylvania. Olivia, Taylor, and I went to hang out in our older teammate Ashley's room, grateful, in this time of awkward interactions with other freshmen, for our built-in friendships.

"Without a doubt, playing basketball has impacted me almost beyond belief," I had written in my application to Davidson. "Though I have only been very serious about it for about five years now, it has taught me patience, persistence, tolerance, heart, and the value of hard work. It has meant more to me than I could ever say; I love everything about it. My favorite part, though, is all the amazing people I have met. A number of my best friends are my teammates and coaches, and friendship is priceless."

2 I Want You to Want Me

When I was in seventh grade I played for my junior high basketball squad in a March tournament at the local rec center. We lost to a team with shiny blue jerseys who called themselves the Johnstown Lady Hoopsters.

Through the veteran coach at the rec center, the Lady Hoopsters' coach, an athletic, curly-haired-dad type, found my parents. "Is your daughter interested in playing college basketball?" he asked them. They told him I was.

"My name's Rick Genday," he said. "I coach this AAU team, the Johnstown Lady Hoopsters. I'd like Amanda to come play for us."

My parents hadn't given any thought to Amateur Athletic Union basketball before Rick approached them and didn't really know what it was. They asked around and found out that he was right to suggest AAU. College coaches would have a hard time finding me in our town of fewer than six thousand in the rolling hills of west-central Pennsylvania, northeastern Appalachia, where I grew up learning country songs on the school-bus radio and where we had a school vacation day at the beginning of hunting season. Traveling with a club team that played in tournaments up and down the East Coast was probably the best way for me to get noticed and then recruited by college coaches. They were allowed to come watch the tournaments when players were old enough. Plus, Rick seemed like a good guy and a good coach. His Lady Hoopsters had, after all, just destroyed my junior high team. He'd played volleyball for Penn State, but the man knew basketball and he knew what it took to compete in a sport at the Division I college level.

For practices we would have to drive an hour each way to Johnstown, Pennsylvania, which would be tough on my parents because they had four other kids at home to take care of. There was also a $450 fee per player every year to cover the team entry fees into various tournaments. My parents would pay for my uniform, plus the cost of travel, lodging, and food during those tournaments. Rick coached as a volunteer. It's a difficult reality of girls' basketball in the United States: the bulk of the college recruiting happens at AAU tournaments. If you couldn't afford to be on a team, you might not get to play in college. I was lucky. I had supportive parents with enough income to make it work.

Unless the team is sponsored or able to fund-raise, AAU parents pay for almost everything. Some parents spent thousands of dollars on personal trainers and dietitians and travel for their daughters. The Lady Hoopsters were relatively cheap. AAU teams with bigger budgets flew to tournaments all over the country, but we usually stuck to regional competitions around Pennsylvania, New York, Ohio, Virginia, DC, Maryland, and North Carolina. We could drive, and the heaviest recruiting took place on the East Coast anyway.

The year I joined my AAU team, 2003—thirty-one years post–Title IX—the women's college basketball recruiting process boasted the highest stakes of any sport for girls in the United States. Twenty-five percent of adolescent girls who play a sport today pick hoops, and many of them dream of playing in college. That was always an option for the girls I grew up with. If we were good enough, we could get a full ride.

Women's hoop teams give out the most full scholarships and garner the most fans of all women's collegiate sports. Every Division I team when I went to college could give out as many as fifteen full scholarships. So there's a lot of money on the line, often hundreds of thousands of dollars per player in tuition, board, food, and textbooks, plus gear and travel expenses. College coaches' livelihoods also hang in the balance. Their jobs depend on the seventeen-year-old girls they recruit and whether those girls can help them win games. The result is a complex, sometimes exploitative, multimillion-dollar business with adults at one end and children at the other.

Of the nearly half-million young women who play high school basketball in the United States, just shy of 4 percent go on to play in the NCAA. Just over 1 percent of high school players make it to the NCAA's highest classification, the full-scholarship level: Division I.

Because playing professional basketball in the United States is not yet a lucrative career option for women, though—the highest-paid player in the WNBA makes slightly more than $100,000 in a season— girls' AAU is still short of the level of corruption that has scarred boys' AAU. There adults jockey to be the one to "discover" the next big NBA prospect while he's still a kid so that they can collect payouts when he goes pro. Rick Genday wasn't in it for that. None of us would be making millions, at least not from playing basketball.

Usually my dad drove me to Lady Hoopsters practices because, as a professor, he was often free after the day's classes. He'd carve out a four- or five-hour block of his evening, bringing papers to grade in the bleachers. Sometimes Coach Genday would ask him to scrimmage with us if we were missing players, which was often the case, since most of us played other sports.

I was a teenager and my dad drove me crazy, but sometimes, in the car, he wasn't so bad. Both of us staring straight ahead at the road, or me gazing out the window, we talked about life, which usually meant basketball—my Hoopsters teammates or my high school opponents, this coach or that trainer. He knew a lot about music, and he'd teach me about songs or artists who came on the radio. Sometimes he tried to sing.

One night he crooned along with Kid Rock and Sheryl Crow as he steered the minivan down the mountain after practice. I reclined in the stench of my own drying sweat. My sweat-damp hair was in a loose ponytail. I slid off my flip-flops and put my bare, blister-scarred feet on the dashboard. My toenails were painted pink, my calluses peeling off.

"Daaaaaaaaad, stop," I groaned, covering my ears. He kept singing. I covered both ears with my hands.

"LALALALALALALALALA," I hollered over him. "CAN WE STOP AT SHEETZ?"

He laughed, steady at the wheel, like always. "Yes," he said.

My dad and I shared a love of all things junk food, all the stuff Mom didn't want us to have. Our favorite gas station and convenience store sat at the bottom of the mountain, and he usually let me get all the treats I wanted for dinner on the way home.

He had picked me up from a two-hour junior high track practice, and we'd driven the hour to Johnstown for a two-hour Lady Hoopsters practice. Now I was snuggled contentedly into the passenger seat for the hour's drive home, holding my Italian sub, a package of miniature powdered doughnuts, and a bag of cheese-flavored chips in my lap, a blue Gatorade in the cup holder, a plastic grocery bag full of ice from the soda fountain perched on each knee. I cracked the window.

"I'll bet you're exhausted," my dad said. I nodded and took a huge bite of my sandwich. An ice bag slipped off one knee. I picked it up and plopped it back on. Because I'd grown so fast and so early—I was already five feet eleven—both knees were chronically sore. Eventually, I'd get a diagnosis of patellar tendinitis, pain and swelling that never really went away, even into my adult years.

"You girls will be in good shape, that's for sure," Dad continued. "I like the medicine-ball work he has you do."

Coach Genday often brought a couple of medicine balls, which weighed ten to twenty pounds each, to practice and had us pass them around a circle or do layup shooting drills with them. You hadn't learned proper layup form until you learned to shoot one with a ball that weighed as much as a small child. It was supposed to help us learn how to go up strong to the hoop when we were getting fouled.

That day we had also run through a ladder on the ground to help us with our foot speed and agility and run a bunch of sprints most everyone called "suicides." Starting at the baseline, we sprinted out to the closest foul line, touched it with a toe—or, if Coach was feeling strict, our fingers—then turned around and sprinted back to the baseline. We turned around there and then headed to the half-court line and back to the baseline, to the opposite foul line and back, and the opposite baseline and back. One of my junior high coaches, in an effort to make this kind of sprint sound less offensive and perhaps more politically correct, once tried to rename them "butterflies," but it never caught on. Butterflies were far too pleasant. "Suicides" stuck.

"I like that Rick has you working on your ball handling, too," my dad said. "You probably won't be a post in college."

My dad and Coach Genday were right. I had been playing in the post, around the basket, all my life, because even though I was scrawny, I was always the tallest on the team. At the Division I level, many guards were my height, and post players were taller and heavier. I hated dribbling, but I needed to be better at it.

I had spent a few summers with the Hoopsters when my first "recruiting" letters came from Tulane University and the University of Iowa. I was in ninth grade. Immediately, I had my fourteen-year-old heart set on both of them, because I didn't know the women's basketball staffs at those schools were sending that same letter, with the same wording and the same stamped coaches' signatures, to hundreds of other girls like me all over the country. The bulk of the mail in these early stages was camp brochures and student-athlete questionnaires that Division I coaches sprayed out to hundreds of young AAU-playing teens who might someday grow to be real recruits. I filled out most of the questionnaires and mailed them back, just in case.

"You understand, right, Manda Banana," my dad explained to me, "that this is not the same as being recruited. You're on a mailing list because you play in AAU tournaments, and that's good, but they're sending these same letters to hundreds of other girls your age."

"I don't care," I said. Most of what he said annoyed me these days.

He called the University of South Carolina's coaching staff. They had been sending me a lot of generic materials. "Just out of curiosity," he asked, "about how many of each of these letters are you sending out?"

"About two hundred," they told him.

I didn't like to listen to my dad, but deep down I understood that he was right. This was big business on both sides, and most college coaches cast their nets wide. The University of South Carolina was sending me three propaganda pieces a week because it was a big school with a staff and resources that could support a steady stream of the exact same mail to two hundred other excited teenage girls.

The attention was pretty cool in the beginning, especially when mail came from the most famous programs. Letters stamp-signed by University of Connecticut head coach Geno Auriemma and University of Tennessee head coach Pat Summitt arrived in the mailbox on the same day. Even though Pat and Geno themselves probably had no idea who I was, I sat on the couch and stared at their signatures and beamed my face off. Those coaches, whose names were often uttered in one admiring breath by young players like me—"*PatandGeno*"—were two of my childhood heroes, titans in the world of women's college basketball, and they coached two of the best teams in the country.

Neither program ever followed up. This was an early lesson in one important reality of Division I women's basketball teams: the levels of competition within the division itself vary widely. There were the girls I saw on TV and read about in books, the ones who went on to the Olympics and played in the WNBA and were coached by legends like Pat Summitt, Geno Auriemma, and Kay Yow. Then there was everybody else. I was going to be everybody else.

I would probably end up at what they called a "midmajor" school, one of the nearly three hundred that competed on the Division I level but outside the top few conferences. I would get a full scholarship, but wouldn't come anywhere near a national championship. If I decided to play Division II basketball instead, I might be good enough to join one of the best DII teams in the country, but I had my heart set on DI. The best I could probably do there would be a one- or two-game trip to the NCAA Tournament. And that, I figured, would be pretty awesome.

The first day of September in my junior year of high school, when I was sixteen years old, I came home from school to a pile of mail. That was the first day the NCAA allowed college coaches to contact a recruit directly in writing rather than with the generic stuff they'd been spewing at her. This begins the official wooing process. The letters said things like, "Amanda—We liked watching you in [specific tournament]. We liked [this] and [this] about the way you play, and we think you'd be a good fit here at [name of college]. Here's what's great about our program: [This], [this], and [this]." I was quickly overwhelmed.

Overwhelmed or not, my parents had raised me to be independent. Now, as I chose a college, independent I would be. They wanted me to go to a good school. I wanted to go to the school with the biggest and best basketball program that would have me, academics be damned. And my college was my decision.

"We want you to keep your options open," my parents kept saying, "and we want you to go to a good school." They even suggested that I play Division II or Division III so I could get a better education, which made me furious. I knew they wanted what was best for me, but I wasn't sure they knew what was best for me. I knew I would be happiest playing for a high-level Division I school, not sacrificing the prime of my playing career for a few good professors. I preferred a good coach. As the recruiting process wore on, my parents and I fought almost every day.

At the same time, Taylor Patton, younger than me by about three weeks, was playing on another AAU team in Pennsylvania, getting recruited, and not fighting with her parents. She figured she'd play midmajor Division I ball, too. She wanted to go to a good academic school but knew she would never make the team at a place like Stanford, which had a strong women's basketball program and competed in a big conference. Unlike my parents and me, Taylor and her dad communicated constantly during her recruiting process. His advice to her was to make the most of a full ride by picking the school with the best academics she could find. He wanted Taylor to get the best value for the money. Use this, he advised her, to get somewhere. Use it to get somewhere that either might be hard for you to get into otherwise or would be too expensive. Yes, the goal is basketball. But the bigger goal, the long-term goal, is a free education.

I didn't know that, for years, my dad had been corresponding regularly with college coaches, mostly by email, without telling me. He was talking to my AAU and high school coaches about me, too. He wanted to make sure he could help me when I asked for it—and also maybe if I didn't. By this point I was having trouble keeping college coaches and schools straight in my head; about thirty different programs interacted with me consistently.

In early October of my junior year, my mom drove me to unofficial visits at three schools. An "unofficial" visit, so termed by the NCAA, is initiated by the recruit and her family. They find their own way to the school and pay for everything. One stop was Bowling Green State University. The Bowling Green coaching staff—including Curt Miller, the head coach, and Jennifer Roos, his associate head coach—had the best rapport I had ever seen. They had also finished the previous season ranked twenty-fifth in the country, which was impressive for a midmajor school. I was looking at other schools with stronger academics than Bowling Green, but their women's basketball program was excellent.

That spring Duquesne University entered the picture. The school had been recruiting me lightly, but they hired a new coach in April and brought on an assistant who had already been recruiting me from his previous job at Bucknell. He vouched for me to Duquesne's new head coach, and they and I began considering each other in earnest. They sent a representative to my high school to look at my transcripts, and that summer I went on an unofficial visit there with my mom. I was enamored. The Atlantic 10, unlike many other conferences I was looking at, was not a one-bid league. In other words, its teams played at such a high day-to-day level that more teams than just the conference winner had a chance to qualify for the Big Dance. I might have my best shot at the NCAA Tournament if I played at Duquesne. Their head coach had played in the WNBA and the Olympics, and I would do anything to play under that kind of expertise. They hadn't actually offered me a scholarship, but they kept saying they wanted to, and I believed them.

I also scheduled an unofficial visit at West Virginia University, where I had been talking regularly with an assistant. The night before the visit, I realized I hadn't heard from him in a while, so I bit back my pride and asked my dad to call. Turned out the assistant had taken a coaching job at the University of Cincinnati and hadn't bothered to tell me he'd moved, and the other West Virginia assistants didn't seem to know I was coming. Annoyed, I canceled the visit.

At the beginning of May my dad set up unofficial visits at two other schools that had been recruiting me, the University of Massachusetts and College of the Holy Cross. I was furious with him for not letting me do it.

The top UMass assistant, Pam Egan, was friendly and exhaustingly outgoing. She talked constantly to my dad, who ate it up, and she had a million questions for me as we strolled through campus. A few weeks later, Pam told my dad that UMass was still "extremely interested" in me but needed to see me play that July to be totally sure I was the right fit. She explained that sometimes coaches had to wait to see what other positions on the team they could fill, what other girls accepted scholarships, before they could see the big picture and figure out how we would all mesh. Coaches tried to be as communicative as they could during that process, Pam explained. But I should have known that they were going to communicate only exactly as much as suited them and no more. They weren't in this to make me happy. This was their job.

"It's poker," one Division I assistant wrote in an email to my dad. "The recruiting game is about not showing all of your cards, a little bluffing here and there, and knowing when to go all in. It is sad. We are talking about young women's lives, but the money has corrupted the game."

I understood that this was a business, but I knew I wasn't a product. I was just a kid. This was my life. It was stressing me out.

"Though there may be some sleepless nights involved in the process (at both ends)," Pam wrote, "generally it all works out fine for everyone."

Duquesne sang the same song that UMass did. They still liked me, and they were my top choice, but they needed to see me play in July, too. It seemed that pretty much everything was riding on July.

For my last AAU summer, since most of my old teammates had already graduated, I joined a new team, the PA Swoosh. I didn't bond with most of them the way I had bonded with the Hoopsters. Olivia was an exception.

Olivia Lowery's high school team had beaten mine when we faced them in their gym earlier that year. Crushed us, actually, 53–34. Olivia and I played the same position, but she was slightly bigger. She pushed me around in the post, played a little dirty. She thought I played a little dirty. When my dad found out that Olivia would be playing on the PA Swoosh too and broke the news, I groaned. I hated my opponents on principle. Olivia felt the same way.

"Do you remember Amanda Ottaway?" her mom asked her. "Her dad just called. She had to switch AAU teams this year, too. She's gonna be on the PA Swoosh with you."

"Isn't this too far for them to drive for practices?" Olivia grouched. "I don't wanna play with her."

Within weeks she was my best friend on the team.

The summer before a female basketball player's senior year of high school is generally the most crucial span of her recruiting process. Most important for us was the July open period, when hundreds of Division I and II college coaches flocked to several huge AAU tournaments to see the players they liked face some of the best competition in the country. At these "exposure tournaments," rows of folding chairs lined roped-off sections courtside. College coaches dressed in team gear, anywhere from a handful to dozens of them, sat and watched with clipboards, taking notes, making phone calls.

Those folding chairs were anxiety inducing for players. The setup could make us feel like zoo animals. Were the chairs full? Were they empty? Which specific coaches were there? Was the head coach there, or had she sent assistants in her stead? Was anyone wearing the gear of (blank) school? Were they there to watch me, or someone else on my team, or someone on the other team? Was that coach who came to my last game also at this game? Did they see me make that great hustle play? Did they see me commit that dumb foul? Did that coach just wink at me?

I didn't play well that July. I wasn't comfortable with the new team, and all the pressure made me nervous. Every game I searched the coaches' chairs for Duquesne shirts.

The thirty schools I'd been talking to since September, and the sixty or so that had been contacting me since I was fourteen, had been whittled down to a list of fifteen, with Duquesne at the top. I felt like I spent all my time that July either on the phone with coaches or on the court, practicing or at a tournament. I was exhausted and burned out, and my looming decision stressed me out endlessly. When I wasn't playing, I lounged for hours in the hot, sticky den of my parents' house in cut-off T-shirts and baggy shorts, watching trashy television with the door closed. I made small talk on the phone with coaches who assessed my every word, trying to figure out if I would fit in at their school, with their program. I asked them the questions I'd learned to ask: Where was I ranked on their list of recruits? Did they see me having an immediate impact on their team and getting playing time right away? What position did they see me playing? Would we be a competitive program in our conference? What was the academic support like for athletes? Would I be able to major in journalism? I didn't know when people were lying to me and when they weren't.

Years later, I wished I had also asked questions like these: Do former players come back for basketball alumni events? When they graduate, do your players ask you for letters of recommendation for jobs and scholarships? How many of your players' weddings have you been to?

My parents and I continued to fight constantly, but they remained patient. I screamed and cried and threw things. When I begged they bought me a small texting plan for my phone so I could text coaches. Other people—relatives, family friends, total strangers—kept telling me this was supposed to be fun. "It's nice to be wanted," they'd say. Or, "I hope you're enjoying this; it'll never happen again!" I wished they would shut up. I had never been so stressed out.

One head coach had been pressuring me to give her a verbal commitment for months after I'd visited, but I wasn't ready. It was too early. "It's like you're waiting around for a better prom date," she finally snapped at me over the phone.

My first thought was that hers wasn't a great comparison, since nobody had ever asked me to the prom. My second thought was that I would be ready to commit when I was ready, not when she wanted me to, even just as a matter of principle. Also, for a grown-up, she was being pretty rude. She and her staff nagged and nagged, calling and texting and emailing me so often that I stopped answering. One day I was climbing into the family minivan to go shopping with my mom and got a call from an unlisted number. Hoping it was Duquesne, I picked up.

"Hi, Amanda," came a familiar voice. It was the coach who'd lectured me about prom dates. I wasn't sure, but I thought they might have blocked their number, or called from a different phone, just so I would answer. The idea made me furious. They were officially off my list.

My family went on vacation in early August before my senior year of high school. Summer tournaments were over, and this was the time of year when coaches called rising seniors and started giving them offers over the phone. I had verbal scholarship offers from Saint Bonaventure, Akron, Miami of Ohio, Siena, Saint Francis, and Bucknell. Duquesne had not offered but continued to say they intended to, and theirs was the offer I was waiting for. But I'd heard horror stories about girls who were promised the same scholarship as one or two others, and whoever claimed it first was the one who got it. If Duquesne was going to offer me, I needed them to do it soon, or I would run out of backup plans.

One day I was sitting outside at the beach house we'd rented, wearing a tank top and basketball shorts. My phone rang, and my heart stopped. Maybe this was Duquesne at the other end of the line. Maybe this was it.

I checked the caller ID—it wasn't any of the Duquesne coaches I had in my contacts, and the number didn't have a Pittsburgh area code. My heart sank.

"Hey, Amanda! This is Coach Deborah Katz down at Davidson College!" came the strongest southern accent I had ever heard and what sounded like three exclamation points after every sentence. I cringed.

"Listen, we really like your game, Amanda," Coach Katz continued. She flattered me for a while, saying how much she liked my athleticism and my hustle. "We saw you play at the Deep South Classic in North Carolina. We're recruitin' your PA Swoosh teammate Miss Olivia Lowery pretty hard, too." (Weird, I thought.) "And lucky for us, that's how we found you! I'd love to chat a bit about Davidson!"

I'd never even heard of Davidson. Coach Katz launched into her stump speech about the school, and I half-listened, strolling barefoot around the pool deck. It looked like it might rain. These little intro rants from coaches were all pretty similar, and they got old after a while—everybody told me their school had great academics, a good professor-to-student ratio, a safe community, an awesome cafeteria, the team was on the up-and-up, I could be a part of its future success and would get a lot of playing time right away, the team would go play in Europe one summer, we would get cool gear, blah blah blah.

"We'd love to get you down here for a visit, Miss Amanda." Coach Katz was still talking. "Would you be interested?"

I hedged. I'd learned to play the game coaches played with me—keeping them on the line while exploring other options.

Back at home in Pennsylvania, the University of Akron called and said they wanted me to come on an official visit. That school was barely on my radar, but sure, if they were going to pay for it, why not?

Davidson called again. Deborah Katz told my parents they would offer if I came for a visit there.

A few days later, I ran into my high school coach Joe Hurd at the dentist's office. He told me he'd learned that Duquesne had made an offer with the scholarship we'd been hoping would be offered to me. The lucky recipient was a Pittsburgh guard and three-point shooter about my size. I wasn't trained as a guard, nor was I a three-point shooter. Duquesne still had more scholarships in my class, though. I wasn't worried yet. Coach Hurd told me Coach Katz had called him, too, to tell him how much she liked me. A few days after that, I got a piece of mail from Davidson. Usually, I didn't share my recruiting propaganda with my parents, but I wanted to share this.

"It's a little disturbing that they found this," I told them, biting back a smile. The Davidson coaches had dug up a newspaper feature in our small local paper from way back in December, when I'd been named

Athlete of the Week and talked about some of my favorite things at the time—cookie dough, Lance Armstrong, English class, a Brad Paisley song. The coaches found pictures of each of the things I named and stuck them all in the envelope.

My dad was always talking about the benefits of liberal-arts colleges because he taught at one. Nobody up our way in Pennsylvania had ever heard of Davidson College or the Southern Conference, the league they played in. My parents had done a little research on the school and learned its academics were excellent. Because my parents loved the idea of Davidson so much, I badly wanted *not* to love the idea of Davidson—but it was growing on me.

Things were getting trickier. Despite the fact that they still hadn't offered, Duquesne wasn't giving up on me, nor letting me give up on them; they kept saying they were still interested and would know more soon. They were like all the boys I wanted to date at my high school—waiting to see what cuter girls might come along. I didn't care. I was desperate for them. I was willing to wait.

I did set up an official visit, the first of five I was allowed to take, at Davidson for the first weekend of September. I was intrigued by their enthusiasm about me and figured I should keep them on the line. My mom and I would fly to Charlotte together. So would Olivia and her mom. So would, we were told, a player named Taylor Patton from the Philadelphia Belles, one of the best girls' AAU teams in the country, and her father.

I also told Akron I'd like to come on my official visit there a little later in September. Duquesne still hadn't invited me for one. With a mixture of excitement and trepidation, at the beginning of my senior year of high school, I prepared for a trip to Davidson.

Olivia and I, old AAU teammates excited to see each other again, texted in the days leading up to the visit. What should we pack? What would it be like? She and her mom were on the same early-morning flight as my mom and me. We met up with Taylor and her dad during our layover in Atlanta. It was just my second time on a plane.

When we landed in Charlotte at noon, all four Davidson women's basketball coaches were waiting at the airport. Taylor had already accepted her scholarship offer to Davidson and was there to hang out and get to know the team better. Neither Olivia nor I had gotten an official offer—just the promise of one—but assumed we would this weekend.

They whisked us off to campus. Over the course of the next two days, we got the royal treatment. Our parents stayed at the guest house on campus. We stayed with the sophomores, Whitney, Alyssa, and Jennifer. We visited a class that afternoon with Erin White, one of the juniors on the team. She was a Spanish major, and it was a high-level Spanish class—Contemporary Spanish Film—so I barely understood anything and spent the hour passing notes to Olivia. We watched a workout in the weight room and a highlight video, played pickup with the team, and went on a boat tour of the lake. We ate Chick-Fil-A for breakfast in the on-campus home of Tom Ross, the college president, where we chatted with him, too. On Saturday evening Coach Katz had the whole team over to her house for dinner.

At one point my mom and Olivia's mom were in Coach Katz's car with her, just the three of them, talking about Rene Portland. Earlier that year Portland—who'd been a hero of mine when I was a kid—had left her head-coaching job at Penn State University after a player alleged, backed up by several other players, that she'd been discriminated against because she was a lesbian. Portland's departure caused an upheaval of sorts in the women's basketball coaching world, and several of the coaches who'd been recruiting me got jobs at different schools.

In the car that day, my mom told me years later, Coach Katz started talking about how she would have a hard time coaching gay players. *This kind of talk isn't okay anymore*, my mom thought. Coach Katz told them she'd had a lesbian on the team in the recent past, and it was clear, my mom told me later, that Coach Katz did not approve. She reminded them that Erin was dating the quarterback of the football team, emphasizing what my mom called an "All-American girls and boys" kind of attitude.

"I just wanna call their mothers up," Coach Katz said, to my mom and Olivia's mom, of her lesbian players. The mothers looked at each other awkwardly but didn't say anything. What could they say? Their daughters both had scholarship offers on the line. What if one of us was gay? What if Coach Katz thought one of us was gay?

On Saturday afternoon, after breakfast with the president, the locker room tour, the campus tour, lunch, pickup, and the boat tour, we had an hour or so of free time, and we were worn out. So Olivia, Taylor, and I crowded into one dorm room to take a nap. Olivia kept us awake. She was in love with Davidson. She wanted to commit right then and there but wasn't sure if she should wait a few days instead. She wound up committing that day, in a meeting with her mom and Coach Katz. Now I was the only one left. If I turned down my offer, the Davidson coaches would call the next recruit in their line and invite her for an official visit. I loved Davidson so far, but I wasn't ready to commit yet.

We all went out to a fancy dinner that night with our parents, hosts, and the coaches, fancy enough that I—still a bit of a tomboy—hadn't brought any appropriate clothes, so Whitney lent me a dress. I ordered meat loaf. Later, we went out on campus with the team. We'd been out with them the night before, too; they asked us if we wanted to see the social scene, no pressure, and we did. It was our first time at college away from our parents—of course we wanted to see the social scene.

We didn't know that Coach Katz had also encouraged our mothers to take a walk around campus that evening to see the social scene for themselves. My mom and Mrs. Lowery didn't see us, but they saw everything we saw—beer pong on balconies, grass littered with Solo cups, drunk students yelling and laughing and running through the night.

"Meet our recruits," the older girls said to everyone we ran into. We were greeted enthusiastically by dozens of Davidson students. "This is Amanda; this is Taylor; this is Olivia." We all went dancing together in a fraternity house on campus. A blast of hot, wet air enveloped us as soon as we opened the door. It smelled like beer and body odor and also a little like farts, and the bass pounded heavy and hard. It was almost completely dark. Once my eyes adjusted I could tell the room was crammed with people making out and dancing, mostly grinding, enthusiastically but not particularly well.

Because Olivia and Taylor were there, too, and because I felt like I already knew them, I could be a little goofy. Otherwise it would have been weird to let loose on the dance floor in front of these other girls we barely knew. So we started bopping around. Before long a guy I'd never met had moseyed over and started grinding on me. This had never happened to me before. He was getting his sweat all over me. It was terrible. What was I supposed to do? I bounced up and down awkwardly and made "HELP" faces at the team. Erin, the one whose Spanish class we'd visited, caught my eye and shimmied over, smoothly cutting in. Erin winked at me, and I scurried away, back to the team huddle, where everyone giggled and hugged me. I felt safe here.

My high school assistant coaches Anita Moore Jennings and Deanna Jubeck, two women who had played Division I, had given me the best advice I'd heard for picking a college: Pick one where you'll be happy with the school and the people if you are injured and can't play, because you will probably get hurt at some point. And pick one where you'll still be happy even if the entire coaching staff leaves, because that happens a lot. Turnover at this level, they warned, is high. But your teammates are in it with you for the long haul.

I knew in that smelly, sticky moment that Davidson fulfilled those requirements.

We went back to the dorm and napped for a few hours and then had to get up before the sun, pack, and ride to the Charlotte airport with one of the assistant coaches. Our flight left at six in the morning.

"So what did you think?" my mom asked me in the airport, glowing. She'd loved it.

I had, too, but I was conflicted. "I'd still verbal to Duquesne," I told her.

I had a lot of thinking to do. I still wanted to wait for Duquesne to offer, but it was beginning to look like they weren't going to. They had now used up four of the five scholarships available for my class, none on me and a few on players who seemed kind of like me.

Coach Katz, on the other hand, told me I had potential to be the Southern Conference Freshman of the Year. She told me the team would play abroad in Europe one summer. She promised that if I came to Davidson, I'd have a scholarship for all four years, even if I got hurt, as long as I stayed academically eligible.

The next morning, while I was at school, she followed up with my parents. They would give me a week or so to make my decision before they had to move on.

I called Akron and canceled my visit there. I didn't tell them I'd visited Davidson. They just weren't the right fit for me, I told the coach.

"How do you know it's the wrong fit for you if you don't visit?" she asked. But I just knew, and her response made me more certain that I'd made the right decision. Akron had always been the wrong fit. I felt guilty for having led them on for so long; they'd been only vaguely on my radar, and somehow here I was turning down an official visit. I felt a little like a bride running away from the altar. How had we gotten this far?

"You don't even owe her an explanation," my high school coaches assured me, which made me feel a little bit better. "When something is right, it's right." And when it wasn't, it wasn't.

The same day the Duquesne assistant called my AAU coach and told him Duquesne was still interested and would know within a week or two whether they could offer me a scholarship—keeping me on their string. Everything boiled down to the next several days.

I had never faced a decision so tough. I stayed up late in the den, watching bad television as usual and thinking hard. I thought about Duquesne and the four girls they had recruited ahead of me and whether I would even play if I went there. I thought about how warmly Coach Katz and her staff had treated my mom and me, like we were a family, like they'd take care of me. I thought about how happy my mom looked all weekend. I thought about how Erin rescued me on the dance floor, how Whitney lent me a dress to wear out to dinner, how tightly Jenni hugged me good-bye, how Olivia and Taylor and I bickered and giggled and pillow-talked like old friends.

About a week later, I sat on my front porch and dialed the number for the Davidson women's basketball office.

"Hi, Miss Amanda!" Coach Katz chirped. "I've got my whole staff sittin' in here with me. Is there anything you'd like to tell us?"

There was, but the way she asked made me uncomfortable.

"Yeah, Coach," I blurted quickly, before I chickened out. "I'd like to come play basketball at Davidson."

3 A Night with the 'Cats

The girl on the dance team was demonstrating a body roll. Olivia, Nicole Cooper ("Coop"), and I tilted our heads and squinted at her, puzzled, trying to figure out how she could move like that. Taylor was busy imitating, and she wasn't bad.

We were all barefoot and wearing T-shirts and basketball shorts. Next to us stood three tall men, also in T-shirts and baggy shorts, gamely practicing their own dance moves.

We were all exhausted. It had been a long first month of college for us freshman Davidson basketball players, three men and four women. Now, after a day that had started for the women's team with a 7:00 a.m. lifting session, included several classes and an intensive small-group workout followed by pickup in the late afternoon, and finally ended with dinner in the cafeteria, it was time for dance practice.

We had to learn how to do body rolls because the first day of official basketball practice was approaching. Every year college basketball programs around the country hold various public events, dubbed "Midnight Madness," to celebrate the NCAA-decreed official beginning of another year of hoops. Activities range from a light practice or scrimmage to goofy player skits and dancing to three-point contests to cheerleader, mascot, and dance-team performances, all designed to get fans excited about the upcoming season. The tradition started with former Davidson men's coach Lefty Driesell, who in 1971—two years after he left Davidson to coach at Maryland—found that eight hundred fans had shown up to watch his team run a six-minute mile around the track just after midnight on the first official day of practice. The tradition expanded from there, and slowly "Midnight Madness" caught on at other schools.

At Davidson we called it "A Night with the 'Cats." Admission was free and open to the public; there were cool T-shirts and an autograph session and a three-point shooting contest, and both teams played an intrasquad scrimmage. Each class of men's and women's players also had to do a themed dance together, as a crowd-pleaser, hence our lessons with the Davidson dance team.

"Being a student-athlete at Davidson is no different than being any other Davidson College student," said the student-athlete handbook. That was hilarious. Yes, we were integrated into the student body in almost all ways, more than teams were at other Division I schools. Athletes and nonathletes—called "nonners" in Davidson slang—shared dorms, classes, the cafeteria, and even the basketball court in Belk Arena, and that was for the most part a wonderful thing. But being an athlete was different from being a nonner in so many ways.

Sure, some nonners worked long hours in labs or coffee shops or the theater. For the most part, though, other Davidson students could stay up all night to study for a test if they wanted to. We were supposed to rest so we could throw weights around in the mornings. Other students got to go home for Thanksgiving and a full winter break. We would spend Thanksgiving on the road and just four or five days at home in December. Our conference tournament often fell during spring break. Other students could attend evening events on campus, get involved in extracurriculars, volunteer, take on internships and outside jobs, and visit their professors during office hours. Everything my teammates and I did to plan for our own futures, we planned around basketball.

Olivia, Taylor, Coop, and I had been on campus as freshmen for a little more than a month. The three assistant coaches who had recruited Olivia, Taylor, and me had all quit after the previous season, and we were not totally sure why. The women's basketball athletic trainer had also left our squad to work with the much larger football team. So Coach Katz had brought in an entire new staff one at a time—one coach in May, one in June, one in July. We also got a new athletic trainer, Meghan Hughes. This was why, I remembered, I had been told not to pick a school for its coaches. A near-full turnaround could happen just like that.

The first time I met Coach Maria Bailey, one of Coach Katz's new assistants, Olivia and I had gone down to the office to say hello and introduce ourselves during the first week of class. Coach Bailey considered me from the other side of her desk, her brown eyes squinted in a sly, thoughtful smile, a look we would come to know well. She had already nicknamed Nicole Cooper "Coop."

"I'm gonna call you 'Otto,'" she declared in a sassy upstate New York accent, so that "Otto" sounded a little like "Aah-Toe."

"Okay," I said, because I was a freshman and she could call me whatever she wanted if it meant I might get playing time. I liked the nickname, though, and I liked Coach Bailey. From that moment on, just about the only people on campus who called me "Amanda" were my professors. Everyone else called me "Otto."

I wore a T-shirt and basketball shorts on the first day of class to let everyone know I was a baller. Olivia and Coop and Taylor all wore sundresses and flip-flops to show people they were ballers who could look cute too. So I did that on the second day of class.

Because Davidson was a liberal-arts school, we couldn't start focusing on our majors right away. As first-semester freshmen we were taking four general education classes apiece—which meant Olivia, who wanted to be premed, was taking a writing class, and I, who wanted to be a writer, was taking premed biology. In order for us to be eligible to play basketball, our GPAs had to be a minimum of 1.8 that year so that we could play as sophomores. We needed a 1.9 our second year and 2.0 our last two years. It didn't sound that hard, but Davidson's professors were nationally acclaimed and notorious for tough grading. We didn't get any of that inflation crap they had at Harvard. If our professors thought we deserved a D, we got a D.

As we'd done in Detroit, we proudly mentioned our sport to everyone we met that fall. "Hi, I'm Amanda, but call me Otto. I'm on the women's basketball team," I said over and over, in one breath conveying my whole identity.

Olivia and I grew even closer. She was loud and outgoing and glamorous and fun, sassy and righteous and stubborn. We did everything together. We ate lunches and dinners together. We walked to workouts together. She had a boyfriend at home but played wingwoman for me. I "shopped" in her closet every weekend.

Olivia, Taylor, Coop, and I had a dozen built-in best friends from the moment we arrived on campus. We were tired and happy. Olivia and Hope, her roommate who ran cross-country, also became fast friends. Hope's parents were both doctors and Davidson graduates themselves. Smart, sweet, and southern, with a knack for lipstick, Hope had the slim waist and tiny arms I longed for but would probably never have. Hope and Olivia bonded immediately over their love of fashion and that they both wanted to be doctors someday, and I spent a lot of time in their room.

We were surrounded at all times by overwhelmingly high-caliber people—high school valedictorians in the classroom, high school hoop stars on the court. I was a decent student but not stellar, mediocre at most everything but English. I had half-cheated my way through high school physics, cried my way through Algebra II. Now I found myself sitting in class next to some of the brightest students in the country.

When workouts started, my teammates and I existed in a constant state of exhaustion, staggering through our weeks to get to the weekend, two glorious days without mandated exercise. Preseason, with its two or three workouts every weekday, was everything I'd been warned about, plus a level of fatigue I could not have imagined.

We did old-fashioned sprint conditioning on the court; ran on the track and on a cross-country course; lifted weights three times a week;

played pickup; had small-group skill workouts with the coaches, which we called "individuals" or "indis"; and sometimes, as a special treat for our aching joints, had spinning class.

Olivia and I rushed into the locker room a few minutes behind schedule before our first class on the spin bikes. Most people had already changed and were tying their shoes and pulling their hair up.

"Just wear your spandy-panties and your dry-fits," our teammates told us. "Spandy-panties" was our nickname for the Spandex shorts we wore under our basketball shorts for workouts, practices, and games, because basketball shorts were so loose. We played our sport in baggy outfits that you couldn't see our bodies in, and I was comfortable with that. I wasn't sure how I felt about anybody being able to see the full outline of my butt, like a cross-country runner, through my skintight Spandex undershorts. I didn't have Hope's body.

"Just the spandy-panties?" Olivia and I asked, confused.

"Yep," said Erin cheerfully, snapping on a headband, grabbing her water bottle, smacking the wall over the door, and whisking into the hall. She wasn't wearing shorts over her Spandex. "No shorts. Hustle up, 'Cats! Don't forget a towel."

So Olivia and I got dressed, grabbed small towels and our water bottles, and shuffled self-consciously to the water fountain to fill them up.

We got halfway to the phys-ed classroom where the spinning bikes were before the upperclassmen, laughing, told us to turn around. I saw that they were all wearing our baggy practice shorts. They must have put them on in the hallway.

"Just kidding!" they said. "We do wear shorts. Go get dressed, freshies."

Successfully pranked, Olivia and I hustled back to the locker room, threw on our red mesh practice shorts, and ran back to the spinning room.

There was an instructor—a good change of pace from having one of our coaches telling us what to do—although they were there, too, just to watch. We spent some time adjusting the height of the bike seats to suit our long legs. Then we hopped on, the instructor blared some music, and we were off pedaling to nowhere.

When we swiped the little knob between our legs to the right, it got much harder to pedal. The instructor periodically yelled things like, "Now, turn up your resistance two full turns." Or "one full turn." Or "half a turn." But we were supposed to watch his legs and keep our legs pedaling as fast as his did. Everyone in the room should have one knee coming up at the same time, he explained, to also match the beat of the music.

Olivia and I rode bikes next to each other, making guttural heaving noises, our thighs burning, sweat splashing in fat droplets on the floor. We'd both turned up our resistance every time the instructor told us to, and we could barely pedal. How was everyone else going so fast? It was like they were biking down a road in Oklahoma and we were biking up Mount Kilimanjaro. We were in slow motion.

Coach Katz strolled through the rows of bikes, hands clasped behind her back, offering encouragement. She walked toward Olivia and me and bowed her head.

"You two," she said to us in a low, discreet voice, "had better start pedalin' faster, or we're gonna get you up on the court running instead." Then she walked away like nothing had happened.

Olivia and I glanced at each other, terrified, and then put our heads down and pedaled for our lives. But I couldn't go any faster. Peeking around to make sure nobody was looking, I gave my knob a tweak to the left to ease some of the resistance. I pedaled faster. I tweaked it again and pedaled even faster. The trick, apparently, was not to follow the instructor's directions, but to make the resistance whatever we needed it to be in order to *look* like we were doing what he did. It was an important lesson.

Afterward, it was hard to walk. I had to hang onto the wall to lower myself onto the toilet. Coop used her hands to lift up each leg under the knee as she walked down the stairs. Even as the soreness lingered, we had a 7:00 a.m. weights session—and it was leg day. This was how all our weekdays went: wake up sore, work out, eat, go to class, eat, go to class, work out, eat, do homework, sleep, repeat.

For players who did not run sprints well, like Olivia and Taylor, the weight room was a place they felt safe. These were workouts they were good at. They were strong girls, solid girls. They'd quickly been initiated into the highly exclusive CLBG, or "Cute Little Big Girls," club, founded by post players a few years earlier. CLBG's message was clear: *We may be bigger than the average woman, but we're still "cute," and we still want to be considered "little," and we still want to be "girls." We still want people to think of us as conventionally attractive.*

Craig Swieton, the head strength and conditioning coach, loved the strong girls. He was a stocky man with a buzz cut and bulging trapezius muscles that made him look like he was constantly shrugging his shoulders. His calves were wide as cereal boxes. He rarely looked anyone in the eye.

We did Olympic-style lifting with Coach Swieton, meaning we were always working toward a "max-out"—being able to lift a lot of weight one time instead of lifting less weight many times. So we'd lift in sets, slowly increasing the weight while decreasing the number of times we lifted it. Coach Swieton was a former football player himself, and we did a lot of the same lifts the football players did: hang cleans, Romanian dead lifts, clean-and-jerks, snatches. All of these lifts involved a free barbell—a long metal bar—with doughnut-shaped weights piled on each end. We picked the barbell up off the ground, jumped to pull it to our collarbones with our elbows out in front of us, jumped again to push it over our heads, squatted while holding it steady on our chests. Our thighs, hamstrings, glutes, core, and back muscles all benefited from these lifts, not just our arms. Coach Swieton interspersed them with agility drills, abdominal work, and muscle-specific exercises like bicep curls.

Squat days were my favorite because I was good at squatting, and so were Olivia and Taylor. Coop was still learning, sometimes getting sent to the wall to practice her squat form with no weight at all. As we got closer to the start of the season, Coach Swieton increased our weight. We would lift as much as we could before our first official practice, and then he'd level it off and taper back down as we started playing games so we didn't tire our legs out too much.

He put us in small groups based on how much weight we could lift, so that players who lifted similar amounts worked at the same rack for convenience. In doing this Coach Swieton had also unwittingly created a quiet competition to see who could get assigned to the rack where players lifted the most. Olivia, Taylor, and I usually ended up together at the rack with the second-heaviest weights. Christina, slim as she was, could somehow lift more. Often Erin and Jenni could, too.

Taylor chalked up her hands from the bin at our rack. Forget how sore our legs were. It was time for her max-rep back squat.

"Okay, here we go, Tay," Olivia and I said to her as Taylor ducked under the bar and positioned herself beneath it so that it rested lightly on her shoulders. "You got this."

"I'll spot," Olivia added to me. She walked into the rack behind Taylor and stood there, a few feet back, waiting. Coach Swieton was watching too, clipboard in hand, ready to check Taylor's name off his list.

"Whenever you're ready, Taylor," he said.

To the weight of the bar, 45 pounds, we'd added 180 pounds' worth of plates. For now, the rack held all that weight. But when Taylor was ready, she would take all 225 pounds on her shoulders behind her head, hold it steady with her hands, bend her knees slowly into a deep squat, and stand back up with it. Just one time. This was what they called a max rep.

"Okay, Lowery, you're spotting?" Coach Swieton asked.

"Yeah, I got her," said Olivia. She stood ready, feet spread apart, hands out, palms up, to grab the weight in case Taylor bent her knees and couldn't stand up again with all that weight resting on her back. The clatter of the rest of our teammates all squatting at their own racks blended with the bass of the music, heavy pop today, and pumped hard through our matching team sneakers. The late-afternoon sun poured through the high windows. Some days we had to squint as we squatted into sunbeams.

"You got this, Tay," I said to Taylor quietly. "Just one time. Piece of cake."

Since I wasn't her spotter, I was supposed to be doing my own exercises—push-ups on an oversize yoga ball—but I had taken a break to cheer her on. Coach Swieton didn't seem to mind. He loved max-out days. He was in his element today.

Standing under the bar, the middle of it resting just below the base of her neck, Taylor slowly tucked her shirt into her shorts. She tightened her ponytail, ran a hand through it to make sure it wasn't stuck under the bar. She shook out her freckled arms, bent each elbow at a thirty-degree angle with her palms facing the sky, and slowly wrapped her fingers, with their blue-painted nails, around the bar, securing it across her shoulders.

"You got this, Tay," Olivia said. "You can do it."

"Come on, Tay!" came a shout from the other end of the weight room. Groups of teammates had stopped what they were doing to watch. "You got this, freshies!"

Olivia put her hands underneath the barbell, and together the two of them lifted it off the rack. Olivia let go, and Taylor stood up straight, holding the full weight of the barbell on her shoulders, and took a few small, steady steps backward. She took one deep breath. She picked up first one foot, then the other, placing them exactly where she wanted them, slightly farther apart than the width of her shoulders. She lifted each foot again. She took another deep breath and slowly bent her knees, sticking her butt out, keeping her core tight, her head and chest up. As she reached the bottom of her squat, her right knee dipped inward.

"Straighten that knee out, Taylor," said Coach Swieton. Taylor puffed her cheeks and expelled a forceful blast of air, and her right knee wobbled back and forth. I winced, but she was fine; she'd just have to work on her form with lighter weight later. Slowly, slowly, she began straightening her legs.

"Yes, Tay!" Olivia shouted from behind her. "You got this. You're almost there."

There is a particular moment in many free-weight lifts called the sticking point, where the body has the least amount of mechanical advantage, when the momentum has run out. If the lifter can push the weight past that point, she is home free and can finish the lift. But if she gets stuck, that's where it happens—usually a few seconds into pushing the weight back. It hit Taylor on her way to stand back up, a couple inches above the lowest point she'd squatted to. She hovered at the sticking point for a second. If she stayed there too long, she would never make it back to a standing position on her own.

"Breathe, Taylor," Coach Swieton said. "You got this. Finish strong." Taylor grunted, scrunched up her face, huffed out the rest of her air, and powered up toward the ceiling until her knees were straight again. Olivia rushed forward to help her place the bar back in the rack, and the room burst into whoops and applause.

"Thatta girl, Taylor," Coach Swieton said, beaming with pride, giving her a high five.

"C-L-B-G!" whooped Erin.

"I see you, Zeus," Jenni hollered.

"Zeus" was Taylor's nickname for her butt. It was a beautiful butt, and it was a strong butt, and it had done her good here.

Most of us, including Jenni and Taylor, had insecurities about our bodies. I had been a gangly high schooler, but in college I grew so sturdy, so solid, that I was practically a rectangle between my wide shoulders and my skinny ankles. In my first two years I gained twenty-five pounds of fat and muscle.

In the weight room and on the court, it was easy to be proud of our strength. But sometimes we remembered that we looked different from other women: in department store dressing rooms, peeling down jeans that didn't fit over our calves; wincing at reflections of our swollen arms in dark car windows; gazing in mirrors at bulky trapezius muscles that swallowed our necks; going up a bra size because our backs had gotten broader.

"It's just four years," Jenni sometimes thought to herself. "After that, you can do what you want with your body."

As the cheers for Taylor rang out in the weight room that day, she grinned and wiped her sweaty, chalky hands on her shorts and then shook out her legs, looking satisfied.

Thirteen hours later, I narrowed my eyes at the dance-team member assigned to teach the freshmen. Sometimes these dance practices started and ran so late that the Baker Sports Complex—the building that housed our gym, Belk Arena, plus the racquetball courts, the locker rooms, pool, and Athletic Department and coaches' offices—was closed by the time we left.

"I don't think I can do a body roll," I announced loudly. My knees hurt. Everything hurt. We were on the hard upstairs practice courts, which were basically wood laid over concrete, and she kept making us do things that required us to bend our knees. We had squatted hundreds of pounds that morning. We could barely stand. Now we were supposed to body roll?

"Sure you can," she said brightly. It seemed like she was losing patience. I was losing patience with her, too. Everyone was trying to be a good sport about it. "Like this." And she did it again, so goddamn cheerful in her cute leggings and tight tank top, rippling her slim body as if all the parts were loosely attached to each other with flimsy rubber bands and not, like ours, with thick, stiff sinew that burned when we moved.

We imitated the dancer, jerky and awkward. Our bodies did different magic than hers. I planted my feet and jutted my hips forward, stiff and robotic as a Barbie doll. "Just loosen up," the dancer advised. Will Reigel, A.J. Atkinson, and Frank Ben-Eze, the three men's players, waited patiently for us to be done with this part.

A few weeks earlier, Olivia, Taylor, and I—we hadn't included Coop—had invited ourselves to A.J. and Frank's dorm room on our first night of freshman orientation. We had seen how close Jenni, Lyss, and Whitney were with Stephen and Bryant and the other guys in their class on the men's team. They had met by walking into the guys' dorm room and saying, "You're on the men's basketball team? We're on the women's basketball team." We wanted that, too.

Frank and A.J.'s room was somehow a mess already, so Olivia and I started cleaning up, congratulating ourselves for taking care of them, while we all got to know each other. Frank, at six feet ten, complained about not being able to fit in his college-standard extralong twin bed. We swiped Gatorades from the case on the floor. It wasn't long after that I learned Frank, whose mom lived in Nigeria, loved snickerdoodles. My mom started sending back homemade batches for him every time I came home.

The athletics marketing and promotions department handled most details of this fourth annual "Night with the 'Cats." They started planning in August, and in early September marketing staff took three of the men's players to dinner to brainstorm ideas. Although they let our team in on the theme idea later, the marketing folks did not invite any women's players to this athletes' brainstorming dinner. It seemed to have been an honest oversight, and it was a small detail, but it demonstrated just how much the event from its beginning was geared toward promoting Davidson men's basketball and how easily even the people whose job was to promote all Davidson sports teams could overlook women's basketball.

Because of the men's Elite Eight run the year before, their team— especially Stephen Curry—still bathed in a bright national spotlight; ESPNU would send a camera crew to tape Night with the 'Cats. The stakes for an endearing and well-attended Midnight Madness performance from Davidson, as far as the marketing people were concerned, were high. Seven months after "Sweet Caroline" rocked the rafters in Detroit, their department was in its post-Cinderella-story element, ready to kick off a new men's basketball season, maybe a trip to the Final Four this year. The marketing assistant in charge of us was young and seemed tense. She was, admittedly, in charge of wrangling two dozen distracted, goofy eighteen- to twenty-two-year-olds into a production that would be broadcast on national television.

Marketing wanted Belk Arena, which sat a little less than six thousand people, to look full for the Midnight Madness cameras. The men's games would be broadcast nationally a few times that season, and after last year their team was used to the attention. The women's team was not. Our upperclassmen at least tried to act like they'd been there before, but the freshmen were unabashedly pumped. We were going to be on ESPN!

The theme was "A Night on the Red Carpet." Olivia, Taylor, Coop, and I called our moms to ask them to ship our senior prom dresses to our campus post office boxes, because that was the freshman women's costume for our class dance. So we were going to be on ESPN, but not in basketball shorts—in old prom dresses.

On the big night, after an early dinner at Commons, the campus cafeteria, our team and some of the guys went to watch the women's volleyball game before they cleared the court for us. The ESPN camera crews had arrived earlier that day and were setting up. Their cords were everywhere. We took pictures of ourselves making faces in the stands while kids came up and asked the men's players for autographs. Then we all headed down to our respective locker rooms to change.

My teammates and I were clean, and our hair was dry. We were not wearing sweatpants or basketball shorts. Our tiny locker room smelled like burnt hair and makeup—two things it did not usually smell like—as we wobbled around each other in our nice shoes, getting ready to be on TV, our trapezius and back and arm muscles bulging out the tops of our little black dresses.

Players' sexuality and appearance are inextricably linked with the sport for many viewers of women's basketball in a way that they are not for men's basketball. This view goes back to the beginning of games as public events, when women were judged more on their ability to bag a man off the court than they were on their ability to shoot a basketball, when watching women play sports was more a performance to ogle rather than a display of athletic feats to appreciate. Some teams required their players to apply makeup right after games. The team sponsored by Hanes Hosiery in the 1940s and '50s doubled as models for the brand's pantyhose.

Especially in post–Cold War America, when anyone who was different was suspicious, nobody wanted to be identified as a lesbian. Female athletes were particularly at risk because they engaged in what were—in what still are—considered to be "manly" pursuits. Gay and bisexual women who played sports, therefore, often dressed and acted like straight women, and straight women didn't want to be misidentified as gay.

Many male sportswriters treated female athletes who acted less feminine, or those with short hair or large muscles, with disdain, regardless of their abilities. "It is a lady's business to look beautiful and there are hardly any sports in which she seems able to do it," wrote acclaimed sportswriter Paul Gallico in 1936.

Women, usually white, whose looks met conventionally approved standards were praised and adored, though often not for their skills on the court. Somewhere along the line, a stereotype built up. In 2007 radio host Don Imus called the Rutgers women's basketball team, which was made up of predominantly black players, "rough girls" and "nappy-headed hos." He later apologized and was fired by CBS Radio and MSNBC, but the damage had been done: he had voiced the stereotype, and his phrasing became famous. I don't know a women's basketball player who ever forgot that he had said it.

"Whatever a women's basketball player is supposed to look like is apparently not straight and apparently not pretty," Jenni said once. Both consciously and unconsciously, and when we presented ourselves on and off the floor, we were echoing what we knew to be appropriate, what society told us was okay. We harbored a constant awareness of stereotypes. In many ways not much had changed since the mid-twentieth century. Girls could play sports, but they were still supposed to be pretty at all times.

Around 2005 Bill Simmons, former ESPN columnist and founder of the sports website *Grantland*, wrote:

> Well, the vast majority of WNBA players lack crossover sex appeal. That's just the way it is. Some are uncomfortably tall and gawky, while others lack the requisite, um, softer qualities to captivate males between 18 and 35. The baggy uniforms don't help. Neither does the fact that it's tough for anyone to look attractive at the end of a two-hour basketball game. . . . Sue Bird is downright adorable. . . . If Sue was walking around at the ESPYs in a cocktail dress, I'm watching. If she's running a pick and roll with Lauren Jackson, I'm flicking channels.

Whether because of societal pressure to subvert people's ideas of what female athletes looked like or because of personal preference, or both, Coach Katz tended to recruit mostly white Christian girls from middle-class families. Her players were less bulky, less visibly tattooed, and presented in a more feminine way—however they identified sexually—than many of the women we played against. One might call us "wholesome." Coach Katz liked to call us "good girls."

"I've been at NC State," Coach Katz told the *Davidson Journal* in 2003. "I loved it there, but I didn't feel like I had any impact on the kids. I feel like Davidson and the girls are more like me. They're family-based, their involvement is heart-felt, they love to play—everything that I believe in."

None of the players on our team who dated women that year were out of the closet to all of us. Years later, I learned one reason: A few years before Olivia, Taylor, Coop, and I arrived at Davidson, two players on the women's basketball team had dated each other. There was no rule against it. Their teammates knew, but the older player, Cassie, was just a junior, not yet out to her parents. Somehow—they weren't sure how—Coach Katz found out. According to Cassie, Coach Katz called Cassie into her office and told her to break off the relationship, or Coach would bench her for the year and make her tell her parents why. The relationship ended. The younger player eventually transferred out of Davidson.

"I realized all the things I'd felt about [Coach Katz] disliking me were true," Cassie told me. "I didn't dress like the other girls. . . . I tried to be what they were. I just wasn't."

She went to Jim Murphy, who assured her Coach Katz did not have the power to take her scholarship away for something like this. Coach Katz didn't call any parents, and the next day she summoned Cassie back into her office to tell her she hadn't actually said what Cassie remembered from their previous meeting. But the incident helped explain Coach Katz's comment to my mom about wanting to call the parents of players she suspected were gay. After it happened some Davidson players stayed in the closet, wary of penalties on or off the court if Coach Katz learned the truth about their love lives.

Our identity was in our sport. But for many reasons my teammates and I—gay, straight, bisexual, closeted—didn't want to be stereotyped into the "butch" identity that seemed to follow women who played basketball. We made efforts to look traditionally feminine in our hair and our faces and our clothing when we could. It was not something we really talked about, just something we understood we were all doing, maybe even subconsciously. We played the same two games that women's basketball players had been playing for decades. Basketball was one. Wanting people to understand that we were not necessarily who they thought we were was the other.

Our appearance, of course, also included our race, and black women who played sports had far more stereotypes to overcome than white women. My black teammates didn't want our Davidson classmates to think they were there only because they were good athletes on scholarships. We all felt pressure to prove ourselves academically, but they felt it most intensely.

That year more than 47 percent of Division I women's basketball players in the country were black—a majority. About 44 percent were white. Our team had one black player, one biracial player, and ten white players. It made me feel good about myself that Coach Katz thought I was a "good" girl from a good family, but I didn't understand until later the deeper implications of talking about players that way. Did "good" also mean "from a stable two-parent household"? Did it also mean "straight"? Did it also mean "white"?

We reflected the rest of Davidson's student body, which was at the time about 6 percent black and more than 74 percent white. One and a half percent identified as multiracial. There were only fifty-one black women on campus. Frank and A.J. were two of forty-four black male students. We had just 4 full-time African American faculty members out of 168.

On this team, at this school, my black teammates were conscious of these numbers. Christina Campbell was premed, on a two-year research grant with a neuroscience professor, writing a senior thesis, and on the residence life staff. She was one of the only black students in her science classes. Outside of practice we barely saw her. She was always rushing from lab to practice, from the end of a road trip back to the lab to check on the rats that were part of her research study. She told me years later that she thought she kept so busy off the court to ward off the stereotype that she was a black athlete who was at Davidson only to play basketball. Most of my black teammates, independently of each other, told me they had felt similar pressures.

Christina had an uphill climb against the stereotypes she felt our Tennessee-bred head coach held against black people, which she thought influenced the kinds of players Coach Katz recruited. Katz had a narrowly defined view, Christina said, of what was acceptable. Christina fitted that "acceptable" view, as did the other black players on our team, and the way she presented herself on and off the court was carefully calculated.

"She didn't want anyone with braids or cornrows, weird bandannas or lookin' like thugs on her team," Christina told me years later. "She wanted the girly girls, the smart girls. I never felt like I could be myself, and I couldn't be too loud, or I couldn't talk a certain way, or I just always had to be the well-behaved black girl. I always had to be the one that wasn't too outspoken, who listened, 'cause if not, I'd be like those other girls. She didn't want to recruit the problem girls."

Another black Davidson player said that knowing she was one of a minority of black women in the Southern Conference imbued her with a sense of responsibility to invalidate negative stereotypes about black female athletes—that they were aggressive, scary, "diesel," rough. She wore makeup, tried to be softer.

Coach Katz did not outright tell us how we should look. We wanted to look pretty and put together because she herself always did, and we got positive reinforcement from her when we did, too. We all would do almost anything for praise from Coach Katz because it might mean more playing time. Christina, who wore braids all the time in high school, stopped wearing them at college. When she pushed her hair into a ponytail instead of wearing it down, she says Coach Katz said to her, "Oh, we can take you seriously now!" By her senior year Christina's personal rebellion was to always wear her hair in an Afro.

On the big night, in our little black dresses and heels and flats, makeup and hair done, we made our way down the hall to the training room, where we were supposed to gather. We would walk out onto the court from the entrance at that end. Coach Katz and Coach McKillop had already been out there, hyping up the crowd. Some of Coach Katz's greatest strengths were her genuine, contagious enthusiasm for women's basketball and for Davidson and her ability to get the community excited about us.

We would be introduced to the court two by two, each men's player, in a white suit with a jaunty matching fedora and cane, with a women's player or two on his arm. I was not yet feminist enough to be indignant about the patriarchal context behind this image. I thought it was cute and fun.

The guys came out of their locker room, and we all milled around, feeling awkward in our dresses and heels and suits. We were two dozen tall, muscular college kids who looked like we were headed to cocktail hour in a place where we all usually wore baggy shorts and sweaty jerseys, cut soggy bits of tape off our ankles, bandaged our blisters.

We listened to the crowd as the players were introduced. I did not know how many people were out there, but it sounded like a lot, a few thousand at least. Marketing had done all right.

"And now, please welcome two more members of your junior class, Alyssa Petteys aaaaaannnnd . . ."

We whooped for Lyss from the back hallway as she and Stephen started walking up the stairs. The announcer paused for dramatic effect, and the crowd responded with an intake of breath, preparing itself to lose its collective mind.

"Stephennnnnnnnnnnnnnnnnnnnnnnn . . ."

Lyss and Steph strolled out of the dark hallway and out of our sight as "Currrrrrrryyyyyyyyyyyyyyyyyy" blared from the microphone and the crowd roared.

Since there were four women's players and three men's players in our class, Coop and I would both walk out with A.J. A few minutes later, it was our turn. Each group was supposed to do something special and silly together when they strode onto the strip of red carpet, like bridesmaids and groomsmen do when they come out at a wedding reception. Coop and I had decided that we were going to fight over A.J. We walked up the stairs when our names were called, me unsteady in my heels and clinging to A.J.'s elbow, all three of us squinting in the spotlight. Little kids lined up behind the ropes on either side of the red carpet, pretending to take our picture, or maybe actually taking our picture, I couldn't tell. This was quite a production. I set my feet and yanked A.J. toward me, hard. Coop yanked him back. I knew I was stronger than Coop, so I pulled A.J. even harder this time, and her response was puny in comparison.

"Okay, Otto," I heard her voice from A.J.'s other side. "Okay, stop." I stopped tugging, all three of us waved and grinned, and we kept walking.

Team lore had it that once, the Davidson women ran out for warm-ups at the College of Charleston and heard a guy in the crowd exclaim, "Wow! They actually all look straight!"

Despite increasing public acceptance of the LGBTQ (lesbian, gay, bisexual, trans, and queer) population across the country, at the time not a single Division I women's basketball coach out of about 350 was openly gay. Many straight coaches across the nation still emphasized their own straightness and the heteronormativity of their programs to recruits and their parents as a recruiting tactic. Some parents worried that if their daughters played for a gay coach or had gay teammates, they would "convert" to lesbianism, and the recruiting world preyed upon this fear. Nobody ever said to me outright, "Don't go to that school because the coach is a lesbian," or, "There are lesbians on the team, and they will turn you into a lesbian, too," but it was clear in retrospect that sexual identity politics lurked in the underbelly of the mid-2000s women's basketball recruiting scene.

Heather Barber, a sports psychology professor at the University of New Hampshire, told *ESPN: The Magazine* in 2011 that "'family focused' recruiting is used as a subtle weapon against programs led by unmarried female coaches: 'When coaches say things like, "We're a family," one aspect of that is "We support each other," and that's good. But it crosses the line when programs talk about "family values," then put a definition on what families look like. That becomes code for "We reflect a straight program."'"

By emphasizing that at least one of her players dated men when she told us about Erin and the quarterback, for example, Coach Katz did not flat-out say that lesbian or bisexual or transgender players weren't welcome in her program. She may, however, have consciously or subconsciously been using code that implied it. She didn't have to say anything at all to recruits about whom her players dated, but she did. Her comment to my mom and Mrs. Lowery about wanting to call the parents of players she thought were gay was outright homophobia.

According to Davidson staff who work with the college's LGBTQ population, North Carolina is also one of the least-friendly U.S. states in which to be LGBTQ. If my gay and bisexual teammates didn't fit the mold, they made it look like they did, hiding same-sex relationships and dressing with feminine flair. As a whole we came off as a bunch of girls who liked dresses and knew our way around a makeup bag, got good grades, wore our hair long and neat, did not want to get too bulky in the weight room, and dated boys.

After the red-carpet introductions, it was time for a quick change in the training room into our costumes. The freshman dance was traditionally supposed to be a little bit embarrassing. For the men, that meant the white suits they had worn for the red carpet with their white home jerseys underneath—hardly embarrassing at all. For Taylor, Olivia, Coop, and me, all white women, it meant something much more flamboyant: our old floor-length prom dresses, sparkly gold elbow-length gloves, and Afro wigs. I hammed it up, especially on the body roll, which I'd never quite been able to master. The next night when the program aired, my parents watched it at home in Pennsylvania.

"Well, that just looks like an example of hazing, right there, with these Davidson freshmen," my mom said college basketball analyst Jay Bilas declared when he saw us. Our ESPN premiere, ladies and gentlemen.

After our team dance in little black dresses and high-tops to Rihanna's "Disturbia," we ran downstairs to swipe off our makeup and change into our uniforms and ankle braces while the men scrimmaged.

Much of the crowd filtered out once the men had played their short scrimmage, so the stands were much emptier by the time we took the court. Eleven minutes later, without fanfare, our own buzzer sounded, a few people clapped, and we trotted to the locker room to shower.

My first college basketball season had officially begun.

4 Heading Home

Ashley made it through Night with the 'Cats, but she was hurting. The team had started to suspect something was wrong with her during our conditioning tests that fall. Two of the tests were to run a timed mile and a timed two-mile. We ran on the Greenway, a long, lightly forested loop around town. The coaches had measured out what they thought was a two-mile course and marked where we should start and stop.

We hustled through the trail, trying to keep up with Jenni and Christina, the two people on the team who had the least trouble with running. As we panted and wheezed, Coach Katz rode a bike along the route, enthusiastically offering encouragement, her strong perfume enveloping us in thick, sickly-sweet clouds as she whizzed by.

The course could not have been two full miles. They must have measured it wrong. I was barely running sub-eight-minute miles at the time but tore through this distance in less than thirteen minutes, beating the required time for post players by more than three minutes. Most of us set personal records.

Ashley failed. Her knee was so unstable she could barely run. It kept popping in and out of place. She walked most of the way, finishing in twenty minutes.

The anterior cruciate ligament, more commonly known as the ACL, is a small tendon that crosses in front of the knee, attaching the femur to the tibia, to help prevent the tibia from moving too far forward. The ACL can tear if the body changes direction and the knee is locked, like in a quick stop and pivot or in landing wrong from a jump, with the weight unbalanced or the body twisted. It's a season-ending injury. Recovery usually involves surgery to reconstruct the ligament and about six months of rehab. Women's basketball players have some of the highest risk of any athlete for ACL tears, which account for about 5 percent of our injuries. They are so notorious they have almost become a cliché.

Ashley had torn hers the previous September, early in her freshman year. She underwent reconstructive graft surgery with a piece of her hamstring, a common procedure, and sat out and rehabbed all year. Not long after the Greenway test, about a year after her first tear, Ashley found out that the hamstring graft had torn, sidelining her for the second year in a row.

As athletes, athletic trainers, doctors, and coaches learn more about the structural and hormonal factors that might help cause ACL tears, they can also work to help prevent them. By the time I arrived at Davidson, our coaches and athletic trainers knew significantly more about ACL tears than they had known a few years before. Many of our workouts in the weight room and on the court were specifically engineered to strengthen our hamstring, butt, and core muscles to support our knees as we jumped, landed, and moved laterally.

Ashley's body might have predisposed her to the danger of this particular injury, though. One day when she was nine, her family, who lived on a military base in Hawaii, went for a hike. She and her mom got caught in a rock slide. Ashley's best friend was walking next to her one second and in the next second had disappeared. She was one of nine people who died in the accident. Doctors amputated about half of Ashley's left foot. She was fitted for a prosthetic and never stopped playing sports. Most of us usually forgot about Ashley's little foot, except occasionally when she was barefoot in the locker room, waiting for the shower. She usually forgot about it, too.

"When I was a kid, I was just like, I'm different," she told me years later. "Nothing's gonna stop me. I'm just gonna be better than people at things so you would never think anything was wrong with me."

But the confirmation early in her sophomore year of Ashley's second ACL tear sent her into a spiral of frustration about the rock slide, an event she had accepted until that moment. After a stellar high school career in which she became her school's all-time leading scorer, Ashley—who had already fought through so much—learned she would have to sit her first two years of college. She was crushed. She was lost. She started checking out.

Erin had torn her own ACL just eight months earlier and was now fighting her way back onto the court, trying to prove herself for her senior year. She wanted Ashley to know she understood her pain. That was the kind of person Erin was.

"We know you're here," we all wanted Ashley to know, "even though you're hurt and can't play right now. We see you."

"Shhhhh," Erin whispered that fall as she, Olivia, Taylor, Lyss, and I climbed the stairs of Ashley's dorm, giggling, dressed entirely in black, faces covered, ninja style. We had just left a preseason workout, so we were freshly showered and a little creaky. Our wet hair dripped down our backs and we all groaned a bit as we climbed the old stairs. Olivia's car was parked outside, ready for our escape.

The five of us crept down Ashley's hall. We burst into her room, growling and yelling and banging on the walls, making as big a scene as we could, diverting from our ninja tactics. There was a small shriek from the back of the room. Ashley was standing by her desk wearing a bra and jeans. Her roommate and our informant, Josie, cracked up in the corner. Josie had told us Ashley was home, but we did not know she was going to be half naked.

"You're coming with us," Erin grunted at Ashley, sticking to the plan as best she could. "Close your eyes and put a shirt on, now!"

"Yeah!" the rest of us chimed in from behind her, making our voices deep and gravelly, puffing out our chests, throwing our arms in the air. "Yeah, put a shirt on!" "Yeah, you're coming with us!"

Ashley's look of frightened confusion relaxed into a grin. She had recognized our team sneakers.

"Yes, sir," she said, glancing around for a T-shirt, finding a red one with Spider-Man on it, and yanking it over her head. Her face popped out of the collar, eyes closed.

"This is a kidnapping," Erin announced with gusto, wrapping a shirt around Ashley's head to blindfold her and then tying her hands together with a headband. Lyss was snapping pictures like a paparazzo.

"Okay," said Ashley agreeably. Without warning Ashley what we were about to do, Olivia, Taylor, Erin, and I surrounded her and lifted her off the ground. Taylor and I each held a thigh, and Erin and Liv supported her from behind. She was so light. Ashley screamed. Josie looked on amusedly. Lyss took more pictures.

We grunted good-bye to Josie and inched carefully back down the stairs. Our vision wasn't great due to our choice of costume, and we carried a rather unwieldy, precious, and already damaged package. Because I was the one holding the leg with the torn ACL, keeping it steady was the most important part of my job. Lyss followed us, still taking pictures, plenty of action shots. After several tense minutes, Taylor and I pushed open the door, and we blasted out into the early-evening light, hustling Ashley down the soft green lawn to our getaway car. Olivia rushed ahead to open the door, and we hoisted Ashley inside.

"Keep that blindfold on," Erin snarled. She climbed into the back-seat, and Taylor and I sat in the middle with the prisoner. Olivia drove. Lyss rode shotgun.

Olivia rolled down the windows.

"Mmmmm, the air feels good," Ashley squealed, turning her blind-folded face to the sun.

"Shut *up!*"

We flew over a speed bump.

"Oops, that was a body," Liv yelled. "I just ran over a body!"

"Didn't we tell you to be more careful about that?" I shouted back.

Erin held Ashley's hands in the air by the headband. Taylor, Lyss, and I were cracking up. Ashley screamed good-naturedly, playing along. We hit another speed bump.

"There goes another body!" Olivia howled.

Finally, we made it to Ashley's favorite restaurant, where most of the team was waiting for us, all dressed in black. We took Ashley's blindfold off and showed her the cake we had made her.

"We love you, Ash," Erin said, giving her a long, tight squeeze.

Ashley beamed all night and thanked us over and over. Inside, though, she felt a little sad. She knew we meant well, but she could barely see herself these days. She had lost basketball and, with it, much of her identity. She was mentally and emotionally so far away. She did not want to be pitied. She did not want to be different. How had we not understood that?

We could have used Ashley's ball-handling skills when we played at the University of South Carolina toward the beginning of that season. This sacrificial-lamb business usually accounted for several of our early games, before we got into conference play, and helped our budget. A big school would often give us, a mediocre midmajor program, several thousand dollars in honorarium to travel to its gym and get stomped in front of its crowd so the team could start drumming up support for the home games that really mattered. Basically, we were their practice squad.

South Carolina's coach was three-time Olympic gold medalist and women's basketball goddess Dawn Staley. I had grown up reading books about this woman. I was impossibly starstruck.

Once Davidson started playing home games, the introduction of our starting lineups fell markedly short of my childhood daydreams. We would play some tinny music and the starters would scuttle off the bench one at a time and high-five everyone, and the two hundred people in the stands would clap dutifully and that would be it.

When we played at the big-time schools, they did it their way, the dreamy way. They turned the lights off in the whole arena so that their starters could run out into a dramatic spotlight while an inspirational slow-motion highlight video with a heavy-hype soundtrack rolled on the jumbotron. Because we were the guests, we were introduced first, to build the suspense—without the jumbotron, the music, or the spotlight, of course.

So we went through our own routine in pretty substantial darkness. Whitney, at six feet two, high-tenned five-foot-eight Jenni and turned away with her arms still raised. Jenni didn't see her. Our starting center's elbow smashed into our starting point guard's nose.

Jenni heard the crunching noise and doubled over, clutching her face.

"And now, the starting lineup for your South Carolina Gamecocks!" the announcer bellowed as spotlights flashed wildly around the arena. Heavy bass pounded from the sound system. Our athletic trainer, Meghan, sprang into action from the end of the bench as the rest of us crowded around Jenni in a confused, stumbling, half-blind clump.

"Starting at guard . . . ," the announcer boomed. The South Carolina player's face and upper body appeared on the huge screen, gazing down at us, cool and intimidating. It was a video. She batted a basketball back and forth between her hands, settled it on her hip, lifted her chin, narrowed her eyes.

Back on the ground, Meghan riffled through her big duffel bag full of medical supplies, pulled out some latex gloves, and snapped them on. She wiped the blood from Jenni's face with a handful of gauze. The nose was clearly broken. Amid the chaos, Coach Katz was trying to give her standard last-minute pep talk. Someone used a sneaker to swipe at the droplets of Jenni's blood on the floor in front of the bench.

"Starting at forward, a six-foot-four-inch senior from Bishopville, South Carolina—"

Jenni set her jaw, and Meghan shoved what looked like a stringless tampon into each of her nostrils, leaving the ends dangling out, stemming the bleeding. They would have to set the bones later. We had a game to play.

"Number 24," the announcer continued, "Demetress Adams!"

Meghan handed Jenni a plastic mask that looked like a clear version of Batman's, without the ears. It would help protect her nose from further injury.

The game started. We could not break their press, and Jenni could barely see through the mask to dribble. There were about 2,200 fans in the arena. They heckled Emma—a shooting guard, not a point guard—as she tried to bring the ball up the court, turning it over nine times by herself.

"Hey, Goldilocks," they shouted at her. "Y'all are terrible. Where's Steph Curry?"

"That's the dumbest heckle of all time," I muttered to Olivia at the end of the bench. "He's not on our team. Why would he be here?"

The final score: University of South Carolina 68, Davidson 47. We had thirty-one turnovers, and at practice the next day we ran sprints for it.

Our next game, four days later, was at seventeenth-ranked Vanderbilt in Nashville, Tennessee. It was a four-team Thanksgiving tournament. The night before the game Vanderbilt hosted Thanksgiving dinner in its athlete cafeteria for us and the other visiting teams, Saint Joseph's and Virginia Tech. It was the freshman players' first Thanksgiving away from home, something we would have to get used to. The coaches made us climb into the hotel's outdoor pool one night as a replacement for a training-room ice bath—the cold water was supposed to help keep our muscles from getting too sore. We huddled together with our hoods up, laughing and complaining.

The freshmen were learning our places on the team and our team's place in the larger order of Division I women's basketball. We lost the game 82–50. The next day we lost the consolation game, 78–68, to Saint Joseph's.

Coop, our walk-on, played two minutes in the Vanderbilt game. She got one rebound. She took one shot and missed it. She didn't play at all against Saint Joe's.

"You're scared to play, Coop," Olivia told her afterward. The visitors' locker room was full of CPR dummies, stacked high on shelves to the ceiling, their frozen faces leering down at us.

"I know my place," Coop responded, exhaustingly self-deprecating. "I'm a practice player. My time to play basketball is at practice and during warm-ups." She made the same time commitment we did, and she didn't have a scholarship.

By the end of the fall semester, we were 4-6 on the season. We'd lost five of our first six games and then snagged a couple of conference wins.

Coach Katz had a wonderful tradition of taking her seniors "home," scheduling an out-of-conference game or two near where they grew up, so that the seniors could, in a way, say thank you to the people and places that raised them. At 7:30 the morning after finals ended, six days before Christmas, we loaded up the bus for our drive from Davidson to Cincinnati for Erin's homecoming trip to play two games there, at Xavier University and the University of Cincinnati.

We were dazed and sleep deprived from weeks of studying and paper writing as we plodded down the bus aisle that morning, freshmen in our seats toward the front, nearest the coaches, upperclassmen in the back. I was bent over, slinging my backpack on my seat, when Erin squeezed down the bus aisle past me, stuck her hand between my thighs, and flapped it around.

"Floppy fish!" she said brightly, the offending hand already on the other side of the aisle, flicking Olivia in the boobs through her team sweatshirt. "Titty tap! Morning, 'Cats." We groaned. Anytime you got on the bus you had to remember to protect yourself from floppy fish and titty taps, an old team tradition Erin had kept alive, but it was early and we were tired and had forgotten.

Erin was goofy and hardworking. She had a wide, warm smile and was quick to riotous laughter and knock-you-backward hugs. She had been our unofficial camp leader that summer. She brimmed with kid-friendly games that were somehow also a blast for us as counselors. She was also devoutly Christian, having discovered her faith her freshman year at Davidson with the help of a couple of her older teammates. She and Emma were both active in Campus Outreach, an organization that trained students to be Christian faith leaders. They both also regularly went to FCA—Fellowship of Christian Athletes—meetings. They usually invited a teammate or two to join them.

Erin had more spirit and more love to give than anyone I had ever met. She made the freshmen feel like we belonged. We felt so cool hanging out with a senior. She lived in a little yellow house just off campus, and she would invite us over to watch *High School Musical* and *The Bachelor* and YouTube videos. We baked pizza bagels and french-toast sticks.

Erin was smart and athletic and a perfectionist on the court. She was also one of the team's hardest workers, a force on the boards, and good at getting up and down the floor and taking charges. She was a tenacious defender. She had fought back from a junior-year ACL tear and earned her way into the starting lineup opposite Whitney at center.

Erin had been a wound-up player in high school. She was so determined to get everything right that she played every game under a high level of stress and once got three technical fouls in one tournament. When she got to college and settled into her faith, as she explained it, she calmed down. Love for her teammates and her sport and life in general poured out of her. It was contagious. After her ACL tear her junior year, she finally understood that her role on the team was not to be the leading scorer. Instead, she was going to be vocal. She was going to be encouraging. She was going to be, as she put it, "the biggest spanker there ever was," which meant enthusiastically slapping teammates' butts when we did something well.

A lot of Erin's friends from high school hadn't left Ohio for college, and if you didn't get out of Ohio for college, she explained, you might not get out of Ohio. I felt the same way about Pennsylvania. Erin was proud to have made her way elsewhere, proud to have gotten a full athletic scholarship, proud to have toughed it out through three and a half years at a difficult school. She was excited to go back to show her people she was thriving, that she was in a good place and was contributing to it.

Tickets to Davidson women's basketball games were cheap—adult admission to our home games that year was $4—but it was still a big deal for us to put people on our "pass list." We each got four complimentary tickets for friends or family per game, so Erin borrowed slots on other people's pass lists to get all her people in for free. Her teammates could not wait to see the place where our beloved Erin had grown up. Many of us were also from the Northeast, so some of our families would be in Ohio to watch the games and then drive us home for the holidays.

The bus trip was supposed to take eight hours, including a stop for lunch. It took eleven. Most of the team slept all morning, through the three back-to-back movies that fuzzed on the tiny bus TV screens. Finals on top of practice had worn us out, and more than one of us had pulled an all-nighter in the past week. The temperature on the bus fluctuated dramatically, from uncomfortably hot to freezing cold. My butt hurt from sitting. I moved my pillow and blanket to the floor. I was more comfortable there, because I could stretch out. At one point I opened my eyes and glanced around under the seats and saw that several teammates had joined me down there. This made getting to the bathroom in the back of the bus an adventure, navigating with much weaving and ducking and climbing the maze of long gray-sweatpants-clad legs strewn across the aisles. The bathroom was out of hand sanitizer.

Sometime after our lunch at Panera, we sat in near-standstill traffic for almost three hours, presumably a result of the holiday season. Our smelly bus bathroom earned a new level of respect when we saw a man ahead of us dash from his car, pee on the side of the road, and sprint to hop back in as the line of cars inched forward.

Finally, we pulled into the bus bay at Xavier's Cintas Center. Our game was the next day at noon. Right now it was time for practice.

Much had been made of the dominance of a few Division I women's basketball teams throughout the 2000s. One was the University of Connecticut. By 2008 Coach Geno Auriemma and the Huskies had won five national championships, including three in a row in 2002, 2003, and 2004. The University of Tennessee Lady Volunteers had qualified for every NCAA women's basketball tournament in its history. Those players and coaches were the ones people had written books about, the books I had devoured during my teenage years. There were a few other successful schools—Notre Dame, Maryland, North Carolina (UNC)—but nobody was consistently on the level of those two.

The five biggest and best conferences for several collegiate sports, namely basketball and football, were sometimes called the "Power Five"—the Big Ten, the Big 12, the Pac-10 (now the Pac-12), the Atlantic Coast Conference (ACC), and the Southeast Conference (SEC). The

Big East (UConn and Cincinnati's conference) was also high up there. About one tier down sat a few almost-as-good teams in conferences slightly below the Powers. One of those next-tier conferences was the Atlantic 10, which both Duquesne and Xavier played in at the time. Xavier's women had been ranked twenty-first in the country just a few weeks earlier.

Technically, we all played under the same big Division I umbrella, but we would be kidding ourselves at little midmajor Davidson if we thought we could compete on a night-in, night-out basis with the UNCs and the Stanfords and the Baylors and the UConns of our world. We were proud to be Division I women's basketball players, but we were also aware of the realities of our situation in the middle and lower rungs of the division and aware of the gap between us. We put a lot of time, emotion, and effort into our sport and loved it intensely, but we didn't have quite the ability the Power Five players had. We also wanted full, diverse lives outside of and after college basketball. Most of my teammates were secure in that decision. After spending my teenage years—my recruiting years—wanting to be one of those girls at the top, I, too, was slowly settling into the reality that my parents had been right: the midmajors were probably a better fit for me.

We walked into gyms like Vanderbilt's and Xavier's and knew a few things deep down: there was always a possibility for an upset, and we were probably better than they thought we were. There was also the distinct possibility that we would get creamed. Mostly, we thought we could be the next big upset. We always thought we had a chance. We could pull it off, come together for this great achievement. We never lost that desire to be the victorious underdog, the nerdy bookish kids beating the five-star recruits, the way our men's team had done. They might be bigger and faster and more talented, but maybe we could be smarter, maybe we could play harder, maybe we could pull it off.

Warming up for the game, though, we did not look like we belonged in that gym. This was in large part due to some of us freshmen, who could not possibly muster the coolness to act like we had been there before. We were a mess. We stood in the layup line and gaped up at our faces on the jumbotron until Erin hissed at us to stop. I tripped and fell during one drill. While she was doing defensive slides in another, Olivia's warm-up pants came unbuttoned at the waist and fell down.

We were losing from the first fifteen seconds of the game, but we managed to keep their lead between ten and thirteen points the whole first half. They had a six-foot-six post player; our tallest player was just six feet two in comparison. On our first possession Erin turned the ball over. Three minutes later, she fouled a Xavier player while crashing the boards on a missed shot by Christina, and Coach Katz subbed her out during the first media time-out. Erin was reverting to her high school self. The steady hustle with which she usually played had been knocked asunder by her nerves at being home. The anxiety of being on the notorious "short leash" came rushing back.

When a player is on a short leash, her coach yanks her from the game the moment she makes a mistake, and it is the most anxiety-inducing possible way to play basketball. It is paralyzing. If a player misses a bunny layup, she should be hustling back on defense, not cringing because she knows she's about to come out of the game. But Coach Katz regularly had about half of us on one- or two-mistake leashes, Erin and me included. I had never been on a short leash in my life until college, because my high school and AAU coaches had always trusted me to work hard and make up for my mistakes, get my game back on track. Deep down I knew I was a good, smart player. Once the short leash came out, though, I played frantically and without confidence. I played to not mess up.

It was easy to see the difference between the short-leash kids and the players who had, for whatever reason—it often seemed arbitrary— earned the freedom to play loose. Some people just walked in the light. The short-leashers, unlike the light-walkers, tried too hard to make a quick impact on the game and prove ourselves so we could stay in. We got selfish. We played tight. In my panic I usually forgot the plays, which I had a hard time remembering even when I was calm. I would try so hard that I shot layups off the backboard like they were baseball passes.

"Am I in the right spot?" the short-leash brain would say. It never stopped:

Should I be here, or should I be a little closer to the baseline? Who am I setting the screen for? Who am I setting the screen *on*? Is there a teammate coming over here to set a double screen with me, or am I supposed to go set a double screen with somebody else? If so, who? Or is it not a double screen at all? What kind of screen is it supposed to be? Is it a flare screen? Is it an elevator screen? What if I set the wrong kind of screen? Am I supposed to take a few steps away and then pivot back and set the screen, or just stand here? Who am I passing it to? Is it supposed to be a bounce pass or a chest pass? What if I make the wrong kind of pass and it gets stolen? After I pass it, do I set a down screen or another flare screen? Then where do I go? Who is supposed to take the shot? Do I take it? What if I miss?

We had dozens of different plays. Basketball had always come naturally to me; I understood what to do on an instinctive, reactive, visceral level, not an analytical one. I wasn't used to having to think this much about every move I made. I could never get comfortable, and I wasn't alone.

As soon as short-leashers knew we'd made a mistake—a turnover, a foul, a missed box out or layup, a crucial pause to remember a forgotten play—our hearts would drop, and we would look immediately to the bench and watch Coach Katz turning her back on the court to pull a player to the scorers' table to replace us. It was a terrible feeling. It was evident in our body language: slumped shoulders, dead eyes, the moment we knew we'd lost our chance, remembered our coaches didn't trust us.

A Jenni three-pointer to start the second half cut Xavier's lead to six. Erin was still playing tight. Then Xavier started pulling away, and fast. The score went from 34–28 at the nineteen-minute mark to 50–30 three minutes later.

Coach Katz was livid. She spun on her high heel and glared down the bench. "Now, which of y'all is gonna go in this game right now and make a difference?"

We all shifted awkwardly in our cushy seats, unsure whether this was a rhetorical question. It was not. Coach Katz yanked four of the five starters and replaced them with all four of the freshmen, leaving Jenni in at the point. We kept that arrangement for about five minutes, and although thankfully for all of us things didn't get much worse, they also did not get better; Xavier's lead hovered around twenty points. With ten minutes left and the score 64–39, Coach Katz called time-out and subbed a couple of the starters back in.

The five girls in the game sat down on the bench, their place during time-outs, and Coach Katz squatted in front of them. The rest of us filed around to stand behind the bench to try to listen to what she said, but she was hard to hear from there. I grabbed my water bottle from Meghan's waiting hand and teethed it glumly.

When my brothers and I were little and our parents took us to Saint Francis games, my brother Zachary, the middle child, always brought his toy cars and trucks to play with in the bleachers. When he was about three years old, he started to perk up anytime the announcer called "time-out." He had no interest in the game itself but always sat up from his toys and watched attentively as the players walked off the court and sat on the bench to listen to their coach.

"Who had a time-out, Daddy?" Zach would ask.

"The green team," my dad would say.

Zach would sit quietly and observe the scene, thumb jammed in his mouth. When the players took the court again, he would go back to his trucks. It didn't take us long to figure out that to Zach, a time-out meant that you had done something wrong and you had to stop playing and go sit down for a while. How right he was.

For the rest of the game Coach Katz played Taylor and me, and a little of Olivia, in a heavy rotation. Xavier's lead ballooned. With fewer than two minutes left in the game, they were up 84–48. The final score was 84–60. They had outscored us in the paint 34–8—and three of the four freshmen spent most of our time in the paint.

"We're never gonna win with Coop playing," the coaches said in the locker room, "try as she might." I glanced at Coop, who kept her face steady, staring determinedly at the coaches. Coach Bailey loved Coop. Bailey got so excited when Coop scored in practice. I knew the loss wasn't just Coop's fault. Coach Bailey had to know that, too. Nobody had been in a position for success today. What were we supposed to have learned here?

"But if you all worked as hard or cared as much as Coop, we'd win," the coaches continued. It was always awkward when they lifted one of us up to put the rest of us down, a motivational tactic they used frequently. Was the player in the light supposed to stand up for her teammates or accept the praise in the hope that she might win more favor with the coaches?

Almost always we bowed our heads and accepted the praise. You let them compliment you. You didn't do anything. Your teammates would understand. It was simple: the coaches had the power, and if you fought the power, you might not play.

Erin told me that once during her sophomore year, when she thought she was playing pretty hard and pretty well, Coach Katz came in at halftime and said to Whitney, "Whit, if Erin had half the talent that you have, she'd be an All-American." It broke Erin's heart to hear that. She felt disrespected. By the end of halftime tears were streaming down her face, but she had at least four hands on her back comforting her. Her teammates knew how she would receive that comment.

Another time in practice five-foot-five Coop had gotten a rebound over six-foot Olivia. "Well, Olivia, maybe I should give your scholarship to Coop," Coach Katz said.

She threatened me, too, when Coop beat me off the dribble to the basket in a different practice. UConn's Geno Auriemma told *Sports Illustrated* that he says similar things to his scholarship players about his walk-ons. It is supposed to be motivational. Katz wasn't going to actually take my scholarship away.

The coaches left the locker room. We undressed quietly.

As long as I had been a member of the Davidson team, we had never showered completely naked on the road. In our home locker room there were four attached but separate showers, each with its own curtain. But most visitors' locker room showers had open floor plans, a couple of poles sticking out of the floor with shower heads all around them, and no privacy.

I didn't know why we never took all our clothes off to shower. No one ever talked about it. I assumed it was some sort of modesty thing, but getting clean was an elaborate production every time. We would strip down to the sweaty red-and-white sports bras and Spandex shorts we wore under our uniforms and shove our soapy loofahs underneath them, then pull them away from our bodies to rinse, and let them snap back into place. When we got out of the shower, we would dry off, wrap towels around ourselves, peel off the wet bra and Spandex from underneath the towel, and then crumple up the soaked undergarments and shove them into a plastic bag and shove that wet bag into our duffels.

That day in Cincinnati we all, especially Erin, jumped through these showers and raced back out to the court to see our families. We needed some loving.

The next day, a Saturday, after a practice in Cincinnati's gym, we all gathered at Erin's parents' house. The men's team was playing Purdue in Indianapolis, and the game would be broadcast on CBS. It was still a big deal for us to see the black-and-red on the big screen, on a big network, so Erin's parents had set up spaces for us to sit in their living room and watch. The men lost. The game wasn't even close.

The next day at 2:00 p.m. we faced Cincinnati, a foe as tough as Xavier. We took an early lead, 11–3, and kept the game close for most of the first half, but ended up losing 60–42. Our record fell to 4-8.

Erin, who had a high school rival playing for Cincinnati, looked much more like herself, grabbing nine rebounds. Coach Katz had thankfully abandoned the notion that playing all the freshmen simultaneously might work, but I still played about half the game. I had such a hard time remembering the plays that I screwed up the offense several times by running to the wrong spot.

The postgame locker room was quiet again, but it had been quieter. Xavier and Cincinnati were both so good—Xavier was at the top of its conference and Cincinnati played in the Big East. There wasn't much shame in losing to them, was there? Anyway, wasn't this good preparation for conference play?

"Our freshmen," I heard Coach Katz say in her postgame speech, "do not want to win."

I frowned up at her, confused. Of course we wanted to win. What was she saying? What was she really saying? I knew I needed to work on remembering the plays. Was that what she meant? If that's what she meant, why didn't she say so? Two days ago she had been blaming the upperclassmen. Now she was mad at the freshmen? Why didn't she just say she was mad at all of us? Taylor, Olivia, and Coop had all played six or fewer minutes that game. Coach Katz could not possibly be blaming them. I had played about half the game. So was this all on me then? That must be what she meant. She meant I had let Erin down.

I had let Erin down.

"Hustle through the showers, 'Cats," Coach Katz continued. "We got a long drive home."

The coaches left. The locker room was silent again but for the sounds of us rustling through our bags for our shower stuff.

"I'm so excited to go home," Coop mumbled. Secretly, I agreed with her. We needed a break. I couldn't wait to have five whole days with my family and no basketball and no coaches.

Christina, who had been leaning over her duffel bag in her sports bra, stood up and glared at Coop. "Well, I'm glad *you're* excited to go home, Coop," she snapped.

Coop started to cry. "I didn't—I didn't mean . . . ," she fumbled. "I'm sorry, Chris. If I could have done more, I would have."

Christina's face softened. She had learned long ago to tune out pre-game and postgame speeches to avoid getting her feelings hurt. Coop had not yet acquired that trick. Freshmen took everything seriously. "It's okay, Coop," Christina said.

Coop started ripping at the Velcro that held her shoulder brace, staring determinedly at the floor, tears welling in her eyes. Christina walked over, hugged Coop, and patted her on the back.

Christina hadn't meant to snap. In fact, she was feeling similarly. She knew we all needed a break. At the same time, as a senior, she also felt a gnawing sense of urgency. We were having a lousy season so far, and it had been a horrible game. As hard as everything was, every time we played, every time we practiced, it cut away at the little time

Christina had left as a basketball player. She needed time off, too, but her career clock was ticking.

The freshmen were supposed to be the last to shower. When I got out there was a strange tension in the locker room. I couldn't tell whether the upperclassmen were mad at us. I wasn't ready to talk to Erin or anyone yet. I gathered up my stuff, went out to the stands, and found my mom and brothers, my chin trembling.

"Can we go home now?" I asked them. I cried in the car for an hour. Then for every day of our quick break at home, I studied the playbook. It was Christmas, but I would learn these plays. I would not let my seniors down.

We kept losing, our record hovering around .500, and a common refrain from Coach Katz was that the underclassmen did not care enough. Erin and Christina sometimes secretly agreed. At the end of January, the freshmen got together and wrote our seniors an email. We wanted to explain ourselves. We wanted them to know that even though we still had three more years, three more chances, we wanted a championship now, for them. No matter a team's record during the regular season, everyone started at 0-0 in the playoffs. We still had a chance.

"Rule #76: No excuses—play like a champion," it began, quoting the movie *Wedding Crashers*.

Erin and Chris–

Talk is shit, obviously, so we're gonna make this quick. But when the people you admire most are disappointed in you—well, that lights a fire, so we just wanted to take a hot second to make sure you guys knew that Coach Katz was dead wrong when she said the underclassmen just wanted this year to be over. The freshmen have talked about this since September—we want anything but. We can't imagine playing with anyone but this exact group of people, especially the two of you. If we could pick any two senior leaders in the world, guess who they'd be?

So we're gonna do it, because you guys deserve this champion-ship more than anyone and hell if we don't do everything we can to get it for you.

Love always,
Tay, Otto, Liv and Coop

A little more than a month later, in early March, a Davidson alum donated his private jet for the day, all white leather and rich wood trim, to fly us and the men's team, separately, to the conference tour-nament in Chattanooga. We felt like NBA players. What was normally a five- or six-hour bus ride became a one-hour flight, during which we tried out every seat, guzzled drinks from the fridge, and took dozens of pictures. Lyss donned a headset and sat up front with the pilots, just because she could.

We were a five seed in the tournament out of eleven and were scheduled to play the College of Charleston in the first round, on my mom's birthday. We had lost to the Cougars twice in the regular season. In our conference it was almost impossible to beat a team three times in a row, so we had been counting on that, on getting our revenge.

Our first-round game was at 9:00 a.m., which threw off our rou-tine; we were used to playing in the evenings. We had a sleepy pregame meal at 6:00. Through most of the first half the lead see-sawed back and forth. Just before halftime we lost momentum. A Charleston three-pointer to open the second half brought their lead to ten. With fewer than eight minutes left in the game, thanks to fifteen straight points from Jenni and Christina, we had cut it to two. But a Charleston player hit two quick three-pointers, and we couldn't catch up. We lost by eleven. We didn't get Erin and Chris-tina a championship.

"You know, it's a hard way for seniors to end and leave, and I really hate it for my two, because they've certainly given a lot to Davidson College," Coach Katz said in the postgame press conference. "I really thought we were ready." Her voice was lower and less steady than usual, sober with emotion.

"These two, Erin White and Christina Campbell, were the last of the group that came in that really have turned our program around, and they're gonna be sorely missed," Coach Katz continued. "Someday you'll look up into the eyes of Christina Campbell as your doctor, and I tell ya, you'll be in great hands."

5 Wet Season

A few weeks later, after consulting with Erin and Coach Katz, Coop quit the team. She had never felt like she belonged.

Mackenzie Lynch, then a sophomore, felt alienated in a different way. She watched Erin and Christina's senior season from the sideline, growing increasingly frustrated. She had been a high school basketball star in Indianapolis, arguably the basketball capital of the United States, and once dreamed of playing in the Big Ten conference.

But by the age of nineteen, Mac had torn her ACLs four times, twice on each side, and three times in a row on December 14, an eerie coincidence nobody could satisfactorily explain.

The last time she went down, Mac was a freshman at Davidson, the same year Ashley tore hers for the first time. She flew home to Indianapolis to get her fourth surgery from the orthopedic surgeon who had performed her other three. She woke up afterward, in a recovery room she had been in before, to see him sitting on the end of her bed.

"Mackenzie," he said, "it's not a matter of 'if,' it's a matter of 'when.' And when it happens again, I'm not gonna do your surgery. I view you as one of my daughters, and I would never let my daughter play again."

If Mac wanted a medical disqualification from college basketball, she had it. Even then the NCAA offered her little scholarship protection; although she had gotten injured while playing the sport she was at school to play, if Coach Katz and Davidson decided to take away her scholarship the following year, they could. She could appeal, but the decision was ultimately up to the school.

Mac's parents had had their doubts about her career since her third tear, but her doctor was the first person Mac really took seriously. She thought about it. She rehabbed for the rest of the school year and got tentatively cleared to play, but every workout that summer caused her pain. She still had so much to prove as a college basketball player, but she had not felt like herself since before her third tear.

"What am I doing?" she asked herself one day. She called Coach Katz and told her she couldn't play anymore. "As much as I don't want to do it," Mac told her, "I know it's the right thing to do."

"Mackenzie," Coach Katz said, "you are still gonna be a part of this team. We are going to find a role for you. Your scholarship's not going anywhere."

True to her word, Coach Katz never pulled Mac's scholarship. Because they never had a real conversation after that about what Mac's new sideline role on the team should be, though, she didn't really know what to do next.

As one player said years later, "I believe providing meaning and purpose to a player's role can go a long way." That applied to all of us—starters, bench players, injured players. If we understood what we should do and why we should do it, we could do it better. But we were all busy, and it was easy not to make time for thoughtful conversations about our individual roles.

On the website Mac was listed as a student assistant coach. We also voted her captain that year, her sophomore year. What those titles meant, especially together, she was never quite sure. She felt weird playing a leadership role without actually being able to play. Why should we listen to her?

College expanded my idea of what a leader is. Mac was one. She hid her private battles behind a wide, contagious smile. She sat behind the scorers' table during practices and on the bench for games, keeping stats and offering constructive criticism and encouragement.

The day the season ended, the players who drank started drinking within an hour of the bus's arrival back on campus. We had a policy of dry season on our team. That meant no player could have a single drink, not even a sip, between the day of the first practice and the day of the last game, no exceptions. Coach Katz had not explicitly mentioned this rule. Seniors and captains passed it down, and we rarely discussed it. Basketball season lasted so long that players who partied in the fall and spring—what we called "wet season"—did so with a wild, intense sense of urgency.

There were compulsory mentions of alcohol during our yearly NCAA compliance meetings with the Athletic Department. But mostly I remembered grown-ups putting the fear of God in us about obscure performance-enhancing drugs and point-shaving, things we weren't going to do anyway; nobody was gambling on Davidson women's basketball games. We had all taken an online course about alcohol use before arriving on campus as freshmen, and of course there were presentations during orientation on how to drink safely. But there was no conversation with athletes that addressed our drinking habits specifically. Each team had its own alcohol policies, designed and enforced mostly by the coaches.

There was a lively drinking culture on Davidson's campus—"Work hard, play harder," students liked to say proudly. Through many of the hall counselors, upperclassmen took on roles as "big brothers" and "big sisters" to freshmen. Officially, your big brother was your mentor. Unofficially, he was your booze deliveryman.

I had mixed feelings about dry season, but mostly I hated it. I understood the main argument—that alcohol is bad for the body, it suppresses the immune system, and it inhibits the ability to perform at your highest levels. It makes people eat food they would not normally eat, it affects sleep, and it affects the brain. Since Coach Katz and Davidson were quite literally paying for our bodies, it made sense for us to keep them functioning at the highest level we could.

We were also college students, though, surrounded by alcohol. The men's basketball team didn't have a dry season, so why should we? We saw it as an issue of trust between coaches and players. Our upper-classmen especially chafed at the rule; they were legal drinkers and wanted to be able to have a glass of wine on Christmas Eve with their parents or a few beers after a win. I followed the rule out of respect not for our coaches, but for my upperclassmen. If the big girls did it, so would I.

We hosted our two top recruits on homecoming weekend in September of my sophomore year. We had received emailed files on both of the recruits who would be visiting, Rory Stokes and Megan Reilly. The coaches instructed us that these were their top two choices, so we should study up for their visit, getting to know Megan's and Rory's likes and dislikes and backgrounds. They stressed the importance of making the recruits feel welcome, like they were a perfect fit at Davidson. This was how the process worked on the college's end—we prepped for recruiting visits almost like we prepped for games.

The team wanted to land these two mostly so we did not have to handle any more recruiting visits for the year. We wanted to make the most of these last few fall weekends on campus with our friends, not with high schoolers. We didn't care much about what they were like or how they played unless there was some egregious issue. We just wanted them to act normally, commit, and then go away until the next fall.

There were a few different groups of girls on our team: those who drank a lot with teammates, those who drank mostly with other friends, and those who did not drink at all. That year the players who drank a lot together made up the majority of the team and dominated its social structure. When we didn't want to be inclusive, we weren't. We could be cliquish. We thought alcohol helped us bond—it lowered our inhibitions, made us more open with each other. We knew we had each other's backs at parties. Teammates who did not buy into this mind-set were not always invited to hang out.

As our teammates and their teammates had done before us, we reasoned that, with the recruits' permission, it made sense to expose them to a college team where some people drank and some people did not. It was a reality of college and of sports teams in college. Alcohol's very existence, and whether we decided to drink it, helped define team members' relationships with each other and the way we interacted with the rest of the student body. These recruits—"kittens," as we sometimes called them, as in "baby 'Cats"—might as well start thinking about how they felt about it. They did not have to drink, obviously, but they should see it happening.

One of Davidson's Athletic Department rules that year was that any athlete hosting a recruit was not allowed to drink while the recruit was in her charge—and the recruit, of course, was not allowed to drink, either. There did not seem to be any rules about what the rest of the team could do, and no one had ever really addressed it, but we figured we should plan to drink responsibly at least in front of them. Separately, various groups of teammates pregamed the team party in their dorm rooms and apartments, so that we could have a drink or two with the team and then be good to go for the night when we separated to hang out with boyfriends, girlfriends, crushes, and other friends.

Sometimes nineteen-year-olds do dumb stuff. I ended up going shot for shot, in quick succession, with a teammate because we were rushing to get to the team gathering. My tolerance had gone down during my underage summer at home in Pennsylvania, and I'd had mostly sushi for dinner. By the time we got to the team party and I slumped on a couch there with the recruits and another drink, I had the spins.

At some point I left the team party with a few people and walked down the hill to the Phi Delta Theta fraternity house, where they were hosting a basement party. We hung out with the Phi Delt guys a lot, because that was the house a lot of the football and baseball players were in. But Phi Delt was officially a dry house—they were not allowed to drink. When they had parties they had them in the basement because they were illegal.

Campus police found out about this one and busted it. When the Phi Delt president came thundering down the stairs, telling everyone to get out, I sobered up enough to realize that I had to make my way back to my room, fast, because I was underage. I tumbled out the back door with the crowd, trying to see straight, trying to orient myself, trying to get home.

All of a sudden Mac and her boyfriend, Michael, a football player, were on either side of me, gently but firmly trying to frog-march me up the grassy hill. Jenni was there, too. We had gotten no more than a few dozen feet when my knees buckled and I collapsed in Michael's arms.

When I came to a few seconds later, a cop was walking toward us.

"She's okay, officer," Mac said. "She'll be fine. She's just gotta go to bed. We're taking her."

"No," the officer said to Mac, Michael, and Jenni. "She needs to go to the hospital."

They sat me in a chair in the front yard of the frat house, and the officer questioned me as Jenni stroked my hair. He was not unkind, and I answered everything he asked as politely and honestly as I could—where I had been, what I'd had to drink. He asked if I played basketball. I said yes. I didn't know if it would help or hurt my cause. I could lose my scholarship over this. I had broken the law and gotten caught.

Despite my teammates' and my insistence that I did not need to go to the hospital, that I just needed to sleep it off, the cop said it was "protocol" and called an ambulance. It pulled up to the curb, making a scene with its flashing lights. Jenni and Mac promised they would meet me at the hospital.

"What's the occasion?" one of the nurses asked me dryly. "It's not the season for Frolics yet, is it?" That was Davidson's big day-drinking and party weekend, which happened every spring. They must see a lot of Davidson College students, I realized, which added to my mortification. What these nurses must think of our student body, a bunch of privileged kids whom they saw only when we were too drunk to stand up.

"No, ma'am," I explained quietly. "It's homecoming." She grunted knowingly.

Mac, Jenni, and their boyfriends showed up at the hospital shortly after I did. They sat in the lobby, trying to figure out what to do, as I lay in bed with my IV. They knew I would be fine—I had already sobered up quite a bit and was more embarrassed than anything. Their next concern, as the two team captains, was how we were going to tell Coach Katz what had happened.

"It's gonna be fine," Jenni's boyfriend tried to reassure them. The football team had seen its share of messy recruiting visits. "This happens."

"We can't hide this from Katz, though," said Mac. "Jim's gonna find out first thing Monday morning."

Athletic departments all over the country deal regularly and quietly with the issues of illegal or excessive alcohol use among their athletes and recruits. At Davidson the campus police department copied athletic director Jim Murphy on its Monday-morning reports. When a student-athlete had gotten in trouble and campus police knew about it, Jim Murphy found out too. Our best bet would be to come clean with Coach Katz before Jim got to her.

Jenni and Mac were also concerned about what was happening back on campus without them. Was everyone okay? Was anyone else as drunk as I was? Who was in charge of the recruits?

"Do you think she's gonna take away my scholarship?" I asked Mac in a small voice when she came in to sit with me.

Mac steadily met my gaze. "I don't know, Otto," she said. "But I don't think she'd do that."

Sleepy and mostly sober, I was discharged after a few hours, and Jenni's boyfriend drove us home. Mac made me sleep in her bed that night and came in to talk to me in the morning.

"Good morning, friend," she said gently, smiling, sitting down next to me. "How are you feeling?"

I was wearing her clothes. I propped myself up gingerly under the covers, trying to gauge how bad the headache was, but I shouldn't have worried; the IV had pumped me full of fluids the night before, and I was totally hydrated.

"Hi," I croaked. "I am so, so, so sorry."

"It's okay," she said, putting a hand on my leg.

"Thanks for taking care of me."

"Of course," she said, beaming that big smile of hers. "Stop apologizing. It happens."

I grunted. "I'm still sorry."

"I know you are," she said. "Here's what Jen and I were thinking. Let me know what you think. We think you should call Coach Katz and ask if you can have a meeting with her this morning."

My stomach dropped into my knees. "This morning?" I exclaimed.

Mac nodded sympathetically. "She's gonna find out on Monday morning from Jim," she explained. "We think it'll be better for you if she hears the news from you first."

I slumped back on the pillows. I knew Mac was right. "Will you come with me?" I asked her.

Mac grinned. "Of course," she said.

We called Coach Katz right then and asked if she could come into her office so we could talk to her. Even though it was a Sunday morning, Mac explained, it was important. We made our way up the hill to Baker Sports Complex.

"What's up, Miss Otto?" Coach Katz asked, cheerful but curious, spinning to face me in her office swivel chair. She'd just had breakfast with the recruits and their families and said good-bye, hoping that they would both commit. She didn't usually have to be in her office on Sunday mornings in preseason.

I took a deep breath and explained what had happened, altering the story slightly so it sounded like I had been drinking with "some girls on my hall" rather than with a teammate. I didn't mention the team party. Jenni and Mac had been responsible captains and good friends by going to the hospital with me, and I was so grateful for them. I was totally fine now, and I had not gotten an official citation. I just had to go to one alcohol counseling session, meet with the assistant dean of students, and pay a $25 fine, plus my hospital bill. When I explained that, Coach Katz visibly relaxed. Then she seemed to remember something, and she tensed again.

"Did either of the recruits see this happening or know this was happening?" she asked. Mac and I glanced at each other for a fraction of a second.

We both knew at that point, from Olivia, that she had been walking with Rory past the Phi Delt house when Rory spotted Mac, Jenni, the ambulance lights, and me sitting down, doubled over.

"Oh, look, there's some teammates!" Rory had said to Olivia. "What is happening? Is Otto sick?"

Liv squinted over, realized it was me, and whisked Rory in the other direction. Rory had been totally sober, so she would probably remember everything.

We also knew by now that I was not the only underage basketball player to have gotten sick the night before. At some point Olivia had also found Megan, our other recruit, hanging out with some of the football guys, seen how drunk she was, and started to take her up the hill to bed. Megan's host, our freshman teammate Amber, was nowhere to be found.

Olivia ran into Allie, another freshman, halfway up the hill. "Can you take her back?" Olivia asked, knowing that Allie lived on Amber's hall.

Allie took one look at Megan and agreed. With the help of a few people she ran into on the way, she got Megan into an elevator and into her room. Megan threw up in the room and in the bathroom, attracting the attention of Allie's hall counselor. Allie assured her that she had everything under control, that Megan was fine. But where had she *been*? How, and when, had we lost her? Nobody on our team seemed to know.

Ashley's good friend was the other hall counselor on that floor. Even though she had been off duty that night, she would talk to her partner on our behalf, so we weren't worried that Megan was going to get written up. Apparently, Megan woke up early in the morning and took a shower; was totally fine; went to breakfast with her parents, the coaches, and Rory; and was on her way home. No one had to know that at some point after the team party, we had somehow all lost track of her.

Mac and I looked back at Coach Katz. "No," we lied. "The recruits don't know."

No need to stress her out further. We would figure out a way to talk to Rory, explain without admitting to too much that we needed her to keep quiet about what she had seen. We had things under control with Megan and the hall counselors. We were in enough trouble as it was.

"Good," Coach Katz said. "These are our top two recruits, 'Cats. We really want them."

"Yes, ma'am."

"Well, Otto," Coach Katz continued, sighing. "You're my first."

I frowned, confused. Her first—?

"I have never, ever had a problem with alcohol on this team," she told me.

It turned out she had never had a player get caught drinking before. This might explain the lack of discussion about our team drinking rules. Maybe Coach Katz didn't think they needed discussing because she didn't think they even applied to us.

Mac and I were bewildered, but knew better than to say anything. Did she truly believe none of us drank, or did she just want to believe it?

"I'm gonna call your mom and dad, Amanda," Katz said in her scariest calm, soft drawl. When she called me by my first name instead of by my nickname, I knew I was really in trouble. "And I want you to explain to them what happened last night."

A rush of heat enveloped my entire body. She pushed her office phone over her desk toward me.

For one wild second I considered dialing a wrong number, but then realized that was crazy. I typed in my parents' home phone number and handed the receiver to Coach Katz. The office was thick with silence as it rang. I heard my dad's voice come on the line, his familiar, "Hello. Ottaways.'"

"Hi there, Mr. Ottaway," Coach Katz chirped. "Coach Katz here. I hope you're havin' a good Sunday morning. I'm here in my office with Amanda. She has something to tell you."

She handed the phone back to me, and I explained to my father what had happened. He was mostly silent. I could feel his disappointment humming through the phone, and it was the worst punishment anyone could have dreamed up. I sobbed, heavy tears. I finished talking, said good-bye, and hung up, shaking. My dad hadn't really said much. Mac rubbed my back.

"All right, Otto," Coach Katz said. "Have you learned your lesson? You gonna do this again?"

I shook my head vigorously. "No, ma'am."

"Good," she said. "I'm gonna give you a few days to come up with a punishment for yourself that you feel is appropriate. When you're ready, let me know, and we can start workin' to put all this behind us."

I sniffled and nodded. "Yes, ma'am."

"All right. C'mere, Otto," Coach Katz said, and we stood up. She was a short lady, which I sometimes forgot because she wore heels so often. She gave me a motherly squeeze. As we pulled away, she sniffed. "Well, you sure don't smell like alcohol," she exclaimed. "Just what were you drinkin', Otto?"

I hesitated, figuring I probably should not tell her about all the different things I had put into my body the night before—cheap vodka shots, a mixed drink for the road, a cocktail at the team party, some watery beer, Phi Delt's notorious Everclear punch.

"Um," I said. "Vodka, ma'am."

"Oh, that's why. 'Cause vodka doesn't have a smell!" Coach Katz exclaimed, clearly pleased with herself for bestowing upon me this punch line of a life lesson.

"Oh," I said, trying to keep my voice light and curious.

"Do you have a headache?" Coach Katz wanted to know. "They call that a 'hangover.'"

Mac ducked her head behind me, suppressing a grin. I fought to keep a straight face and felt a rush of affection for Coach Katz for trying to teach me about hangovers.

"No, ma'am," I said. "I feel pretty good, actually."

"Oh, well, I guess that IV you had last night would've fixed you right up," she reasoned, talking herself through it. I shrugged, as if this was all news to me. We arranged to have a team meeting that night in Mac, Jenni, Lyss, and Whitney's apartment so I could apologize to everyone. Coach Katz herself would be there.

That afternoon I went to Walmart to grab a few things and try to clear my head. Emma, who wanted to make sure I was all right, rode along with me. When we pulled into a parking spot back on campus, she took the keys out of the ignition and we sat next to each other in silence. I was a mess of guilt and anxiety and terror. Coach Katz still had every right to take away my scholarship for this.

Emma had recently overcome a bout of swine flu, and her mother had broken her out of the on-campus quarantine. She hadn't been invited to the team party the night before, but not because she was still sick. I realized she had not even known we were having a party. She was deeply Christian, and she didn't drink.

Her absence at the party was an unintentional exclusion. No one had ever said, "Let's not invite Emma." But sometimes the players who didn't drink didn't get invited to team activities on weekends, because in the fall and spring those activities tended to revolve around drinking. Some people who drank felt judged by some people who did not drink, and vice versa.

I didn't know or ask whether Emma's feelings were hurt, but she was focused on me.

"Can I pray for you?" she asked suddenly. I glanced at her, her huge blue eyes wider than usual, her face open and earnest.

"Sure," I said.

She grasped my hand in hers and bowed her head and closed her eyes, and I did too. With the Walmart bags in the backseat and the September sun beating through the windshield, Emma prayed for the team and for peace and strength for me. I did not often pray myself, but I knew Emma's faith meant a lot to her, and I appreciated it.

A few hours later, it was time for the team meeting. The seniors and captains had warned us not to mention Megan, the recruit. Coach Katz never had to know about that. It had been handled.

The whole team, plus Coach Katz, sat awkwardly in a circle in the living room and looked expectantly at me. I gave a short speech, saying how badly I had messed up, how sorry I was, how grateful I was to have the teammates I did, and how much I loved them. I meant every word. The meeting broke up without a word about Megan.

The next morning, a Monday, I was sitting in class when my phone buzzed. It was a text from Olivia.

She knows.

My heart and stomach dropped into my lower extremities for the second time in two days, and I could no longer pay attention to anything the professor was saying. When 11:30 classes ended, I raced to Liv's room and found nearly half the team there; we had gravitated to the same place without communicating about it. Everyone looked grim.

"How'd she find out?" I asked.

"We think the other hall counselor on Allie's hall must have written Megan up after all," Lyss said. "Ash's friend couldn't convince her not to."

"Fuck."

"So she found out from Jim Murphy?"

"We think so."

"Fuuuuuuuuck." We were in so much trouble.

Coach Katz spent the day in her office trying to piece together the story, calling in the captains and other members of the team, including the hostess of our team get-together that night, who was worried she would get kicked off the team. She was underage herself, and her older girlfriend had bought the alcohol. Players who had graduated years earlier texted us to say that Coach Katz was calling them to ask if they or other players had drunk alcohol on their official visits. Of course they had, they told her.

"If she kicks you off the team, I'm quitting," Lyss declared to the hostess.

"She kicks you off the team, she won't even have a team!" the rest of us exclaimed, although even as the words came out of my mouth, I wondered if I believed them myself.

I had broken the rules, too. If I really did quit—or, for that matter, lose my own scholarship—where would I go? My family depended on it. My parents had four other kids to worry about. I was supposed to be helping them out by being here for free. As much as I wanted to be a supportive teammate, I knew I couldn't just quit and give up my $200,000 scholarship on shaky principle alone. I was lucky to still have a scholarship.

I could maybe get tuition exchange at Saint Francis, since my dad worked there. Or maybe I could transfer somewhere and play basketball, but I would have to sit out a year, and I didn't know if anyone would even want me after this.

We all felt a little ill before our team conditioning session that afternoon. It had been on the schedule for a while, but we had a feeling it was not going to be any ordinary workout.

We had the concrete upstairs practice courts that day, since we shared the main court both with volleyball, who had first dibs since they were in season at the time, and with men's basketball. We got dressed nervously and clambered up the stairs, where the coaches were waiting for us.

"Line up on the baseline, 'Cats," Coach Katz said, in an eerily calm voice, that familiar, dreaded phrase more ominous than it had ever been. In silence, we did.

"I want you," she continued quietly, strolling down the line with her hands clasped behind her back, "to take a step forward if you drank alcohol while recruits were present this weekend."

There was no point in lying. She had found out about everything so far. All but a small handful of players stepped forward in silence, our heads bowed. I looked down the line at my teammates, shifting their weight nervously, watching Coach Katz, waiting for a verdict. We had always known there was an unofficial, mostly amicable divide on the team between those of us who drank and those of us who didn't. In that moment the divide became physical.

I'm different, Emma realized suddenly from the baseline, overwhelmed with loneliness, gazing at the teammates standing in front of her. In those few seconds a thousand thoughts flew through her mind. Should she step forward, too, even though she hadn't been drinking, just to be in unity with her teammates, to show her allegiance to us? Would that make her a good teammate? But would she be being honest to herself and who she was and to the decisions that she made if she lied and stepped forward?

Amber, Megan's host, did not step forward either. Amber had been on campus as a freshman for only two weeks, and she didn't drink. But she had hosted a recruit and lost her, and then the recruit got in trouble. The main issue for the coaches, it seemed, was that the team had been drinking, not that we had let a recruit get drunk. But they had never made a rule about either.

"How dare you?" Coach Katz said, her voice low. My own infraction had apparently been forgotten, swallowed up by the team's larger sins. "How dare you neglect your responsibilities to your coaches and your team? How dare you lie and not tell me about this yesterday when we learned about Otto?"

Coach Katz had called Megan and revoked her scholarship offer. The coaching staff worked hard to bring recruits to campus for official visits. They did so much planning and talking, spent so much money and time on it. Now half of that work had been wasted, and we had lost one of our top two recruits for good. If Rory found out what had happened, we might lose both of them. The coaches would have to move down to the next girl on their list and start over again.

But the coaches' verbal rebukes were nothing compared to what happened next.

"When I blow the whistle," Coach Bailey said, "you sprint toward the opposite baseline, touch it, and come back. When I blow it again, you jog. When I blow it again, you sprint again. If we can't distinguish between your sprint and your jog, you're gonna keep going. You're gonna do this until we get sick of watching you. Understood?" She blew the whistle, and we were off.

We were in good shape, so the first twenty or so down-and-backs weren't bad. My mind wandered, to my poetry class, to the transfer on the men's basketball team I had a crush on. We kept going, the whistles still shrieking. Sprint. Jog. Sprint. Jog. Sprint. Jog.

The coaches excused the players who said they had not been drinking. Emma walked slowly down the steps and entered the quietest locker room she had ever felt. Upstairs, the rest of us kept running. The whistle shrieked, again and again. Sprint. Jog. Sprint. Jog. The coaches had set up trash cans around the court for us to throw up in. Olivia stopped and heaved over one for a while.

I felt the hardness of the concrete under the court shoot up through my feet, my ankles, my shin bones as I ran, felt it pound harshly in my hamstrings and my hip flexors and my butt. Running on the upstairs practice courts hurt more than on the main court. The pain throbbed clean and hot in my head. My lungs ached as I gasped, then wheezed, for air. My asthma was kicking in, and my bad knees were giving out. I focused on putting one foot in front of the other. My eyes went slack, my sight blurry and unfocused. We had started out yelling encouragement to each other as we ran, but now we didn't have any extra air to do that with. My sprint was now a slow jog, my jog slower than a walk. I seriously considered stopping at a trash can, more for rest than anything, but resisted.

After about an hour Coach Bailey blew her whistle several times in quick succession. We staggered to a stop and gaped at her, gulping for air like fish out of water, hands on our knees, not daring to believe that this might be over. We were not supposed to ever put our hands on our shorts or knees because it was a sign of fatigue, which was a sign of weakness, but I physically could not hold my body upright anymore.

"Stand up," said Coach Bailey. We heaved and shook, still doubled over.

"Stand *up*," she snapped. We straightened slowly.

"That's it for today," Bailey continued. "Be back here at 5:45 tomorrow morning. We'll be doing workouts like this every morning until we get tired of watching you."

These punishment runs happened on top of everything else we were already doing that preseason—weight-lifting sessions, small-group on-court workouts, pickup, and our regular conditioning, two or three workouts a day. My personal punishment seemed to have been forgotten in everything that had happened since Saturday, so as much as I hated the running, I felt like I deserved it. I set my alarm for 5:15 every morning so that I could get dressed, walk over to the gym, and wait. We didn't have card access to Baker Sports Complex, so to get into the building we were dependent on a coach. Every morning we stood silently outside the arena in the chilly predawn, the hoods of our sweatshirts pulled tightly around our faces, stomping our feet to keep warm, waiting for someone to arrive with a key.

The seniors and Mac were furious. As far as they were concerned, they had done nothing wrong. They were of legal drinking age, and we weren't in dry season. There were no rules about not drinking with recruits on campus if you were not a host. It was a Saturday night. It was homecoming. Two of them had gone with me to the hospital. We still didn't know if we were being punished for drinking, for letting a recruit get drunk, or for not telling Katz that a recruit got drunk.

We did a variety of sprint drills on those mornings, some tougher than others. One day Coach Bailey brought an Egg McMuffin and ate it on the sidelines while she watched us run. The thick, greasy smell of it made us want to throw up. Another morning, presumably to preserve our joints, we worked out entirely on cardio machines in the gym of the student union. On a different day we had been doing the sprint-jog-sprint drill for twenty minutes or so, and I was having a mild asthma attack, when Coach Bailey suddenly looked over at Coach Simmons and exclaimed theatrically, "Coach Simmons, did you forget to start the clock?"

"I believe I did, Coach Bailey," Coach Simmons said brightly, and we started over. Gosh, they were mad. A few minutes after that Olivia reached the baseline and kept on running, off the court, down the stairs, into the hallway by the training room, and disappeared.

The coaching staff sent letters home to all of our parents, explaining what we had done and how serious it was.

"I write this letter with a heavy heart," Coach Katz began. In vague terms she explained what had happened. "Over the next few weeks our players will engage in additional exercise; enough to move oxygen to the brain and this has proven to increase exam scores and prevention of memory loss as they age."

Translation: We'd be runnin'.

My parents had still hardly said a word to me since I'd called my dad from Coach Katz's office. The Davidson College dean of students had written to them, too.

My roommate Brooke's birthday fell a few days later, while I still had 5:00 a.m. wake-up calls. I was falling asleep early every night from pure exhaustion; between our three workouts a day, I could barely stay awake in class. Brooke stayed up late that night doing home-work. Her phone went off at midnight, a text message from someone wishing her a happy birthday. My eyes flew open, and I leaped out of bed, thinking the sound was my alarm. I was yanking open dresser drawers and pulling off my pajamas to change when Brooke, who had been sitting at her desk with a small light on and her headphones in her ears, glanced over at me.

"Amanda," she said, yanking a headphone out of her left ear. "Amanda. What are you doing?"

"I gotta go," I muttered, trying to shake the hard sleep out of my brain. "I can't believe it's time to leave again already."

"Leave for . . . ?" Brooke touched my arm, looking genuinely bewil-dered. "Amanda, it's midnight."

I paused, standing there in my sports bra, a T-shirt dangling from my hand, and glanced at the clock. "Oh."

"You can go back to bed now," Brooke said gently. "You're fine. You've got five more hours."

"Thanks, Brooklyn," I said, already walking back toward my wonder-ful warm bed. "Happy birthday. Let's celebrate more later."

One morning Coach Bailey gathered us in a circle around her and, holding a yellow notepad, listed all the costs involved in bringing a recruit to campus. Our program budget paid the travel costs for David-son coaches to see her play in AAU tournaments and their salaries for the time they spent recruiting her. Davidson women's basketball footed the bills for her transportation to campus with a parent for the visit, her meal costs, her entertainment costs, her per diem costs. We had all gone out to a hibachi-style team dinner that Friday night. Bailey made Taylor add it all up. All that money and time for Megan, the recruit, gone to waste.

"Y'all better pray Stokes commits," the coaches warned. We did not want to know what would happen to us if we lost our top two recruits over this.

So we sent Rory a barrage of Facebook and text messages, telling her how much we liked her, how we were here to answer any questions she might have, how much we wanted her to be a part of our Davidson family. We couldn't tell her that we were in trouble over what had happened that weekend, but we somehow had to convey to her not to mention to the coaches that she had seen me sitting by the ambulance or they would know we lied about that, too.

The exhaustion among the members of the team doing the extra punishment workouts—a vast majority of us—stood in stark contrast with the energy of the couple of girls who told the coaches they had not been drinking and were excused. Those players shone in our small-group workouts. They seemed fast and fit and healthy, not raggedy and desperate—and preseason was the time of year to start impressing the coaches. I didn't really feel like I was impressing anyone. I was just trying to get through it, stumbling through workouts, struggling through class, and wolfing down as much food as I could find.

The coaches wasted no time in setting up another official visit for the next recruit on their list, a high-scoring guard named Samantha Pidart. She came that Friday with her mom, who was out by the track for a run herself one morning and saw us walking zombielike to breakfast from our early punishment workout.

"Boy, you girls sure do get up and get in the gym early," Sam's mom exclaimed.

"Yeah," we mumbled, laughing nervously. We hoped she didn't know we were actually being punished, that if it were up to us we would not be working out quite so early or often.

The captains had made an official rule that nobody was allowed to drink with a recruit on campus again. We were too tired to anyway. One of the eating houses was holding its annual toga party the next night, so we decided that our team get-together this time would involve decorating cupcakes and donning bedsheet togas. Sam, we could tell, was incredibly bored by us. She sat by herself on her phone the whole night.

"So," she asked us at one point, "do you guys do this every weekend, or, like . . . ?"

We all laughed awkwardly.

We took her to F, the apartment complex where seniors lived and where most of the parties happened. Every weekend F looked like a movie about college—drunk students hanging out and laughing on balconies with Solo cups, playing beer pong, streaking through the front lawn.

"Meet Sam, our recruit," we said to everyone, and they wrung her hand enthusiastically. People kept asking us why we weren't drinking. We wandered up to a party. Someone there tried to hand Sam a drink.

"NOOOO!" a teammate howled, leaping over and theatrically smashing the drink out of Sam's hand. It landed hard on the ground and splashed everywhere.

"No! Do not let her drink anything! No one is drinking anything!"

Ashley was driving Sam and a few other teammates to a pizza place for team dinner one evening when she got a phone call. She picked up. The letters the coaches had written home to our parents had started to arrive.

"The letter came?" she said. "Can you hide it? Yeah, pretty please, just hide it from my mom, okay?"

Sam started to suspect something was up. Eventually, she got the truth out of us and committed in the locker room before she left campus. One down, one to go.

When we finally got word from the coaches that Rory had also committed to Davidson, Olivia and I ran whooping up and down our hall. I felt like crying with relief. The coaches also must have decided we had been punished enough. One morning when we showed up outside the gym in the dark, the coaches weren't there. Instead, there was a stack of papers attached to the door. It was a written test about basketball.

We huddled up, confused. We weren't sure whether we were supposed to take this test and then go home or take the test and then do some running without the coaches. Maybe it was also a test of whether we had the discipline to punish ourselves.

In the end we took the written test and went home. And that was it.

6 Knocked Out

It happened at full speed, as injuries often do. During our last practice of the preseason of Olivia's, Taylor's, and my sophomore year, weeks after our drinking punishment, our hard, bruised bodies ached for real action. Rory and Sam had both committed, the recruiting-weekend disaster was behind us, and now it was time to get down to the business of the season. We were in the best shape of our lives and ready to kill each other for playing time.

We were running a one-on-one full-court defensive drill with screens on the hard, concrete upstairs practice court. I dribbled in zigzags up the right side of the floor. Liv was on me tight, shoving a little, so I jabbed back at her with my free arm. Coach Katz strode alongside us, watching closely, shouting encouragement.

"Good job, Olivia," she was saying. "Keep working hard."

Olivia scowled with concentration, keeping her eyes focused on my belly button so she wouldn't get faked out, spurred on by Coach Katz's enthusiasm. We kept banging into each other, both of us grunting.

Whitney stood waiting to set a screen on Olivia. Olivia was supposed to get around it. Instead, off-balance and moving fast, we made contact. Three big bodies clashed. Six long legs tangled. I lost control of the ball and fell forward onto my stomach, catching myself with my hands. A few feet away Olivia fell backward. I watched the back of her curly-haired head smash into the court with a loud, grotesque thud and bounce up faster than a snapped rubber band, so fast that at the hospital that night they would evaluate her for a broken neck from the force of the whiplash. Textbook concussion.

I got to my feet and reached to help her up, but Liv rolled over and buried her face in her forearm, shielding herself from the gym's bright lights. She could not bear to hear them buzzing. "This is bad," she thought.

None of us liked to think about it, but we all knew we risked serious injury every day we played. In addition to ACL tears, women's basketball players are at particular risk for ankle sprains, concussions, and stress fractures.

Micky Collins, PhD, the clinical and executive director of the University of Pittsburgh Medical Center's sports concussion clinic, describes concussions using an egg metaphor: The brain is the yolk, and the skull is the shell. When an outside force rocks the shell hard enough, the yolk shifts and hits the inside of the shell. That's what happens when you get a concussion: it is not your head hitting something else; it is your brain hitting your skull. That's why helmets don't always help.

Coach Katz was squatting at Olivia's side within seconds, her face white.

Our full-court drill stuttered to a halt as players realized what was happening, straightened up, tucked basketballs into the crooks of their arms, and traipsed hesitantly over to the scene. Olivia, her face still jammed into the crook of her elbow, did not move at all. Whitney and I hovered awkwardly nearby, not sure what to do or where to be but knowing instinctively that now was a time to keep our distance. We could not tell if Olivia was unconscious.

Jenni appeared at my side. "What happened, Otto?" she asked. "I heard her head hit the ground."

I explained briefly, and we stood in silence. I did not feel guilty, because I knew it could just as easily have been me who fell backward that day. We all knew the risks of what we did for a living.

There was sometimes a certain bizarre, backward, ephemeral relief to getting hurt on the court. It was a break. We got to sit down. We had time to absorb things. The other aching parts of our bodies had a chance to heal. People paid attention to us, at least at first. We were presented with the strange privileges of watching the gears from the outside and of missing basketball, which helped us remember that we loved it after all. I had reached a point the year before when I was so frustrated and embarrassed by the season and my lack of playing time that I found myself wishing for an injury. I wanted no choice but to ride the pine, as if sitting hurt was preferable to sitting healthy, because at least then I had an excuse. I knew I wasn't the only one who occasionally felt that way.

As we loitered over Olivia that day, I was having a hard time gauging the severity of her injury. We were all hurting, and we had little patience for people with low pain tolerances. Neither Olivia nor I had played much as freshmen. It had been a long and exhausting preseason for everyone. There was that time Olivia dropped out of the conditioning drill during our punishment week. Maybe this incident was a plea for attention from a coach she felt didn't pay her enough. Maybe she just needed a break from the drill. Maybe she was upset about something else.

"Olivia. Olivia," Coach Katz was saying in a low, steady voice, squeezing Liv's hand. "Stay with me, Olivia."

A small crowd of concerned onlookers had gathered around our practice court. As was standard with an on-court injury during practice, our assistant coaches herded us to a different part of the floor to continue playing, but we could hardly tear our eyes away from Olivia, especially when the paramedics arrived a few minutes later. They strapped her to a stretcher and carried her out the door to the waiting ambulance. Meghan, our trainer, and Mac—who by this point in the school year must have been getting pretty used to hospitals—went along with her to the trauma center in downtown Charlotte, almost thirty miles away. Practice resumed in earnest. We had a season to prepare for.

In the back of the ambulance one of the paramedics, a man, introduced himself to Mac and Olivia as Ashley. But in the South we called everyone "sir" and "ma'am." Liv, strapped tightly to a stretcher because they were worried she had broken her neck, thought that was the funniest thing in the world—a man named Ashley.

"Stop calling me 'sir,'" Ashley told her. "My name is Ashley."

Eyes closed against the harsh ambulance lights, Olivia lifted up her right arm and used it like a sword. "I now dub you," she slurred, "Sir Ashley." She started giggling uncontrollably.

Coach Katz drove to the hospital when practice ended. She pulled up a chair at Olivia's bedside, and Olivia, turning to say something, threw up on her by accident. The second time it happened, Coach Katz was ready with the bedpan. She stayed until Olivia was released late that night, making periodic phone calls to Liv's worried parents to update them. Coach Simmons joined them and took Mac home.

A CT scan revealed nothing wrong with Liv's neck, but doctors diagnosed a concussion and prescribed meds for the pain. Coach Katz drove Olivia back to campus late that night, stopping at multiple pharmacies until they found one that was open. She refused to take Olivia home without her medicine.

"I'm happy you're here," Olivia murmured to her as they waited in the drive-through lane of an open pharmacy. "I didn't think you cared about me. But now I really think you do."

Olivia's roommate, Hope, and I were in their room, waiting for her to get home, when Hope's phone buzzed. It was a text from a delirious and panicked Olivia. "She's coming in," it said. "Clean up the room now."

Coach Katz sure had made a lot of unexpected appearances in players' living quarters that fall. We went down to the parking lot behind the dorm to meet Olivia and Coach Katz when they arrived to try to intercept Olivia without Coach Katz's having to come inside.

"Hi, Coach," I said as she opened the door of her big black sport-utility vehicle. "You remember Liv's roommate, Hope?"

"I sure do," Coach Katz said. "Hi there, Hope."

Olivia was slowly extracting herself from the passenger seat, wincing, and all three of us rushed to help her. She still had on her practice gear; her face was pale, her hair stiff with dried sweat. Even though it was dark outside, her eyes were half-shut, squinted against the parking lot lights.

"We can take her from here, Coach," I said to Coach Katz. "Her room's right there." I gestured vaguely.

"That's all right, Otto," Coach Katz said. "I want to make sure this girl gets safely in her bed. She took a hard fall today."

So Hope, Coach Katz, and I, all three of us in mom mode, slowly walked Olivia the whole way inside and helped her climb into bed. Hope, Olivia, and I all held our breath until Coach bid us good night and left. Hope watched Olivia through the night, waking her up every couple of hours to make sure she was still conscious.

Olivia's parents drove down the next day. That night was Night with the 'Cats, which she had been looking forward to all year. Our class dance theme this time was rock and roll. We were supposed to wear fake tattoos and fingerless fishnet wrist gloves, tease our hair, and rock out on neon air guitars to Aerosmith. The costumes were deliciously campy, Olivia's masses of curly hair were perfect for the occasion, and this year's dance would be fun and maybe even cool, not embarrassing like last year's. We had been practicing for weeks.

The flashing lights, loud music, and excitable crowd made Belk Arena a virulent cesspool of concussion stimuli that night. Olivia went to the locker room and threw up. Her parents took her back to her dorm, and she puked three more times there while the rest of us hammed and scrimmaged for the crowd. Afterward, she barely remembered anything.

For several days after that Olivia barely came out of her room, which she and Hope had darkened like a cave. Hope, who had been raised by two doctors and still wanted to be one herself, continued to wake Olivia up periodically to check on her.

Olivia did not go to class. She did not shower. She did not eat. She had lost, at least for the time being, much of her ability to taste and smell. Mary Marshall, our sweet soccer-playing friend who lived on the hall a few doors down, went over and spoon-fed her oatmeal.

Family friends of the Lowerys picked her up, and Olivia slept at their house for five days. She ate two bowls of Ramen noodles. The family drove Olivia back to the hospital in Charlotte for an MRI. Afterward,

Olivia got a voice mail from the hospital, saying she needed to admit herself into the trauma center in downtown Charlotte immediately. Our friend Bryce drove, flying down I-77 with Hope in the passenger seat and Olivia in the back. A brain surgeon and a wheelchair were waiting for Olivia at the trauma center.

The MRI had shown three contusions on her brain, which meant Liv's brain was bleeding. If they had seen this the night she hit her head, they would have drilled into her skull to relieve the pressure, but the doctors had been focused instead on her neck and whether it was broken. They sent her back to campus, and she spent the night in the student health center, where nurses woke her up every thirty minutes to check her heart rate. When Olivia woke up in the morning, her mom was there.

In the weeks following Olivia's fall, Coach Katz asked her to come to practices and sit in the gym so she could keep up with the plays and scouting reports. Concussion science was still new, and coaches didn't know much about the countless ways this kind of brain damage could impact their athletes. But being around a sporting event is a profoundly uncomfortable experience for many concussion patients and for people whose brains are bleeding. A basketball court teems with painful stimuli—the sounds of the bouncing ball, the whistles, the crowd, the buzzer, the bright lights, the back-and-forth nature of the sport. Being at practice or games made Olivia physically ill, so she would go down to the training room and sit there instead. She was not well enough to travel to away games with us, although injured athletes often didn't travel anyway because our budget was so tight. Eating in Commons, the school cafeteria, overwhelmed her. We almost never saw her.

The rest of us had plenty to keep busy and only so much extra capacity to support our teammates, and now Liv was one fewer person with whom to fight for playing time.

Doctors diagnosed Emma with a stress fracture in her foot, and she sat out the exhibition game. She wore a cast for a week, followed by a boot. Ashley, finally healthy from her back-to-back ACL tears, did not feel like herself, like the player she had been in high school. Even though she was a junior, she had never officially played in-season col-

lege basketball before. So she was in the awkward position of simultaneously being an upperclassman leader and a wide-eyed "freshman."

Because her first tear had happened when she landed from a layup
on the right side of the court, Ashley now had a phobia of that side.
It was a mental block that became a physical one; she couldn't figure
out which leg to lift, which hand to shoot with. The footwork didn't
make sense anymore. She started doing left-handed finger rolls on the
right side of the basket, which she had seen the men do. She could go
off her strong leg this way. It drove the coaches crazy because if she
always went left, she was much easier to defend, but Ashley was defiant.

Ash had a wicked handle, quick feet, and a keen eye for passing. She
balled out when she came to Davidson for camp the summer before
her freshman year, and the upperclassmen started worrying for their
spots. Ashley's first love was baseball, though. She played both sports as
a kid and loved being the only girl on her baseball team. When she got
old enough that practices started to overlap and she had to choose—
baseball or basketball—she reminded herself that girls did not play
baseball in college. Ever since her accident, she had wanted to be a
doctor. Ashley, valedictorian of her high school, knew medical school
was expensive, so she wanted to go to college for free. Only basketball
could help her do that. She quit baseball cold turkey.

Now, though, Ashley felt slower and more tentative than she had
before the two ACL tears, like a different player. She wasn't excited to
get on the court anymore. Our loud, giggly, spunky Ash, whom Coach
Bailey had nicknamed "Hot Sauce" for her sass and speed and handles,
whom we had seen be so outspoken and outgoing, turned inward. She
didn't talk much, didn't smile much. Off the court she was so busy,
we barely saw her outside of mandated team time. In order to distract
herself from her injuries for those two years, she had gotten involved
in a bevy of extracurriculars on campus and made new friends, moved
on with her life.

Once Ashley was cleared to play, she and I were often on the same
team at practice, a group of substitutes whose prescribed job was to
make our starters better. Often we played offense in the half court as
our starters worked on their man-to-man defense.

"Force them baseline" was the constant refrain from the coaches to the defense. "Cut off the middle. Whatever you do, do not let them go middle."

The middle of the court, they explained, was the easiest path to the basket; if a defender angled her body in such a way that the ball handler had to dribble sideways, toward the sideline or baseline, instead of toward the middle of the key, the handler could not go toward the hoop. Coach Katz's most obvious coaching strength was defense, and it was our primary focus as a team. Keeping a player from going middle attracted high praise. Letting a player go middle was the most cardinal of sins, sometimes punishable by a personal character attack. A poor defender didn't care enough about her teammates to hustle. She didn't care about her scholarship. She was selfish, selfish, selfish.

Allie, a freshman, watched the rest of us internalize the criticism and drown in guilt. *I don't think she didn't get there on defense because she didn't have the heart to*, Allie thought as somebody got reamed out. *I think she didn't get there because she didn't get there.*

Ashley's flashiness as a player was highly functional, but she was the only one of us who played with any, and we were not all accustomed to playing together yet. Her passes were much quicker than we were used to, and sometimes she threw them without looking or behind her back, something none of our other guards did. When Ashley put her head down and drove right, shifted her weight, pulled back her dribble, slipped it between her legs, and whipped a left-handed no-look pass at me in the post, all in a matter of a second and a half, I didn't see the ball coming, and it hit me in the shoulder.

"Otto!" Ashley shouted. I fumbled for it, but I was too late. My defender, Whitney, had the steal.

"Turnovers for Otto and Ashley," Coach Katz said flatly to Mac, who marked it down, wincing. "Steal for Whitney. Get it together, 'Cats."

"Otto, you gotta be ready!" Ash exploded. "You gotta be looking. You're open, I can see your numbers, I'm gonna get it to you."

"You gotta yell my name sooner than that, Ash!" I shot back without thinking. She was right, though. It was not her responsibility to tell me when I was open. I should have been ready. And if the guards and the posts didn't get along, the posts would never get the ball.

We all wore knee pads and mouth guards in every practice and game that year—coaches' orders. I wished Ashley's pass had hit me in the knee and ricocheted out-of-bounds, as passes into the post often did that year due to the springiness of our knee pads. Better than giving Whitney the steal.

Another practice we were working on our full-court press. Freshman Leah, on one team, was assigned to guard junior Ashley on the other. Leah was riding her, harassing her, all over her. Ashley, who was, at her quickest, quicker than Leah and easily the best ball handler on the team, could not get the ball past half court. We had run the drill a half-dozen times and turned it over almost every time. Our starters' press could not possibly be that good.

"Again," Bailey intoned.

I was supposed to inbound the ball and then hover near Ashley, across the court but parallel to her, in case she needed to pass the ball off. Taylor was waiting down near our hoop to make a cut toward half court for another possible pass. Leah positioned herself on the left side of Ashley's body so Ashley would have to dribble right, something she had been avoiding because of her injury-induced phobia.

"You got this, Ash," I muttered, standing on the baseline, tossing her a firm bounce pass around Leah and trotting inbounds alongside her.

Leah was on Ashley immediately like a koala on a tree branch. Ashley took a few dribbles left, and Leah cut her off. Ash expelled a forceful spout of air—"*Heeeeeeessssh.*" She dribbled between her legs and tried to go right. Leah cut her off again.

"Ash, I got you," called Taylor, sprinting to half court, holding out her hands for the ball.

Ashley picked up her dribble and faked a pass to me and then tried to throw the ball to Taylor. But Leah was a smart defender. She didn't go for the fake, and she jumped up and intercepted the pass to Taylor. Ashley's whole body—her shoulders, knees, head—slumped as Leah dribbled in for a fast-break layup with nobody near her.

Coach Katz blew her whistle. "You can't just let her go like that, Ashley," she warned. "You make a mistake, you get back on defense." Turning to Mac, she said, "That'll be . . . seven points for Leah and minus three points for Ashley."

Mac winced and made some notes at the scorers' table. She was in charge of keeping track of the complex points system Coach Katz used during practice. Players gained points for things like offensive rebounds and steals, but turning the ball over or not boxing out earned negative points. If a player didn't have a certain number of points when practice was over, she had to run.

"Nice defense, Leah," Coach Katz said. "Ashley, get it together. Y'all have one minute to get yourselves some water. Hydrate, 'Cats!"

Mac started the countdown clock. Ashley slouched over to Coach Bailey, who had been a college point guard herself.

"What am I doing?" Ashley asked Bailey, hands on her hips. "Why can't I get the ball past half court?"

"Well, Hot Sauce," Coach Bailey said, "sometimes someone just has your number."

Ashley walked slowly to the sideline for her water bottle. A few teammates, including Leah, patted her on the back.

"You got this, Ash."

That day was a turning point for Ashley, the day she realized she did not want to use the NCAA-permitted fifth year of eligibility for injured players, a medical redshirt. She was not mad at Leah. She just had no confidence. If this was what basketball was going to be like, she could not handle an extra year of it. If she couldn't play at the high level she had once been capable of, she didn't want to play at all.

We didn't know why it was taking Olivia so long to get better, and more than one teammate suspected that she was milking it. She had come in from the summer a little out of shape and had a rough preseason. The coaches were mostly ignoring her, so we took their cues. Plus, we were emotionally occupied—we started that season with six straight losses. Lucky Olivia, she didn't have to run around the court and lose; she could stay home in bed.

We got killed at both Nebraska and Creighton on Lyss's homecoming trip to start off the year. Then we lost big time at NC State, where Coach Katz used to coach alongside their head coach, Kay Yow.

We were in Commons eating dinner one night after that, plastic cups of yellow-and-blue-mixed sports drink on our trays. Most of us also had a cup of chocolate milk and a cup of water and three or four different plates of food. We were playing our usual game: talking through the coaches' actions and puzzling over their motives. There were no freshmen at the table.

One of the freshmen told her upperclassman roommate in the hotel at NC State that Coach Katz had held a secret meeting with the five freshmen. Word quickly got around the bus: Katz had told the freshies that they were the future and the coaches were relying more on them. It was like a game of Telephone. By the time the rest of the team heard and discussed the news, we heard that the freshmen were Coach Katz's Super Class and that she had given up on the rest of us, and we were pissed.

"I mean, it's not the freshies' fault," somebody said. "They're in a really awkward position. But still."

It was a large-scale example of Coach praising one player by putting down her teammates. What were the freshmen supposed to do about that—stand up for us or let her adore them?

"I can never tell if she's pissing us off to motivate us or if she's just pissing us off because she can," someone else said.

"God, the freshies have been walking in the light all year. From the Megan incident on. What are they, the class sent down from heaven to rescue us? They're really not all that."

"It's because they're the first recruiting class for this group of assistant coaches. The assistants want the freshies to show out so they can show Coach Katz what a good job they did. So they're gonna keep giving them opportunities."

It was like a grown-up game of "Hey, look, I did the best on my homework!" except the homework was alive.

"If she's done with us, why not have a conversation about it? Why not talk to us, too, and not just them? And in secret!"

"If they think the freshmen are outworking us," I added, "are the coaches looking at the same court we're looking at?"

I had been a freshman once, but I wasn't anymore, and I was old enough to declare them babies. I didn't think they were outworking the rest of us. I thought some of them were lazy. It wasn't totally their fault—most freshmen were lazy. It took a while to get used to the level we played at in college, more intense than we could have dreamed as high schoolers.

At the college basketball level, as one teammate said years later, "the highs are higher and the lows are lower. And you're exhausted, so it's that much more intensified." Players didn't know what working hard was, what "tired" was, or fully understand that college-level pace and intensity until they had been a part of it. They had to learn by doing.

"The freshies have no idea how to finish a play. Ball's going out-of-bounds, they just let that shit go. They inbound the ball and jog up the court. Maybe you do that in high school, AAU, whatever. Not here."

"Allie told me the diagnosis for that stress fracture in her foot is 'play as tolerated.' Who gives that diagnosis to a freshman? Or anybody, really, but especially an underclassman? That's so confusing. She has no idea what 'tolerance' even means at this point. How is she supposed to know how hard to push and how much it's supposed to hurt before she stops?"

Sure enough, in our game at William and Mary, three freshmen started: Allie, Leah, and Alanna. Whitney and Lyss, both seniors, came off the bench. So did Taylor and Ashley. The freshies, to their credit, played pretty well, but we lost 74–63.

When we did see Olivia these days, which was not often, she was miserable and no fun to be around. We let her drift. She wasn't physically present anymore, and when she was she remained too sick and cranky to make much conversation. So Liv's situation was easier for us to forget about. We were in full-season mode now and constantly overscheduled and overwhelmed, trying to balance classes, labs, and schoolwork with scouting reports, practice, rehab, travel, and coaches' demands.

Kathy Bray, the associate dean of students, arranged for Olivia to have a note taker in each of the classes she missed. The basketball program also covered the cost of tutors, which Olivia desperately needed. By this point professors, coaches, Olivia's parents, and several doctors had advised her to drop the entire semester, to take a leave of absence and focus on healing. Liv refused. She wanted to graduate on time.

Beth Hayford, the head athletic trainer and resident women's basketball mother figure, didn't think Davidson athletes recovered from concussions as quickly as athletes did at other schools and suspected academics were partly to blame. Olivia, and several other players on the team, had been struggling in school anyway. Nobody ever slipped into academic ineligibility, but once any student fell behind at Davidson, it was incredibly hard to catch up.

Beth wanted the NCAA to develop some large-scale means of making academic provisions for athletes with concussions. At Davidson, student-athlete or not, concussion or not, the strict class-attendance rules were pretty firm. Although a lot of professors were understanding, some were less so, and according to Beth one even demanded doctors' notes to have concussed players miss class. Because most concussions don't require a doctor's diagnosis and are diagnosed and treated in the training room instead, a doctor is often an unnecessary expense for players whose parents foot their health insurance bills.

The NCAA doesn't usually provide accident insurance for its student-athletes. We were not its employees, and it had little legal responsibility toward "workers' comp." The NCAA helps with medical expenses under its Catastrophic Injury Insurance Program, which kicks in when an athlete's injury costs match or exceed $90,000. It is easier and cheaper for the NCAA to be sued later by individual players over health-care bills than it is for them to cover insurance costs for all four hundred thousand–plus student-athletes. For $89,999 bills and below, the financial responsibility for health care related to sports injuries lies with either the school or the student herself.

Student-athletes get free care like initial diagnosis and therapy in the training room, but someone has to pay for MRIs and CT scans and bone-setting and surgery and specialized protective equipment.

For the most part it's up to individual colleges to decide whether to provide health insurance for their athletes. No Division I school at the time was required to cover the cost of full primary insurance for student-athletes, so most who came in covered under their parents' insurance plans remained on those plans (and had to make sure those plans covered collegiate athletics) or under the rules of the school had to buy their own insurance before they enrolled. This meant that the player and her family were responsible for any costs that insurance did not cover, like if they had a high deductible or saw a doctor out of network. The policy frequently resulted in confusion and irritated parent phone calls to the Davidson training room.

As time went on and Olivia did not seem to be making much progress, Mama and Papa Lowery got her an appointment with Dr. Collins, the sports concussion expert. They had great insurance, which covered the visits, and they could afford to fly Olivia back and forth between Charlotte and Pittsburgh for appointments. They are an exception.

Coach Katz had started treating injured players strangely, making a rule at one point that they were not even allowed to come upstairs and watch practice. They had to stay in the training room and do their rehab instead. That meant they missed out on new plays, scouting reports, and bonding with the team during water breaks. They also had to stay home on road trips, because our team was on a tight budget and injured players were an extra expense.

Olivia was lonely and lost. She sat in Coach Katz's office one day crying. "But basketball is who I am," she said tearfully.

"Olivia," Coach Katz replied gently, "you are not just a basketball player. You are so much more than that. You love helping people. You love kids. You need to remember that basketball is not who you are. It's a part of your life, but it's not who you are."

We could have beaten William and Mary, but we didn't. We should not have lost both games at the Thanksgiving tournament in Wilmington, but we did. The first loss was to the Duquesne team full of girls my year who had gotten scholarships I wanted and were coached by the woman I had wanted so desperately to play for. The second was to Monmouth, one of whose new assistant coaches was my old high school coach Anita Jennings.

Emma broke her nose in the Duquesne game, which we lost by three in overtime. (The first girl to get the Duquesne scholarship I wanted, the three-point shooter, scored twenty points.) We were half-court pressing and trapping them, and Emma, part of a successful trap, forced a Duquesne guard to pick up her dribble just over half court. The girl got stuck and, panicking a little, started trying to create space for herself, pivoting with her elbows out. One elbow clocked Emma across the face.

Emma blacked out for a second. None of us even noticed that she had lost consciousness because she stayed standing. When she came to, the ball was on the ground right in front of her. She picked it up, dribbled to our basket, and finished the layup, blood streaming down her face. Our bench went from screaming, "Yeah, Em, nice finish!" to, "Hey, she's bleeding, ref!" The Duquesne coaches were also pointing at Emma and yelling, "Blood, blood!"

Emma touched her face, and her hand came away red. The refs blew their whistles, and she walked to the sideline and stood, dripping, over a trash can while Meghan scrambled to get her treatment kit together, as she had done for Jenni at South Carolina. Em got patched up and went back in the game. She played forty-two minutes that day out of forty-five, including overtime.

Emma had to wait until we got back to Charlotte before she could really get herself fixed up. Fortunately, her mom was in town and held her hand as the doctor shoved needles up her nose to numb it before they set the bones while she was awake. She had to wear a mask afterward to play, but it was a free one from the training room—possibly the same one as worn by several broken-nosed teammates, including Jenni. It didn't fit right, it smelled bad, and Emma, like a horse with blinders on, could not see down or to either side.

"We could get you a custom one," Coach Katz offered, like the kind NBA players wore. But Emma and her parents would have to pay for it and were told it would cost several thousand dollars. She stuck with the smelly blinder mask instead.

When my teammates and I were choosing a college, our future access to health insurance in case of injury never crossed our minds. First of all, we were never going to get hurt, and second, to a seventeen-year-old, what even is health insurance? The lack of coverage was also, to my knowledge and my parents' knowledge, never mentioned by any of the coaches who recruited me for any school. It was not a question my family thought to ask, and of course in many cases it's not information that's in the best interest of a recruiting coach to volunteer. I didn't find out until I arrived on campus and we had our annual meeting with Beth and the other athletic trainers that Davidson wouldn't cover my sports-injury bills, and even then I didn't totally absorb the information.

According to Beth Hayford, head athletic trainer, since 1994 Davidson College had been one of a small number of Division I institutions with no insurance policy at all for its four hundred–some student-athletes, who are at a higher risk of injury than nonathletes. Beth told me secondary health insurance for all of us would probably have cost an additional $160,000–180,000 a year on top of the school's athletic budget. Many other schools do provide secondary insurance policies, which supplement the athletes' primary health plans and usually help to lessen or eliminate out-of-pocket costs for athletes and their families. When we were at Davidson, though, our school did not. Wildcat sports were not exactly lucrative ones. Unlike larger, more successful football and basketball programs that also make arguments for student-athlete health coverage, we did not bring in much revenue.

For Ashley's, Mac's, and Erin's ACL tears; Olivia's head injury; Em's and Jenni's broken noses; Allie's stress fractures; and all the other injuries on our team, any outside-the-training-room treatment, surgery, and gear were paid for by their parents' insurance and sometimes, when insurance didn't cover it, by thousands of dollars out of their parents' pockets. In at least one instance our team doctor wasn't covered under a family's health plan, and the player got her surgery elsewhere. According to assistant athletic director Katy McNay, there was extra money from the NCAA in a special pot for students who really needed it, but most players did not know the special pot existed.

Part of the reason the Davidson athletic administration hadn't yet seen the need to make as big a purchase as insurance was that because men's basketball was technically our only fully funded sport and most Davidson athletes paid some chunk of tuition, the school attracted a lot of kids from well-off families who could afford the extra health-care costs if their kids needed surgery or a special mask or brace. But many women's basketball players, full-scholarship athletes whose families often depended on those scholarships, fell through the cracks.

Olivia still was not traveling with us much or showing up at practices or team meals. We had so much doubt about the severity of her condition clouding our own minds at this point that we weren't receptive to her often irritable expressions of frustration and loneliness. We all continued to slip further away from each other—players from players, coaches from players.

We were furious when we found out Olivia had been at parties on campus while the rest of us were on a road trip. She was supposed to be in her room by herself, healing, not partying. We thought that had to be the worst possible thing for her head.

But social distractions may actually have been exactly what Olivia needed at that point. "Athletic identity" is the slice of a person's identity that she relates to her sport. Division I athletes tend to have high athletic identities. But what do you do when the thing you love to do most becomes your job and then when your job takes over your life—and then all of a sudden you can't do your job anymore? Almost immediately, Olivia started reducing her athletic identity, mostly as a survival tactic, since being around basketball was physically and emotionally painful. She went to parties so she could have social interaction, since her team no longer gave that to her.

Concussions affect everyone differently, and they're hard to describe and understand unless somebody has personally experienced one. When Liv got hers I had had one concussion, a much milder one. It was a freak accident our freshman year. A thick, bumpy piece of plastic we had been using as a rim cover to practice our rebounding broke and fell off the rim. Coach Katz asked Coach Bailey to put it back on.

The second time the plastic fell, it landed directly on my head. I knew what it was like to feel a little off, a little headachy, a little out of it, a little unwanted, but it was still easy to think Olivia was being dramatic. Her injury was invisible.

Concussions build on themselves. Usually, the symptoms for a second concussion are worse than they are for the first, and it takes longer to heal. A third concussion could take even longer, and so on. It is important to catch them when they happen and treat them right away and to make sure they are completely healed before the athlete takes the court again. After my first concussion I was back playing within a few weeks. For Olivia it had been a few months. It wasn't looking like she would be healthy in time to play at all that year.

7

Sisterhood of the Traveling Sweatpants

January was always a hard month. It was like the Tuesday of basketball season. In November we were excited about the beginning of another year, another quest for a championship. In December we had a few days off around the holidays to look forward to. February and March hummed with the anticipation and adrenaline of the playoffs. But in January we were tired, our bodies hurt, the overuse injuries started to set in, and we still had a solid nine or ten weeks left in the season. We had just spent nearly a month living in a hotel with our teammates over winter break, seeing almost nobody but them and the coaches, and we were all sick of each other. We could finish each other's sentences. Little things pissed us off that didn't ever piss us off before.

One day in mid-January we were somehow losing by twenty-one points to the College of Charleston. Even though they rarely made the top half of the league standings, we never seemed to play well in their gym. We were holding their best player scoreless from the field, but two others had stepped up and were killing us. They had scored thirty-four points between them already, and we didn't have an answer. The Cougars had also hit eight three-pointers and scored almost fifty points as a team. It wasn't even halftime yet.

In the locker room Coach Katz fumed that we were playing so poorly it was clear to her we didn't appreciate our expensive scholarships. Typical coach move.

The NCAA has rules about how many full scholarships a Division I school can provide in each sport. For example, a women's basketball program is allowed to have as many as fifteen full scholarships to give out, if it can afford to. Not all schools can; Davidson, a particularly small and expensive private school, supported only thirteen full women's basketball scholarships that year (up from twelve the previous year), and even fewer in most of our other twenty sports. Men's basketball, with thirteen out of an NCAA-permitted thirteen full scholarships, was technically our only fully funded sport.

Coaches of other teams often split up the money and gave out smaller amounts to partially cover more athletes. Parents or grants or other financial aid picked up the rest of the tab for our field hockey players, men's and women's soccer players, volleyball players, and everyone else. Olivia and I knew a women's soccer player who received $20,000 a year out of the $45,000 school cost, which was a lot for that team. She told us they averaged $10,000 to $15,000 in scholarships per player. We knew a volleyball player who got $30,000 a year.

That men's and women's basketball were so well funded meant that there was much more money on the line for our programs than for any other Wildcat sports. Thirteen full scholarships at Davidson that academic year cost $585,390, just more than $45,000 apiece. On top of that came the costs of all our books, gear, and travel. We were an expensive bunch, and our coaches may have felt more pressure than most on campus for us to do well.

We wanted to show Coach Katz that we not only were, in fact, grateful for our scholarships, but flat-out wanted to win. We did not give up that day. We poured in almost fifty points ourselves in the second half, outscoring them by thirteen in those twenty minutes. We continued to hold Charleston's best player scoreless from everywhere but the foul line. Lyss was a force, hitting five three-pointers, and four others scored in double digits. We outrebounded them by twelve. We never could quite close the gap, and Charleston won, 84–78. I watched all but five minutes of the game from the end of the bench.

Every minute I sat on the bench hurt my soul. I had never spent much time there before college. None of us had. We learned hard lessons there.

I had been a four-year varsity starter in high school. Now I wanted to get on the court so badly I cried. The pain of playing mostly in practice, hardly ever in games, was wearing on me. It made me tired and sad. It made me care less about our losses, because I had practically nothing to do with them. It made me care less about our wins, too.

As my playing time stagnated and our losses piled up, I started looking for ways to stop thinking about basketball. It hurt too much. I sat on the bench thirty-five or thirty-eight minutes per forty-minute game, watching us lose over and over. I would go in, make my one or two mistakes, and get yanked. I could never get in a flow. I was gaining weight. My grades were not good. I called my parents crying once a week, asking if I could transfer. I had heard of the sophomore slump, but hadn't expected it to be quite this devastating.

That fall I took an Introduction to Writing Poetry class. One of our assignments was to attend a poetry event on campus and write about it, so even though I had no idea what slam poetry was, I went to a show. I was hooked. I tried out for the team that January and made it.

That same fall Clint Smith, a men's soccer player two years ahead of me, had founded FreeWord, Davidson's slam poetry team. When I tried out my self-confidence was at an all-time low. My identity was in basketball, and as I realized that I was not as good at basketball as I thought I was, I felt increasingly lost. But I felt a connection to Clint. He hadn't been getting much playing time in his sport, either, and had found something else he loved and was good at.

FreeWord changed my life. Being in the group introduced me to Davidson students I probably never would have met otherwise, many of them sexual or racial or ethnic minorities, all brilliant and funny and in tune with politics and art and activism. We were all appreciative of the safe, supportive, collaborative space our weekly workshops created. I remembered how much I loved writing, and I found solace in it again.

The real beauty of Davidson's student body lies not in who is admitted, but in what they do when they get there and after they leave. Most of my teammates had not been valedictorians, although Ashley had been, or gone to swanky private high schools. But we were gritty and competitive, and we refused to fail. Not one women's basketball player was ever deemed academically ineligible during my four years at Davidson.

I learned how to turn off the "basketball" part of my brain, making myself care less about it so I could focus on my homework. As I took on more activities, my grades improved. I spoke up in class. I began to feel more like I fitted in academically at Davidson. Maybe I wouldn't have gotten in without basketball, and maybe I wasn't actually as good at basketball as I had thought I was, but maybe I could cut it here anyway. I was finally starting to figure myself out.

We were all disappointed after the Charleston game as we waited in the locker room for the coaches, but we were proud of how we had not given up and cautiously enthusiastic. Giving up would have been bad, but this was a good sign. It showed we had heart.

Coach Katz crashed in, clutching the stats sheet, eyes fierce and red hair wild, and let us have it. It was all a numbers game today, like so many other days in college basketball. Our record had fallen to 8-9 overall, 6-3 in the Southern Conference, and she was not pleased with our turnover rate. We had had twenty-three, and Charleston scored twenty-seven points off of them.

Never mind the fact that we had made a big comeback, that my teammates had left their hearts and a few bits of skinned elbow out on that floor. I was proud of the way Lyss and Jenni had hustled that game, the way Alanna, just a freshman, had held her composure and finished with a double-double. But Coach Katz didn't see it like that.

"Better make your showers quick, 'Cats," she said.

Even warm-ups had made my bad knees sore that day. I was getting pretty good at scooping ice into plastic bags, putting the bag around my mouth and sucking out the excess air so the ice made a flat pancake, and then using a roll of clear plastic wrap to secure a bag to each knee. I made a couple of extra bags in the locker room because nearly half the team needed some, too. We hustled through the showers and onto the bus.

The restaurant where we ate our postgame meal was a southern barbecue chain that we patronized often on road trips, because it was cheap and fast. By the time we got there, it was almost five o'clock, and we hadn't eaten anything since our pregame meal at ten that morning, after shootaround. I was so hungry while we waited for our food that I poured out drops of each of the six different kinds of barbecue sauce—Memphis Original, Carolina Sweet, Habanero Hot, Tennessee Whiskey, Carolina Classic, and Memphis-Style Dry—and licked it off my fingers.

Coach Katz had told us we were not allowed to talk during dinner that day. Silently, I wolfed down my barbecue sandwich and fries and immediately started scavenging for more food, but there was not a crumb to spare. Within a few minutes we all slouched over our empty plates in silence, staring hungrily at the coaches' table, where they sat discussing the game intensely in low voices, loudly enough for us to sort of hear. Hopefully, since we had had only two meals that day, we would be able to get more food in a few hours. We would stay overnight in Charleston and head south the next morning for our game at Georgia Southern on Monday.

My ice bags started leaking down into my socks, which was how I knew it was time to throw them away. I ripped through the plastic wrap and plucked them off, and a small parade of teammates, all holding their own dripping ice bags, followed me stiff-legged into the bathroom, where we dumped the melting ice into the sink and threw the empty bags in the trash, a postgame restaurant routine of ours.

We normally had boxes of snacks on the bus for every road trip. The assistant coaches or Terry, our administrative assistant, bought them ahead of time—pretzels, granola bars, apples and oranges, fruit snacks, trail mix. That day the coaches hid the bus snacks, saying they were rationing them for our trip to Georgia the next day. When the bus pulled back into the hotel parking lot, Coach Katz stood and turned around, and we all sat up, waiting for her to address us about plans for the evening.

"Film in my room, 'Cats," she said. "And y'all can take care of your own laundry tonight."

Instead of lugging the bag full of sweaty uniforms and socks and sports bras to the assistant coaches' rooms that night for them to wash, the freshmen had to figure out something else to do with it. Katz gave us her suite number, which was strange. Normally, we watched film in the hotel conference room. Maybe they had forgotten to book it ahead of time. I was already wondering when our next meal was going to be, but figured we would just eat after the film session.

It was always exciting for us when the coaches stood at the hotel check-in desk, announced the roommate pairings, and passed out keys, which they had done the night before when we arrived in Charleston. We slept two to a room, one to a bed on the road, better than the volleyball team, which had three to a room, or the women's soccer team, which had four. My roommate this trip was Allie, gentle and low-maintenance.

We all had our road habits. Ashley talked on the phone. Taylor talked and smacked her mouth in her sleep and vehemently denied all of it. Mac taught me to rinse my face with cold water after washing it to close my pores. Several people had reputations for taking huge dumps in the bathroom at inconvenient times, like when you needed to brush your teeth. Others preferred to use the public bathrooms in the hotel lobby before games.

Once you got through Alanna's shyness, she had a wicked sense of humor. Erin had liked to play practical jokes in hotels; she and I once stood on my bed and gave Christina a heart attack by hysterically pointing in different directions at an imaginary bug running around the room. Christina taught me about the singers the Temptations when we watched something about them on TV. Jenni and Mac worked incessantly, sometimes at the desk in the room, sometimes in the hotel lobby. It was almost easier to focus on school from the road, away from the distractions of campus.

Some of us used the time away to download pirated music, since on Davidson's campus that was considered stealing and a breach of the Honor Code. Olivia had once shaved the calluses off her feet into our tub, and when I turned the shower on a flood of dead skin chunks came shooting out of the drain. On that same trip I couldn't find my tampon string, and she yelled advice and laughed at me through the bathroom door and would not let me out until I succeeded.

I usually tried to do my homework on the bus so I could sprawl out in my big, soft hotel bed and watch TV. We had twin beds on campus, so hotels of the midrange chain brand we generally stayed at—Marriott, Holiday Inn Express, Springhill Suites, La Quinta—were a welcome luxury.

Allie and I banged into our room at the Holiday Inn and threw our duffel bags on the beds.

"It's weird that we're scouting Southern already," I said. "We have all day tomorrow to do that." I wanted the rest of the night off to relax.

Allie shrugged. She was one of the most easygoing people I had ever met, and she didn't mind film, because she was one of those women who could watch a scout film about another team and learn from it and then remember what she had learned when she got on the court later. Not everyone's brain worked that way, which drove the coaches crazy. I had good basketball instincts, but a weak mind for analysis. Coach Katz and Coach Bailey had brilliant minds for analysis. If I had my way, we would have only two or three set plays. Instead, we had dozens and dozens and dozens of them. Further complicating my situation was that I played both guard and forward and had to learn every play from two different positions.

"Don't forget to leave your phone in here," I reminded Allie. She was injured—stress fractures in her foot—so she hadn't played that day. Even though she normally played more than I did, I was older, so I took charge. "The last thing we need right now is for someone's phone to go off during film."

We tossed our phones down, pocketed our hotel keys, and galumphed down the hall in our team sweats and unlaced sneakers.

Coach Katz had a whole suite in the hotel. The players sat on the floor around the TV as the coaches perched on the couches around us, and Coach Romero popped in a DVD.

"All right, ladies," Romero said. "We're gonna watch today's game."

I was surprised. We had never done this before. Especially in our tight SoCon schedule, where we played a Saturday-afternoon game and a Monday-night game every week, when a game was over, it was over. Then we moved on to getting ready for the next one. This week we would spend Saturday night talking about Saturday afternoon.

The sound on the TV was off, and the room was silent. No one fast-forwarded through free throws, dead balls, or time-outs, the way they usually did. Huddled on the carpet, the team kept quiet the entire first half, cringing at our missed shots and defensive assignments. We looked sloppy and tired. This was the point. The coaches weren't going to tell us we sucked; they had already done that. Now they were going to show us.

By that point in the season I had taken on the role of encourager. In the negative environment our losses dragged behind us like a heavy cape, and we needed all the positivity and energy we could get. I figured that since I could not do much else, I was going to be the source of some positive energy. I always kept up a running stream of complimentary commentary during film.

As my teammates and coaches and I sat in tense, hungry silence and rewatched the game I had just watched from the sidelines that afternoon, I felt a burn of anger in my chest and a ringing in my head. I decided to fight the power a little. I barely played anyway, so the stakes were low.

In the second half things visibly picked up. Jenni made some beautiful plays. Whitney scored nine straight points. Lyss went on a tear, too, and Emma hit some well-timed three-pointers. I complimented them out loud, the way we normally did when we watched film and somebody did something good.

"Good hustle, Whit," I murmured, my heart beating fast, when Whitney read a passing lane perfectly and earned a steal. Or, "Nice finish, Lyss," when Lyss laid it in off the backboard. Or, "Great pass, Jen," when

Jenni had a pretty assist. We had agreed as a team that the comeback would be something to build on. These plays were building blocks.

A few minutes later, I heard Coach Katz's voice behind me. "Otto, who's your roommate tonight?" she asked. I whipped around to face her, startled.

"Uh," I said. "Allie."

"And do you have a key to your room with you?" she asked.

"Yes, ma'am."

"I'd like you to go wait there, please," she said evenly.

My teammates gaped at her, then at me, baffled. Most of them thought I had sneaked my phone in and gotten caught when it buzzed, but I knew exactly why she was kicking me out of the room. By complimenting my teammates during what was supposed to be a punishment, I was sassing her, bucking her authority. I pulled myself to my feet and walked out the door.

As soon as I got back to my room, the facade of coolness shattered. I burst into tears and called my mom.

Later, I heard the buzz of the key in the hotel room door, and Allie came in tentatively. "Are you okay?" she asked. She had always been a favorite of the coaches; I never had. Allie was a light-walker. I was a short-leasher. We saw the same ocean from different shores.

"What happened?" Allie asked. "Did you have your phone?"

I rubbed my eyes. "Nah, I was talking back," I explained.

Allie looked confused. "That stuff you were saying?"

I nodded.

"She wants to see you in her room," Allie continued.

"Right now?" I asked.

"Yeah," she said.

"Are we getting dinner?"

"Doesn't look like it."

So Katz really was serious about that. They had never flat-out refused to feed us dinner before. After previous losses on the road, sometimes the coaches had canceled our meal reservations and given us each five bucks to spend at McDonald's instead, a trick Tennessee coach Pat Summitt had pulled, too.

"'Get in and get it to go,'" Coach Summitt apparently told her players after one loss in the early 1980s, pulling the team van into a McDonald's parking lot. But our college coaches had always made sure we ate *something*, no matter how greasy or small portioned, no matter how mad they were. Not today.

I think Coach Katz tried to model a lot of her coaching style and techniques on Coach Summitt's. I think she saw a little of herself in her. I saw it, too. Coach Summitt was another strong-willed southern woman who grew up working on Tennessee farms and spoke in a drawl and loved hoops. Summitt was seven years older, but both women were born in the 1950s, both part of a generation that came of age during the slow adaptation of Title IX, women crucial to the formation of women's college basketball as we know it today. Both were likable, passionate, and outspoken ambassadors for their programs, for the sport, and for women athletes.

When Tennessee suffered its first loss at Vanderbilt in 1985, they made that trip home without dinner. Coach Summitt also once pulled a no-stopping-to-eat-after-a-loss trick with a team after a loss in Mississippi; she drove the team bus all night and would not even let the players out to pee. She had made her teams do their own laundry as a punishment. She held them to high standards, and when they didn't meet them, they paid up.

One-on-one conversations with Coach Katz tended to go better for me, and for many of my teammates, when we cried in front of her or when she could tell we'd been crying. I stopped in the bathroom on my way out to check that my face was appropriately red and blotchy. Then I knocked on the door of Coach Katz's suite and gingerly pushed the door open.

"Come on in, Otto," she said cheerfully. It was strange and ominous to hear that cheerfulness when you knew you were in trouble, but that was Coach Katz. The four coaches sat me down on the couch and told me calmly they had been trying to make a point and that my sass was not appreciated. I protested that I had been looking for the silver lining. They reminded me what time the bus left in the morning and said I could go.

The sun was setting over Charleston, and it was officially dinnertime. My stomach grumbled, informing me that it was confused.

Women's college basketball in the United States had come a long way in just a couple of decades. When Pat Summitt started her coaching career in the early 1970s at age twenty-two, she drove the team van herself. Vivian Stringer, who coached at Cheyney State in Pennsylvania when she graduated, and then at Iowa and then Rutgers, did the same, except it was a prison bus with defective brakes. At Kay Yow's first coaching job at Elon College (now Elon University) in North Carolina, wrote Pamela Grundy and Susan Shackelford, quoting Yow in their book, *Shattering the Glass*, the players and coaches "paid for [their] own gas and food, bought their own uniforms and ironed the numerals on." Before that women during the Great Depression "practiced in their socks, saving their precious basketball shoes for games." One team in the 1950s, the Arkansas Travelers, kept a gun with them on the road, and they "weren't afraid to use it," one of them said, as a group of single women traveling together was seen as an easy target.

Then–Davidson College athletic director Thom Cartmill told a campus publication in 1974 that he thought "women probably differ[ed] from men in the amount of time and dedication they want to devote to a sports program, as well as being less interested in the competitive aspects of a game."

Over the next three and a half decades, Davidson's female athletes had proved him wrong. Now in the late 2000s, we had full college scholarships, which included tuition and food and beds and books and pens and calculators. We had two different sweat suits to travel in, two sets of practice gear and uniforms, and warm-up jerseys that people washed for us. We had matching sports bras, socks, Spandex, sneakers, shower shoes, countless T-shirts, and two pairs of basketball shoes per player, all free. We had an athletic trainer who took care of our bodies during the season, including on the road, and our own locker room, small as it was. We had four coaches who didn't coach any other sports or work any other jobs to make their living. On special occasions we flew to games instead of taking the bus, which had working brakes and was driven by a trained bus driver, not by a coach. A member of the school's sports information staff, Gavin McFarlin, covered all of our games and traveled with us on the road, and the athletics marketing and promotions department spent time and money trying to get people to come watch us play. All of our food, both on campus and on road trips, was paid for. In fact, we had access to so much food, all the time, that the lack of it in Charleston had come as an especially harsh shock.

This was all just the basic package for a Division I women's basketball program—we knew girls at bigger schools got way more swag—but it was still a lot. Free gear, free food, free school, free travel with your best friends—what more could a teenager ask for?

We even had a team shrink. Early on that season Coach Katz had hired a young male sports psychologist named Troy, himself a former Davidson student-athlete, to meet with us. We all knew we had a lot of potential that year that we were not meeting. Coach Katz was visibly beginning to grasp at straws. The year before had been disappointing too, and at the Division I level head coaches don't keep their jobs if they don't win games. She presumably wanted to make sure we tried everything we could.

Maybe our coaches realized that we wouldn't come to them with our basketball problems because they controlled our playing time. Maybe they thought we would open up to an outsider, but I was not the only player who had already shut myself off emotionally. Troy was just another mandatory time suck, just another adult we were supposed to trust.

At the end of October, after we'd had a few sessions with Troy, the entire team had gotten an email from Coach Bailey. It was immediately clear that this message was intended only for Troy, not for us. That we had received it had to be the result of a rather calamitous mistake by the coaching staff. It contained the coaches' detailed thoughts on each of us as people and as basketball players, apparently to give Troy some background information before he spoke to us individually. Coaches assess their players all the time. We knew that; we were their job. But usually we weren't privy to the dirty details.

What I saw affected me for the rest of my career. I read the email at my desk in my dorm room with my jaw hanging open.

"Amanda Ottaway—She works extremely hard and genuinely cares about the success of this team. She probably loves the game more than anyone, however, when it comes to performing she freezes. Otto is a very intelligent young woman in the classroom but her learning curve on the court is non-existent. She has all of the ability, but, doesn't know how to use it/get there/see the big picture etc. . . . Once one mistake happens she plays tighter and tighter and generally never recovers."

I appreciated that they recognized how much I loved hoops. I wished that meant they'd give me more of a chance to play.

Other evaluations were much worse. Amber got called "high maintenance" and was accused of cutting corners. Emma was described as "selfish." Ashley was apparently "very selfish in the same way as Emma, except ten times worse." Whitney had been "working extremely hard, but, has displayed selfishness."

"It's like all the worst things you think about yourself," Emma said years later, "and you're seeing them in print."

Olivia's evaluation, which we read about a month after that awful day when she hit her head on the upper courts, was telling. "Olivia Lowery—Olivia is struggling in every way possible. She came into preseason far behind everyone else. It's questioned if she loves the game or if she cares about individual and team success. She has been very removed from the team because of an injury and it will be hard for her to catch up. Olivia has a hard battle ahead of her that will no doubt trouble her along the way."

There was now no question of knowing how the coaches felt about Olivia and her injury. We had read with our own eyes what we already questioned ourselves.

Because everything was always provided for us on road trips, most of us didn't even bring our wallets. There was no need. For planes we needed our IDs, but we never needed any money. Everything, from food to lodging to transport, was always covered. So even if we found a way to buy our own food—if we sneaked out to try to find a restaurant or grocery store within walking distance in Charleston—we wouldn't be able to pay for it. Washing our own uniforms and practice gear would be tricky simply because nobody had change for the hotel washers and dryers. We were lucky Jenni's parents were around to donate some cash to the cause.

On this trip, thankfully, Ashley had brought a credit card. The team quietly gathered in her hotel room, sprawled on the beds and the floor, and listened, practically drooling, as Ashley ordered a stack of pizzas. We would all owe her money later, but for now we at least had a snack. We could not stop giggling. My tears from that afternoon were forgotten as I explained what had happened while we wolfed down the pizza straight out of the box.

That the act of feeding ourselves had become an act of rebellion, something we had to do in secret, was both funny and sobering. And so it was that night, crammed together on the two beds and the floor in that Charleston hotel room, eating pizza in our baggy sweatpants, when we started taking notes. We had been saying for months that we should tell the athletic administration about how discouraged we were with the program, but we were scared. We didn't want to sound like a bunch of whiny, tattling kids, and even more than that we knew word got around fast among the adults in the Baker Sports Complex. If Coach Katz found out we'd gone to Jim Murphy about her, we were scared to think what she might do. We had legitimate concerns, and we wanted to be taken seriously. We had tried to tell Troy these things, but we spent so much time catching him up that there was no time to brainstorm solutions.

We were unhappy. Punishment was valid, we weren't perfect, and sometimes, like that fall with the drinking incident, we deserved it. But Coach Katz took punishment to physical and emotional extremes. Playing for her had become both emotionally and physically exhausting in a way that we couldn't take anymore.

My teammates and I were mostly the types of people who internalized every bit of criticism we got. With Coach Katz criticism was generalized, or aimed at our character, rather than being something an individual player could act and build on—we were lazy and selfish, or didn't appreciate our scholarships, rather than we'd been missing too many box-outs lately, for example. We would rather get screamed at on the court for a mistake than ignored off it. Maybe that tactic worked for some players, but it did not work for us, and it was part of the reason we were losing so much. We were so deep in our own heads that we barely remembered how we had once been able to play.

The hotel we stayed at in Charleston had a restaurant but no free continental breakfast. The next morning Allie and I packed up our duffel bags and dragged ourselves to the bus for the two-and-a-half-hour drive southwest to Georgia Southern. Despite the pizza I was hungry enough to be irritable; I could not even imagine how hungry the girls who had played the whole game the day before must be.

The bus snacks were still hidden in the storage space underneath the bus, so no breakfast for us. We rode in near silence, most of us listening to music or staring out the windows. The coaches said we could eat when we arrived in Georgia in the early afternoon, and they kept their promise. By that time it had been more than twenty hours, including part of a game day, since we had eaten a team-sponsored meal. We had a fairly normal practice in Georgia Southern's gym that day. It seemed like the mind-set now was to look forward instead of back.

The hotel staff in Georgia kept a bowl of lollipops on the front desk. We took so many they hid the bowl. We beat Georgia Southern by almost twenty points. We brought our record to an even .500 at 9-9 and rode home to spend the rest of the week in Davidson before heading to Boone, North Carolina, the following Saturday to take on Appalachian State.

8 A Postgame Surprise

Appalachian State's athletic program was famous because its football team had beaten Michigan a few years earlier, in 2007. What people outside of Boone didn't talk about as much was App's women's basketball team, which was perennially at the top of our conference and incredibly tough to beat in its home gym. App's campus sat in—confusingly—the Blue Ridge Mountains, and the court in the Holmes Center was built at an elevation of approximately 3,333 feet, a number plastered all over the gym, presumably for intimidation purposes. That elevation really did make a difference. The town of Davidson sat at just over 1,000 feet. We got tired and breathless more easily in the mountains.

Boone—named after explorer Daniel Boone—is a snowy city nearly twice the size of Davidson. Appalachian State had a much larger student body than ours, 17,000 to our approximately 1,700. Their fans were loud and crass and callous, and although we professed to hate them, it was kind of fun to play there and actually pretty cool that some people cared about women's basketball enough to come out on a Saturday afternoon and trash-talk an opposing team. More than 1,500 fans showed up at our game that day, an impressive number for midmajor women's college basketball. We usually got a third of that number at our home games, and we averaged more fans than any other Davidson women's team.

Davidson was a progressive town, and the college was the center of much of its social life. Some parents, as mine had done, brought both their little boys and their little girls to watch us play. Tickets to our games cost less than tickets to men's games, spectators were guaranteed a good seat, and the kids still saw Division I basketball. We babysat for some of these families, who knew we'd have some free weekends since we didn't party during the season. Our professors could often be counted on to catch a game or two. Sharon, one of the Commons cafeteria employees, was a fixture at both men's and women's games, as was an old guy named Fred, who always sat by himself with a huge DAVIDSON WILDCATS flag. We felt comforted by the sweet, steady presence of the folks who rode vans in from the Pines, the retirement home up the street, with their red sweaters and puffs of white hair, several orderly rows of glasses glinting under the game lights. Usually, a couple of unmarried, middle-aged men showed up who seemed to genuinely enjoy basketball but also stood a little too close to us when we came out to the lobby after games.

We had a small, loyal posse of student fans. Some were practice players who started showing up to every game with signs and posters. Others were our friends from church or from our halls or classes. Many played football or other sports. The men's basketball team showed up to most of our home games when they could my first two years. After that their support started to trickle off.

People sometimes stopped us on the street and in restaurants and asked about our season. Little girls adored us. Their parents thought we were stellar role models. For the most part, though, when people talked about "Davidson basketball," it was safe to assume they were talking about the default: the men.

Coach Katz, in her ninth year at Davidson, was three Southern Conference wins away from reaching one hundred for her career, and the assistant coaches and the sports information office kept talking about it. Maybe that was partly why she had been acting so strangely lately, not feeding us in Charleston the week before and all. Maybe she was nervous.

We had outrebounded Charleston and Georgia Southern, but we had trouble boxing out the tall, nimble App State players and their massive center, whose width measured about three of Alanna. They got offensive board after offensive board, their rebounding total almost doubling ours. Their press suffocated us and forced a couple of key turnovers. It was ugly.

I played a startling twelve whole minutes in this game because a couple of our post players got into foul trouble. But I was not in game shape. I had gone from playing almost every minute of every game of my entire life to barely seeing the court at all, and I had gotten comfortable on the bench. Being in practice shape, being able to run a bunch of suicides in a row, wasn't the same. There's something unique about the kind of fitness a player needs to sprint up and down the court over and over, push people around, and run plays at both ends.

I had had an ache on the top of my right foot for a few weeks, and it intensified that day, shooting pains through my foot and up my leg. I knew about the warning signs of a stress fracture, a tiny crack in a bone usually in the foot or leg, because Emma, Amber, Whitney, and Allie all had them in their feet that year. So did Lyss, who played with incredible heart that day, despite the pain.

A small number of stress fractures was normal on a women's team. We put intense, repetitive strain on our bodies. It is possible to play through stress fractures if you're willing to wait longer for them to heal, but not good to play too much. Often, players with stress fractures rode the stationary bike on the sideline during practice and then suited up for games.

But as we moved through the season and a total of six of us developed stress fractures in our feet, Beth started to suspect that something more might be wrong. She and Coach Katz thought our team shoes might have something to do with the issue. They called athletic trainers and coaches at several other schools whose women's basketball teams wore the same team shoes we did. Those teams were having the same problem. There was no definitive proof the shoes had contributed to the stress fractures—and we had done a lot of running that year—but we ditched them immediately anyway. The damage had been done. Over the course of the season nearly half our team clomped around wearing the training room's clunky black Velcro boots on their injured feet.

She might not have been a captain, but Lyss was our soul leader, our scrapper, the inspiration for the rest of our team to dive on the floor for every loose ball and go after every rebound. She wore a boot every minute she was off the court, and when she was on the court she tore shit up. She scrapped that day at Appalachian State more than usual. She started over freshman Leah because she had been playing well lately. She put up sixteen points, four rebounds, three assists, and two turnovers. She was all over the place.

Lyss hated losing more than almost anything. She was one of the most competitive people I had ever met. Even in an intramural softball game or a card game, she would work her butt off to win, sometimes to the point where playing with her stopped being fun for everybody else. She liked being good at things, and sports were something she was good at. She wanted to earn people's respect by impressing them with her athleticism. She wasn't sure she knew how to earn respect otherwise, she told me years later.

Unbeknownst to most of us, by this point Lyss and Whitney were regularly breaking dry season. In order to hide it from their roommates and captains, Jenni and Mac, the two of them would sit in Whitney's car in the dark parking lot behind the soccer field and chat while they split a bottle of wine. They were past the legal drinking age and past caring about this particular team rule. That time became sacred to the two of them, their time to relax and bond. On those nights they left the stress of the court and our many losses behind and nurtured their own quiet little rebellion.

Lyss and Whitney, both seniors, had not been voted captains in our team voting process that season. The previous year we'd had four captains: both seniors, Christina and Erin; a junior, Jenni; and a sophomore, Mac. This year we had just two, Jenni and Mac. That meant two of the three seniors were not captains. Lyss went home and cried on the day the coaches made the announcement. Maybe this was because she had been injured a lot, she thought. Maybe the coaches believed she was making up excuses about her injuries so she wouldn't have to play.

She never talked about it, but privately Lyss was shocked and hurt. She did not feel trusted. She felt snubbed. Whitney was a regular starter, and Lyss either started or was first off the bench. Since Mac couldn't play, Jenni took on the full weight of captaining on the court.

Appalachian State opened the second half strong, taking a twelve-point lead by the first media time-out, the game stoppages that occurred every four minutes so the TV and radio stations that covered us could go to commercial. By the next media we had closed the gap to three. At the 11:06 mark, Lyss hit one of her five three-pointers—she'd really found her shooting touch lately—and brought us within one, 47–46.

We could never quite catch them. They'd be up twelve, and then we would cut their lead to four. Then all of a sudden it was back to eight, then nine, then eleven. We just ran out of time. The final score was 71–62, App.

We had outrebounded our opponents in eight of the last nine games, but App's size and quickness were too much for us today, and we did not box out well. They grabbed an embarrassing forty-six rebounds to our twenty-eight.

Quietly, wet-haired, ice bags wrapped onto various creaky joints, we heaved ourselves onto the bus, ate our boxed lunches, and sat in near silence for the two-hour trek home, looking forward to hanging out in Davidson on a Saturday night. My foot was bothering me so much that I was actually excited to spend my evening looking for over-the-counter orthotics at Walmart. I hated that we all had to wear the same shoes. We didn't all have the same feet.

Emma's boyfriend's parents were in town, and they were all supposed to have dinner together. Allie's mom was visiting, too. There was a winter party and concert in the student union that Mac and a few other people were looking forward to. We had another game Monday, but at home, so all we had the next day was practice. We didn't have to travel anywhere.

We pulled into the bus bay alongside the gym and stopped. The bus driver flicked the lights on. Heads started popping up from behind seats and out of headphones and from behind books.

"Okay, we just pulled up. I gotta go," Emma said on the phone to Noah, her boyfriend, a football player. "I'll meet you at your house in a few minutes." Allie texted her mom, telling her we had just gotten back and that she would see her soon for dinner.

We waited for Coach Katz to turn around in the aisle and address us from the front of the bus before we got off, as she always did. She surveyed us coolly, the wrinkles that snaked across her pale face highlighted like rivers under the fluorescent bus lights.

"Y'all have fifteen minutes," she said softly, "to get your gear on and meet me on the court." She turned and walked off the bus, her spray of red hair the last part of her we saw as she descended the stairs.

We ducked behind our seats to gaze at each other in openmouthed amazement. I almost laughed out loud. *Practice?* Now? After a shootaround and a game? This could not be legal with the NCAA. I glanced back at our captains, Jenni and Mac. They looked as confused and astonished as the rest of us. We hobbled off the bus and filed back down the hallway to our locker room in disbelief, muttering quietly to each other.

"Is she serious?"

"Why?"

"Did we really play that bad?"

"Well, there goes my Saturday night."

"My hair's still wet."

"My mom is here!"

"I'm hungry."

"We still have another game on Monday, right?"

Two freshmen each grabbed a handle of the heavy laundry bag and hauled it to the locker room with us, one of their "freshman duties." We tied up our still-wet hair; yanked on our next set of practice jerseys, shorts, and socks; grabbed our moist ankle braces, knee pads, and shoes; and hustled back to the training room to get taped and wrapped for the third time that day.

Meghan was quiet as she taped our ankles. Beth was there too, because the football team was doing a workout on the upper courts. My teammates and I wondered aloud if this was an NCAA violation. We were allowed to play only a certain number of hours on game days. We had already had an hourlong shootaround that morning and played a full game.

But we couldn't spend too much time analyzing whether Meghan and Beth were worried as we rushed to get back on the court. At least the coaches let us stretch first. As we trotted the bus ride out of our cold muscles, Coach Katz started talking. Tonight, she announced, we would practice our rebounding.

"Mac, can you keep score, please?" Coach Katz asked. Mac nodded and slipped behind the scorers' table, silently resenting us for not having won the game, for keeping her at practice even though she'd had nothing to do with our loss that day. It was a terrible feeling.

She kept it quiet from us, but Mac was crying almost every day that year. Over time the little jabs, the small exclusions, the feeling of not knowing her role on the team—it all added up. She felt like some of her teammates didn't respect her because she was supposed to give them orders, but couldn't prove herself on the court. She felt like the coaches did not always respect her, either, asking her to do menial tasks, like fetching water bottles. We had managers, but we couldn't afford to bring them on the road with us, so they came only to home practices and home games. Otherwise, Mac and the freshmen took over some of those logistical duties.

Jenni, our other captain, was exhausted. She was our floor general, the only captain who could play, and the primary liaison between her teammates and the coaches. She had a tough job, because she knew we were getting a lot of mixed messages from the coaches. Katz had always been a great defensive coach, but now, after years of drilling into us that we had to force the other team's offense out of the middle of the court, she had suddenly changed her mind. Now we should force our players to go to the middle, because that was where the help was, where our teammates stood waiting with their arms up. It made sense in a way. But because it was the exact opposite of what she had always taught us, we needed some time to adjust, which she seemingly kept forgetting. We started to trust her court coaching less and less.

The practice court is a sacred, gritty place of swallowed tears and small triumphs, the place where the ultimate prize—playing time—is both earned and taken away. It is a place of exhaustion, disappointment, and satisfaction; there was no feeling quite like leaving the practice floor after you had impressed the coaches and none as crushing as feeling your performance at a practice spiral out of control. But on some days, like today, practice was only about survival.

The coaches split us into three-on-three teams and pitted us against each other like dogs in a dogfight: Losing teams would run. Players who allowed offensive rebounds would run.

We were all drained. I had played only twelve minutes, and I felt like I was running underwater. I couldn't imagine how my teammates who had played almost the whole game felt. Because we were tired and desperate and sprints were on the line, we got sloppy fast. We played the kind of aggressive, dirty way we usually saved for our nastiest opponents. We grabbed jerseys, pulled hair, threw elbows, scratched and shoved each other. We fell hard, our knees and elbows thudding heavily on the court. We dove into pileups and slid around in our sweat. We snarled.

At my basket six players, a grunting, slippery, twelve-armed monster, writhed on the floor like a football pileup without any pads for a good eight or ten seconds before a coach blew a whistle to stop the play. Slowly, one or two at a time, we stood up, mouths hanging open, breathing hard, extricating ourselves from the mass of tangled limbs, adjusting torn-out ponytails, swiping dirt and ripped skin from our elbows and sweat from our foreheads, glaring at each other. Jenni picked up the ball, her mouth a thin line, her sweaty bangs torn out from under her headband, her jersey sliding off one shoulder. As I walked past Taylor on her way to reset the play, I purposely bumped her hard with my shoulder.

"Is anyone gonna call a foul?" Whitney howled, her voice cracking with frustration, as Alanna decked her for a rebound on a different court. The coaches let it go. Mac sat at the scorers' table, frantically tallying and subtracting as over and over and over we threw each other to the ground and pounced wildly on top of the skittering ball.

We all ended up running sprints at one point or another, for one reason or another. If a team lost a round, or allowed too many offensive rebounds or had too many turnovers, those players sprinted. We ran suicides, double suicides, down-and-backs, and sixteens—sixteen sprints side to side across the court in sixty-eight seconds. Those who did not finish a sprint set in time ran it again.

Out of the corners of our eyes we saw some people not touching lines with their feet on sprints, and we tucked our anger at those teammates away, where it might explode later. Touching lines was a big deal. Early in the season, not long after the coaches named Jenni and Mac captains, we were running 3-2-3 sprints at practice—up and down the court six times, a few seconds' rest, then four times, a few seconds' rest, then six times again.

"Alyssa," the coaches said, "you didn't touch the line. Run it again." Lyss ran the sprint set again. Sometimes, especially when we were tired, it was hard to tell whether we had touched a line during a sprint set. The coaches watched our feet carefully because as far as they were concerned, it was a matter of principle, but as a player I definitely didn't want to waste any extra energy going too far over the line. So most of us usually cut it close. When we were unlucky or misjudged the distance or didn't try quite hard enough, sometimes we fell just short.

After that practice one of the coaches told Jenni and Mac that Lyss had continued to miss the line and that they should address it with her. They asked their friend and teammate and roommate if she would go back up to the court and run the sprint again.

"Look," Lyss said to them, wondering if they really believed that she hadn't touched the line—or even whether the coaches had just made the whole thing up to help establish the captains' authority over the other seniors, also a possibility. "If you guys ever seriously think that I'm intentionally cutting corners, tell me. But if not, no. No."

She knew that Jenni and Mac were only trying to do what the coaches had told them to do, but on top of not being named captain, this was a slap in the face.

"I'm not going out there and running another 3-2-3," Lyss told them. "I'm sorry, but no." And she didn't.

Belk Arena was not empty as we huffed around the court that evening after the App game. It was dinnertime on a Saturday, and other athletes had the upper courts, also patrolled by their coaches and a few athletic trainers. I saw some of the football staff gazing curiously at us staggering around, shoving each other. I registered all these witnesses somewhere in the back of my mind, behind the pain and exhaustion and Katz's voice, calm and dangerous in my ear, to box out.

Pat Summitt's postgame practices were the stuff of movies. If Coach Summitt did it, it had to be an acceptable coaching move, right? After one loss at Ole Miss, she made her team take the floor—in Mississippi—and run twenty suicides, despite the Ole Miss fans still leaving the gym. After a loss at Vanderbilt and a bus ride home to Knoxville, she made them get dressed and back on their own court for a practice at two in the morning. When they lost at South Carolina, they had to put on their stinky uniforms the next morning when they got back and play as she yelled, "Now you're going to play the half you didn't play last night."

Coach Katz kicked us out of our locker room during a rough streak my freshman year; Pat Summitt had famously pulled that trick for five weeks with her 1989–90 team. We spent a week or so changing in the general locker room with whoever else happened to be in there and showering in the referees' locker room. Coach Katz also told us that because we were an embarrassment to our college, we were not allowed to wear any Davidson gear, so we all showed up to practice in ratty, mismatched cutoffs from high school.

There were important differences between Coach Katz and Coach Summitt, though. The most obvious was that Coach Summitt's teams went to the NCAA Tournament every year and sometimes won championships, and Davidson women's basketball did not compete on that level. We had never qualified for the NCAA Tournament or won even a league championship. Having read every book about Coach Summitt's teams I could get my hands on as a teenager, I suspected that their success—partly due to their superior talent—also came, in part, because they felt loved. Maybe they felt like all the punishments, awful as they were, came from a place of powerful shared competitiveness and deep love. Maybe they understood there was a purpose to each punitive action and that there could be redemption.

I believed that Coach Katz loved us in her way. I just didn't think she knew how to show us. So a lot of the time her competitiveness came off as plain old hurtful. We were competitive, too, and we didn't need her love to cushion the blow, but we did need to know that the anger we saw was founded in something rational, in a sense of belief in us and that we could be better. We needed to feel like we could be forgiven for our screwups, not that people held grudges against us. We needed to understand that each punishment was legitimate, that it was for a purpose, and that it would end.

The assistant coaches loved us, too, but they had very little job protection. And because the world of women's Division I coaches is so small, as I learned during my recruiting process, if a fired assistant complained to an athletic director, she might be branded a tattletale and have a hard time getting hired elsewhere. So our assistants, overworked and underpaid as many Division I women's basketball assistant coaches are, tended to side with Coach Katz. We didn't begrudge them that.

I envied players at other schools who seemed to have tight bonds with their coaches. We never could quite seem to get there. There was a reason we hadn't called any of them the night I had gone to the hospital and Megan got sick. We liked our assistants, but many of us felt there were no adults in our program we could fully trust.

We had our moments, though. Coach Romero had arrived at one morning practice during winter break a few weeks earlier, bursting with news. The men's team had an out-of-conference home game that night against the University of Pennsylvania.

"Y'all!" Romero exclaimed as we puttered around the court, practicing our foul shots, wearing long-sleeved shirts because the gym was freezing. They usually kept the heat pretty low in Belk Arena over winter break. "Guess who the ticket office just told me is coming to the men's game tonight?"

"Who?" we asked, knowing the answer would be big. After all, LeBron James had come to watch the guys play in the NCAA Tournament. Our men's team had a convenient habit of attracting celebrity fans.

Romero paused dramatically, her eyes lit up behind her glasses, her mouth spread wide in a toothy grin. "Den. Zel. Washington," she announced.

"Denzel Washington?" we squealed. "Holy shit."

Remember the Titans had been one of the most popular movies in the country when we were kids. By now we knew Denzel was famous for some other stuff, too.

"Yup," Romero said. "His people just called and bought a bunch of tickets. His son's the backup point guard at Penn."

"Oh, my God," Olivia exclaimed from the sideline. "Dude. We gotta go. We can go, right, 'Mero?"

"Should be fine," said Romero. "You should be able to swipe your CatCards like usual, but let me see if I can get you better seats."

"Can you get us seats near him?" Whitney asked.

"I'll try," said Romero. "I'll let y'all know."

She managed to procure first-level seats for every one of us who wanted to go see Denzel—ahem, the men's team—in person that night. With our CatCards, Davidson's form of student ID, we had free admission to all the college sporting events. The free student seating at men's basketball games was subprime, if we didn't want to go early in the morning and wait in line for a good seat. Most students got shoved high in the second-level bleachers on the far side of the court, in the rafters way behind the visitors' bench. Not that night. Since it was three days after Christmas and most students except our team and the men's team were off campus, we would be able to watch from the section behind the basket where the pep band usually sat.

Denzel's son Malcolm Washington was a short kid who saw some playing time but not much. He wasn't bad, wasn't outstanding, but he was cute. We spent most of the game observing Denzel's every move and reaction. He smoldered behind the visitors' bench in a dapper black conductor's cap. We might not have known it was him if we didn't know it was him.

I sat with Jenni, Olivia, Marie, and Emma. We spent the game giggling and taking pictures of the Oscar winner in our midst. Poor Penn never had a prayer. Our guys, somehow unfazed by Denzel's magical presence, jumped out to an 8–0 lead and never looked back.

"Somebody's gotta go ask him for an autograph," I said, dipping a nacho in hot melted cheese and shoving it into my mouth, an open bag of peanut M&Ms in my lap. John and Pam, who worked in the Wildcat Den—the sandwich spot and concession stand outside the gym—could usually rustle up free snacks for us, as long as we were discreet about it. John, or "Big John," as we called him, was famous on campus for knowing the name of almost every student he served food to. Pam always told us to have a blessed day.

"I'll do it," said Taylor.

We watched her closely, grinning with anticipation, as she marched purposefully around the lower bowl of arena seating and down the steps to the row where Denzel sat. She bent over and said something. A few seconds later, she turned around and started back toward us.

"What happened?" we exploded as soon as Taylor was back within earshot of us.

Taylor shook her head. "He's not doing autographs," she said.

Malcolm Washington played nine minutes. The Wildcats won, 79–50.

Coach Katz wanted us to be able to rest as much as possible over that winter break. She didn't want us shopping; she wanted us sitting down. Our bodies had taken more of a beating that season and preseason than usual, and we were dropping with injuries faster than Meghan could get us back on the court.

We were allowed to spend our per diem money only at certain restaurants preselected by the coaches, and the restaurant employees would cross our names off a list when we ordered a meal there. A few times the coaches bought us movie tickets, which I thought might be an NCAA violation. We spent night after night at those same couple of restaurants followed by the movie theater a few miles away, usually in jeans and sweatshirts, sometimes wearing 3-D glasses.

Olivia had not been allowed to travel for most of the season, for many reasons—it was physically painful for her to be in the gym with us, and she was also behind on her schoolwork, barely hanging on academically after all the class she had missed fall semester. She had trouble with even the most basic functions, like reading. She bought the audio versions of her textbooks and listened to them with her eyes closed. She lived in constant pain. Coach Katz helped arrange a couple of private tutors for her. Olivia had spent winter break in the hotel with us, but mostly catching up on schoolwork. She had gotten some "incompletes" that fall semester.

The way we talked and laughed with Liv over Denzel and his lack of autograph made things seem like they were back to normal for a moment, but they weren't. Not like they used to be.

We finally finished our postgame practice an hour and twenty minutes after we stepped on the court, some groups having run well more than eighty punishment sprints—Emma counted. We staggered back to the locker room to shower, too tired and angry to speak to each other, our arms and necks spangled with fingernail scratches, blooming with finger-shaped bruises. Emotions ran high from all the elbow throwing. I showered, dragged myself to my dorm, and went straight to bed. When I woke up the next morning, it took me a few minutes to figure out how to walk properly again. The dull ache in my foot sharpened into a shot of pain every time I took a step. We still had a game the next day.

By some miracle we pulled out a ten-point win over Western Carolina, one of the worst teams in the conference. It was the ninth game in the last eleven—the App game being one of the two exceptions—where we had outrebounded the competition.

We had a day off. The day after that Coach Katz did not show up to practice.

"Where's Coach Katz?" we asked in our prepractice huddle.

"She's out recruiting," the assistant coaches told us. One of the managers stood poised in the stands with a video camera, ready to film our practice.

This was definitely weird. Coach Katz had never missed an in-season practice for a recruiting trip before. Preseason or postseason, occasionally, but never this.

Wherever she was, we had one of our best practices of the year. We played hard but loose, controlled, and natural. Coach Bailey was tough on us, proving that just because Coach Katz wasn't there didn't mean we could fuck around, and we rose to her challenge.

Coach Katz wasn't at practice the next day, either. Lyss, who because of her various injuries was in and out of the training room several times a day and knew all the gossip, had heard that the football coaches who saw us practicing after the App State game had reported Coach Katz to the athletic administration, and she had been suspended for it.

Since 1991 it has been an NCAA violation to hold a practice after a game. In season a coach was allowed to require twenty hours of participation in the sport per week. That included practice, weights, film, and basically any workout we did with a coach. However, "countable athletically related activities may not be conducted at any time (including vacation periods) following competition," said the rule.

Immediately, I felt a rush of gratitude toward the rest of the Davidson community for looking out for us.

Lyss wrote an email that she addressed only to Coach Katz. Her message: Suspension? Fine. Lying about it? Over the line. "For future reference," she added at the end, "I'd appreciate the truth."

Coach Katz came back to practice two days later and called a meeting in the team room. She was upset that our postgame practice had been discussed outside the team, even though we hadn't been the ones to report her. She told us she was loyal to us and that people outside the team were trying to tear us apart.

"I didn't know I couldn't practice you," she continued. "And I have almost no NCAA violations." She genuinely might not have known that a postgame practice was against the rules. The rule was almost two decades old, though.

She seemed to be trying to prove to us that she followed the rules and did not maliciously try to break them. That fitted with her personality: she liked order and good manners. We didn't know what we were supposed to do with this information, though. We did not know how many violations she had or how many coaches were allowed to have before they got suspended or fired. The athletic director and assistant athletic director, Jim Murphy and Katy McNay, were the ones to have that conversation with. Coach Katz seemed scared.

Because of the email she had written to Coach Katz, Lyss, just like that, went from being a favored hustle player into the doghouse.

About a month later, Lyss watched practice from the sidelines, because she was supposed to rest her foot whenever possible so she could get through the season. She was so competitive that she hated sitting out more than maybe anyone, and she was a talker. Lyss was shouting encouragement during a drill when Coach Katz snapped, "If you can't play, you shouldn't be saying anything, Alyssa! No one cares what you have to say."

Wide-eyed, wiping sweat from our faces, the players on the court gazed at Coach Katz, shocked.

I care what Lyss has to say, I thought. I didn't say it out loud.

It was the worst thing anyone could have said to Lyss at that point. Coach Katz had struck a chord with her she had never hit before. Lyss's career was weeks from being over for good, she was stuck on the sidelines, and now it didn't even seem like she could be appreciated there.

She refused to give Coach Katz the power of seeing her cry. So Lyss strode off the court in her big black boot and clomped down the stairs into the hallway. Mac followed her and, after a few minutes, got her to come back to the court. Lyss barely said a word the rest of practice.

9 A Team in Transition

Troy, our team psychologist, had basically given up on us. In our last group session he gave us a speech along the lines of: "I can't do anything to fix this situation with your coach. I'm convinced that the problem does not lie with you. I'm not really sure what to tell you guys to do at this point. Let's just try to get you through the season."

How much did you get paid for this diagnosis? we thought. *We already knew all that.*

And he disappeared as quickly as he had come. When your shrink quits on you, that's when you know you've got issues.

We had agreed as a team not to give up, though. We knew we still had the raw talent for a championship, and we wanted to win one—not for our coaches, but for each other. This goal was a deep bond, a quiet acknowledgment, a rebellion. We were tough. We could handle being Davidson athletes, so we could handle anything. We could still do this.

But the rebellion was not flawlessly unified, either. It never had been.

Olivia still wanted to be around us, but our relationship with her was awkward and strained. She had barely traveled with the team at all. By the time we left for our longest conference road trip of the season, though—to mid-February games against the University of

Tennessee at Chattanooga and Samford University in Birmingham, Alabama—Olivia thought she would be able to go. She was feeling a little better, and she had been working hard to catch up in class. She had finished her fall semester over winter break and gotten off to a decent start in the spring. She still wasn't allowed to attend practices because she was supposed to be focusing on schoolwork, but Coach Katz had told her that if she put her head down and worked until that weekend, annually our most important in-conference trip, she would be able to come with us as a reward. Her boyfriend was a little miffed that she would be spending Valentine's Day with the team, but Liv wanted to.

So she set her heart on it. The morning of our departure Olivia pulled on her team sweats and packed her team duffel bag and backpack. She started lugging her bags across campus to the gym, where we caught the bus. It was pouring cold rain, because in North Carolina in February we got rain instead of snow. Her phone rang.

"Hello?" Olivia said, blinking raindrops out of her eyes.

"Hi, Olivia," Coach Simmons said at the other end of the phone. "There's been a misunderstanding." He explained, in his gentle, fatherly voice, that she would not be allowed to travel with the team that weekend, or for the rest of the season.

Olivia's bags slid off her shoulders and fell, with two sodden, heavy *plumphs*, on the sidewalk in front of the student union. She burst into tears. The rain was relentless, soaking her team sweatshirt, seeping through her team sneakers, deflating her triumphant mane of curly hair.

It was her breaking point. It was her breaking point with the coaches; she hated that Coach Simmons, with whom she never discussed her injury, had been the one to give her this news. She assumed Coach Katz had asked him to, but did not understand why. It was her breaking point with her teammates, the moment she knew she had truly lost us all. She knew that even though this exclusion was the coaches' decision, her teammates no longer valued her as part of the team as we once did. She knew we wouldn't fight for her to join us on this trip. She had been shut out of the family from the top down. We barely saw her for the rest of February.

The Southern Conference Tournament was in Charlotte that year, so we didn't have to travel far. Our first game was in an arena called the Bojangles Coliseum, named after the fast-food chain, which we kept giggling about. We would face Furman, a team we had beaten comfortably just four days earlier.

We disembarked in the bus bay outside the Coliseum, dressed in our matching travel suits and sneakers. We bunched around the side of the bus to grab our duffel bags from the storage space underneath and entered the yawning underbelly of the arena.

There was a walk we affected when we entered an arena as visitors for a game or even a shootaround or practice. The romance of the big entrance was ruined for the freshmen who had to carry the large, unwieldy laundry bag, the ball bag, and the water bottles, but the rest of us were free to look as cool as we wanted. Duffel bags slung diagonally across the body, hands shoved in pockets, headphones in ears, we blasted whatever motivational music—Eminem, Beyoncé–worked for us at the moment. We swaggered.

Before bigger games between better teams, ESPN focused its cameras on this headphoned parade from the bus bay through the dark bowels of arenas. Even though nobody watched us, we imitated the purposeful stomp of the NBA and WNBA players we saw on television. It didn't matter how badly we might lose in that arena. What mattered was that we entered it like we had already won: with attitude.

We stared straight ahead, faces cool and set. We were presumably focused on the game, although I was usually thinking either about the hours I had spent in the gym at my childhood YMCA or about whatever boy I liked at the time, wishing he could watch me move like this, hoping there were men out there who found this walk sexy. Years later, when I realized this was also how I walked down dark city streets alone, desperately hoping men did *not* find it sexy, I called it the "like-you're-about-to-kill-somebody" walk.

Furman's players thought they were pretty clever with their little "F-U" huddle chant. They had won only six games all year, just four in the conference. Usually, they were at least a threat, but this year they were terrible. We had beaten Furman the last four times we played them. They were the eleventh seed out of eleven teams. With a 12-8 conference record, we had a six seed. By all accounts except perhaps Furman's, we were supposed to win. And although we focused on that day's game, we were also thinking ahead. We couldn't help it. Four games. Four days. Anything could happen.

I felt my heartbeat quicken as the powerful, delicious adrenaline of the playoffs, which had been coursing through my body for a few days now, picked up its pace. This feeling had come back faithfully every year since my junior high–playing days. No matter how exhausted we were, no matter how sick of basketball or the coaches or losing, no matter how little playing time we actually got, the playoffs were rejuvenating. Nobody's records mattered once the playoffs started. Anybody could win; anybody could lose. Every year, like clockwork, the beginning of the playoffs helped us remember why we loved our jobs.

Olivia dressed for that game and warmed up with the team. Jogging through the layup lines, she felt torn—happy to be back on the court, but also strange, like the coaches were doing her a favor by letting her run around with us.

With fifteen minutes left in the game, we were up fifteen. Then Furman started to chip away. We lost by six points, and just like that our season was over, our final record 14-15.

The coaches didn't say much in the locker room afterward. All of us were stunned and disappointed.

Jenni sat with her face buried in the neck of her jersey, holding her head with both hands. Her bangs, soaked with sweat, hung limply over her headband. The ends and underside of her ponytail dripped onto her thin, muscular, shaking shoulders.

On her way out, Coach Katz patted Jenni on the back. "Go take a shower, Jennifer," she said softly.

Jenni, slumped deep inside a locker, was crying too hard to even untie her shoes. I wanted to sit down next to her and pull her shoes off, unlace her ankle braces, ease the headband from the wet tangle of her hair, gently help the warrior transition from battle.

That's it, Jenni thought over and over. That's it. It's over. I'm not a basketball player anymore. It's over. I'm not a basketball player anymore. After eighteen years, just like that, she was done. She was not a basketball player anymore.

Whitney was numb, quiet, her face blank. She couldn't feel anything because the things she needed to feel were too big for her to feel. Lyss stared around at all of us, her bright-blue eyes glazed over in shock. The locker room in that moment felt like a funeral home. Something—something beautiful and draining and excruciatingly loved—had died, somewhat unexpectedly, and nobody knew what to say to make it better.

Although many of our parents had hotel rooms in Charlotte, the players had to ride the bus back to Davidson and stop for an agonizingly long and quiet sit-down dinner on the way. Coach Katz let Taylor's mom drive Taylor and Mac, who were sick with a stomach virus, home in her minivan, which Mac threw up in. When they got back to campus Mac lay in bed by herself and cried for Jenni, Lyss, and Whitney and their finished careers.

While we sat silently around a restaurant table with the coaches, waiting miserably for greasy platters of sandwiches and fries, our families sat together at an expensive Charlotte steak house. My parents had made the eight-hour drive down to the tournament with my younger brothers, Luke, Zach, Jesse, and Casey. The boys, who had never been to a restaurant so fancy, were overwhelmed by the prices on the menu. They squirmed in their chairs, these three teenagers and a ten-year-old, hilariously underdressed for a place where professional athletes brought dates to dinner, and said they didn't want anything.

"It's okay, guys," our mom told them. "It's a special occasion." Indeed, it wasn't every day a kid got to sit in a car for eight hours and watch his big sister ride the bench while her college basketball team lost to the worst team in the league.

At the end of the meal Olivia's dad picked up the bill for the entire table.

We grabbed our cars from campus and drove back to Charlotte to hang out with our families or, if our own families weren't there, to nuzzle for love from our teammates' families. I watched Jenni sipping a cocktail at the hotel bar with her parents, her face a blur of melancholy and relief, her long hair drying down her back.

I was jealous of her. I was jealous that she was drinking a cocktail, and since I was only twenty I couldn't drink at hotel bars yet. But mostly I was jealous her career was over. I would have maybe two weeks off, and then it would start all over again. How was I going to get through the next two years, especially without Jen, Lyss, and Whitney?

I pulled up a bar stool next to Jenni and slung an arm over her shoulders. We were both pale, no makeup, hair still wet, draped in our soft, baggy black team sweats. She looked bone-weary.

Jenni told me years later that she had wanted to be sad that day, but it was bittersweet. She loved us, but she was tired. She was exhausted from being the only on-court liaison between her teammates and the coaches. She was ready to be in charge of herself, her own time, her own body, her own actions.

Jenni's mom got up and wrapped her arms around me. My family was there too, but this was the last time I would see Mr. and Mrs. Hughes for a long time. They had come to every game for the past two years. It would be strange to look up in the stands next season and not see them sitting there, decked out in their Davidson gear. They made us all feel loved and seen and appreciated.

"We love ya, Otto," Mama Hughes murmured into my shoulder.

I was devastated to not be Whitney, Lyss, and Jenni's teammate anymore. Ever since our official visit Olivia and Taylor and I had been closer with them than with anyone else on the team. But I felt a powerful relief at the ending of the season. Plus, we still had meals and parties and late-night study sessions and a week at a beach house in South Carolina after finals. This was not good-bye. Not yet.

Back on campus a few days later, our entire team sat in the room Davidson used for press conferences, the same room Stephen Curry had used to announce he was leaving early for the NBA, where he became the seventh pick in the 2009 draft. But the reason we were there wasn't quite as fun. Jim Murphy and Katy McNay, the top two athletic administrators, sat there too. Our coaches did not. Many of us brought notes that we had been taking all season.

We explained to Jim and Katy what had been going on with our team, that season and before it, and how much we were hurting. We did our best to describe our complicated, volatile relationship with Coach Katz. All three seniors had shown up to this meeting, which meant a lot to the rest of us. It meant they cared enough about the situation that they wanted to see it addressed, even though they would graduate in two months.

"My teammates are like my family," one of the seniors had written in her notes, "but my coaches aren't even sort of friends. They don't invest in us as people, but merely as commodities that either produce or don't."

More than half the team cried. It was cleansing, cathartic. Katy and Jim listened intently, rarely stopping us to ask questions. They seemed to recognize that it was our turn to talk.

The bottom line, we explained, was that we had decided that year that we wanted to play as hard as we could for each other alone. We determined that together over our secret pizza in Charleston. We tried to unite as a team, but we had united against our coach, and as much as we genuinely, desperately wanted to win a championship, no matter how many times we told each other that in the locker room, we could not do it without her.

"Why didn't you come to us sooner?" Jim asked. We were scared she would find out and use it against us, we told him. Davidson was a small campus. Word got around.

Coach Katz had many strengths. She was a good face for the program. She was enthusiastic and well spoken in public, and she loved and appreciated Davidson for the tight-knit community and rigorously academic place that it was. She made sure we kept our grades up, and she had built relationships with our professors. She was a solid strategist and a good defensive coach—until this year, when she started making decisions we didn't trust, seemingly out of desperation that we weren't winning more with the talent we had. Most important, she recruited players who adored each other.

Our problem wasn't what had happened to our bodies or our record that year. It was that the LGBTQ women on our team had not felt safe being fully out of the closet, that black women on our team had never felt comfortable in their own color and hair and culture. It was about how our coaches knew almost nothing about who we were as people off the court. It was about what playing the sport we loved was doing to our minds and spirits, how ready the seniors were to graduate and get out. It was about how some of us had forgotten that we loved it.

Jim and Katy thanked us, saying they would be able to tell us more soon.

Not long afterward, still in the break period between the season and our spring workouts, Coach Katz called a meeting in the team room. She told us that she was resigning from her position as head women's basketball coach at Davidson. She cried. Taylor, who had always gotten along with Coach Katz, also cried. The rest of us watched stonily as Coach Katz bowed her head, walked out the side door of the team room, and left us there, stunned into silence.

We walked to Commons together for dinner, feeling like survivors of a war, stumbling in dazed from the smoke of the battlefield. We explained to our friends in the cafeteria what had happened. It was all very civil. Jim Murphy wished everyone "great success going forward." Coach Katz's resignation meant all three assistants had to leave their jobs too, unless her replacement decided to rehire them. We were coachless. No one had technically been fired, so they should be able to find other jobs elsewhere.

"A national search for a replacement will begin immediately," the press release said. Nobody publicly gave a real reason for the resignation. Coach Katz simply said it was the "right move for her and the program," ESPN reported.

Most of us, especially the upperclassmen, had found bright spots elsewhere. Jenni got into graduate school. Lyss, Whitney, and Taylor all had close friends outside the team. Ashley had STRIDE—a college program where she was a mentor to young students of color—and the sorority she and a few other women were secretly trying to bring to campus. Emma had Campus Outreach and Athletes in

Action. Mac was professionally ambitious and widely loved, friends with pretty much the entire football team. I had FreeWord and the college newspaper and my English-major friends. About half the team had a serious significant other. We liked school, and we worked hard in class. We had found things we enjoyed besides basketball, and maybe if I had been enjoying basketball more or felt like it was worth it to spend more time in the gym, I wouldn't have looked for other activities that made my soul happy.

"If nothing else," my mom said wisely when I called my parents to break the news, "Coach Katz brought you to your teammates. She brought you guys together. She knew how to recruit girls who would get along. You love them so much. You have to credit her for that."

And I did.

I finally got an X-ray on the foot that had been bugging me all season. The Charlotte orthopedists found what they called a "stress reaction" and scar-tissue evidence that I'd had a stress fracture earlier, possibly in February, when I started to suspect that was the problem. The training room put me in one of its infamous clunky black walking boots, which I promptly christened Betty Boot. I was supposed to wear Betty all the time, except on the court.

As the coaches prepared to move out of the office, Coach Bailey called our new recruit Rory to tell her about the coaching change. Rory was driving when her phone rang.

"Stokes," came Coach Bailey's voice. "I have something to tell you."

She explained that Coach Katz would not be returning to Davidson next year. None of the coaches would. If Rory wanted to get out of her scholarship, Bailey would help her. Since incoming recruits weren't technically students yet, they would theoretically have an easier time transferring than the rest of us, although they would need Davidson to release them from their National Letters of Intent. Bailey was sad she would not have a chance to coach Rory.

Rory felt a little scared—the outgoing coaches were the people who had recruited her, the ones she had a relationship with. She held her commitment, though. Davidson, the place, was where she wanted to be.

Our other recruit, Sam, was sleeping over at a friend's house without cell reception, so she missed Coach Katz's call. Katz left her a voice mail and said she was resigning. Davidson would be putting a new coach in place. She apologized for not being able to see Rory and Sam through their careers.

Sam didn't understand how the process worked and thought she might lose her scholarship. She had signed her National Letter of Intent with Davidson College, though, not with Coach Katz, and that document protected her for her first year. While a new coach can technically come in and clean house if she wants to, Sam wouldn't lose her full ride just because Coach Katz had resigned. Instead, it would be up to the new coach to decide whether he or she wanted to let any of us returning players go by not renewing our scholarships that summer. We were aware of this danger, but assumed Jim Murphy and Katy McNay would protect us if the worst happened. We had the right to appeal.

While the administration started combing through résumés for the new head-coaching job—Jim said they received 125—we continued with our lives, and that meant, for everyone but the seniors, beginning the postseason. Every year seniors joked they were going to put booze in opaque water bottles and sit in the stands and get drunk while they watched our spring workouts. One of the men's assistant coaches, whom we called T.I., and the team's director of basketball operations, Billy, who was still a student at Davidson, led these workouts for us.

Billy and T.I. put us through some of the same workouts the men's team did, which were fun and intense but not grueling. Olivia was finally cleared to play at that point, but she couldn't do any contact drills. Springtime was mostly for fundamentals anyway. Billy and T.I., accustomed to working with players who wore their hair short, seemed genuinely bewildered the time Liv's hair tie snapped and she went running off the court to the locker room to grab a new one, her thick mane flying behind her. It was good to have her back.

We really liked Billy and T.I. Some of us wondered now whether we might prefer to have a male coach—a desire that went against almost every feminist principle I was learning I believed in. When Title IX first passed in 1972, nearly all women's basketball coaches and administrators were female. Women's sports were often run by the women's physical education department at universities in a "separate-but-unequal" kind of way. But when the NCAA took over women's college basketball from the Association for Intercollegiate Athletics for Women in the early 1980s so the sport would have more publicity and make more money, jobs in the field became more appealing to men because of that increased publicity and money. In 2008 about 64 percent of Division I women's basketball head coaches were women, down from 90 percent in 1972.

As female players we were not sure whether we had a duty to advocate for female coaches because they were at a disadvantage in our country's hiring market, especially in sports, where men coached women but women didn't coach men. We didn't know which was more feminist: to support women for coaching jobs no matter what or to simply want the best coach we could get, regardless of his, her, or their gender, because we knew we deserved the best.

Probing the reasons years later for our somewhat bewildering preference, some of my teammates and I wondered whether we liked male coaches better because of the experiences we'd had. We had been coached by men from an early age, starting with our own fathers and moving through high school and AAU, where we were often coached by other girls' fathers. Coach Katz was the first female head coach many of us had worked with, and college, with these two straight losing seasons, had not been as positive an experience for most of us as high school.

It was a funny, kind of backward result of progressiveness: as sports for girls became more popular with each generation, more dads who liked sports wanted to be involved with their daughters' athletic careers. Maybe we liked those male coaches because we were valuable to their squads, and it was easier to like coaches who gave us praise and playing time. Maybe part of the reason I had liked Coach Genday and Coach Hurd so much was that I was a starter and valued contributor on both of their teams.

Maybe it wasn't fair for my teammates and me to let our college experience sour us on female coaches. However, we had just seen firsthand a woman coach who was unable to leave court drama on the court. Jenni, a psychology major, pointed out later that perhaps we were conditioned by the patriarchal society we had been raised in to accept male boss behavior as the norm, and when a female boss behaved in the same way—by yelling or through verbal abuse or throwing things—we deemed her inappropriate. Maybe we liked Billy and T.I. so much because they were in charge of us only temporarily in the off-season and therefore didn't have to make rules or dole out real punishments. Or maybe we really did prefer for men to be in charge of us. It was impossible to know.

I decided that regardless of what kind of feminist it made me, I did want Davidson to hire a male head coach for the women's basketball job. I had simply had better personal experiences with male coaches. The Athletic Department picked three finalists for the position, two women and one man, and brought them all to campus separately for daylong interviews. Our team met with each prospect for an hour or so, without Katy or Jim or any other adults present. Katy told us to email her after each meeting with our thoughts, if we chose. We had some idea what we were looking for, but, more important, we knew what we did not want.

My teammates and I were overthinkers, internalizers, and people-pleasers. Generalized, passive-aggressive criticism like "y'all don't care" was devastating for us, because it wasn't true, and we couldn't parse it out and physically address it on the court. We needed constructive, straightforward advice like, "Box out. You should have gotten that rebound. I need you to be big for us on the boards," or, "Get the ball inside. Use your fakes; use your dribble; use your pivot foot. She's open. Don't be selfish."

One selfish play did not a selfish human make. I had always responded well to coaches yelling furiously at me. They could scream in my face all they wanted as long as I respected them, felt they respected me in return, and understood that their words were constructive and not personal.

More than anything, we wanted to be loved. We wanted a coach who was going to get to know and love us as human beings and work with us from there. If that was all our new head coach did, we would be happy.

"Sitting in this room are fourteen girls ready and willing to run through a brick wall for a coach they respect and who respects them," one of the seniors had written in her notes for our postseason meeting with Jim and Katy. We were still ready. Still willing.

Women's college basketball was such a small world. The first candidate was Jennifer Roos, the associate head coach at Bowling Green State University who had recruited me when I was sixteen. On my unofficial visit there I had admired her rapport with her fellow coaches and players. Plus, if she got the job, I reasoned, I might actually get some playing time.

Turned out Coach Roos was an alumna. She had played basketball on the Davidson club team in 1991–92 and then again when the school brought the varsity program back the following year. Then she stuck around to help coach for eight years after she graduated. She was businesslike, assertive, and goal oriented. I loved her.

The next candidate was a man whose name nobody could remember after he left. He had been coaching at an Ivy League school, which made sense for us academically. He made clear to us that he would prioritize his family life over his coaching, which in theory sounded reasonable, but we'd never had a coach with kids before and didn't know whether his promise would work out or whether we wanted it to.

The third coach we interviewed was Teresa Harris. Tall, stooped, and soft-spoken, she had been an All-American at Northwestern. They told us she had been an assistant coach at Cornell and Tulane, but had never been a head coach before. She seemed nice, but painfully shy. Ashley was excited that she was black, which was—we all knew—a rarity for Davidson. There were not many black women in positions of power at our school. Only about 8 percent of Division I athletic directors in the country were women, of any race. Our Athletic Department staff, overwhelmingly white, had just two women in high-level positions.

Recording artist Akon came to campus that spring for a concert in Belk Arena. Akon had been big when we were in high school; Olivia and I spent hours crooning along to his whiny, irresistible, vaguely reggae hit "Don't Matter" in the car and in hotel rooms when we were

AAU teammates. His music was catchy and misogynistic, lightly Auto-Tuned and just exotic enough to be incredibly popular. But Akon was decidedly out of fashion by then, stuck in the awkward stage between being a pop star on the Billboard charts and the point where nostalgic twentysomethings giggled over his songs on road trips.

The basketball court my teammates and I had laughed and cried and sweated and bled all over was gone, covered by an artificial floor and an elevated stage at the far end by the home bench. A scattering of people sat in the lower bowl of the arena, but the majority of the crowd—a few hundred students and townies—gathered on the floor in front of the stage. It was a sad showing. Akon, the international pop star, could not fill our small college gym the way Stephen Curry and his teammates had once filled it.

Stephen was around for the weekend. He had come back to his hometown of Charlotte to visit. As an NBA rookie and the starting point guard for the perennially lousy Golden State Warriors, Stephen was substantially more famous now than he had been when he left school a year earlier. Most people in the gym already knew him, though, so they mostly left him alone, except for quick hugs and catch-ups. The Warriors' season had ended in mid-April with a record of 26-56. We thought we'd had it bad losing fifteen games that year; I couldn't imagine losing fifty-six. But Steph was his usual cheerful, goofy self, and he seemed happy to be with his college buddies again.

We stood coolly with the men's team in the back, on the court we all loved, and made fun of Akon. I had been flirting for a few weekends with one of the men's players, James, and he and I kept exchanging glances as Akon gyrated, lip-synched, and flashed his disturbingly white teeth at the crowd. James came over to chat.

Occasionally, men's and women's basketball players hooked up with each other or dated, but for the most part we were all just friends, like brothers and sisters. I had crushes on a bunch of them, including James, but the guys I liked usually liked different girls, smaller girls. Although I was accustomed to boys not wanting me because I was tall and strong and awkward, it still stung every time.

Later that night I ran into James again, at a party. We danced together, me working hard not to stomp on his feet with Betty Boot, which I still wore everywhere. He bent at the waist to put his mouth near my ear, the rare man who was that much taller than me. His scruffy cheek, his strong jaw, brushed against mine. God, he was gorgeous. My heart did a little hiccup.

"Wanna get out of here?" he said over the noise. I looked up at him and grinned.

"Yeah!" I shouted back. He grabbed my hand, and we walked outside, Betty Boot clunking loudly along with us. We fumbled in the darkness, chatting and giggling, through a patch of trees and popped out onto the soccer field. No way were we allowed to be there.

The sprinklers sputtered on. We definitely were not supposed to be there. James pried off his shoes and shirt and sprinted away, his arms flung wide, his bronzed back and shoulder muscles bulging, into the spray.

"Come on, Otto!" he shouted. "Hang the fuck out!"

"Hold on!" I yelled back.

Betty Boot could not get wet. I plopped down in the grass and started yanking at the Velcro that fastened her around my leg. I wasn't supposed to put any weight on my foot without her, but the doctors had carelessly failed to consider that a cute shirtless boy might invite me to run through sprinklers with him.

After a minute or so of fiddling I finally yanked off the boot and tossed it aside. I took a few cautious steps. Little pangs of pain shot through my right foot from the tiny, delicate bones near my second toe. I started jogging, and the pain clanged up the foot into my shin. It was worth it.

"Take your shirt off!" James hollered from across the field.

"Nope!" I yelled back. I didn't like how I looked with my shirt off. Plus, I was wearing a bra that didn't fit anymore and made my back and pectoral muscles bulge like sausages.

"Hang the fuck out!" he yelled again.

I left my shirt on and ran faster toward him, trying to keep most of my weight on my left foot, just barely touching the ground with my right, squealing and ducking in the sprinkler spray. We stood barefoot in the kickoff circle, blinking water droplets out of our eyes, laughing. He put his hands on my waist and kissed me.

A few minutes later, lying inside the goal, my shirt still on, we heard a car door slam and saw a light bouncing toward us.

"Fuck," James muttered, scrambling off me. I stood up and straightened my skirt, swiped the wet grass from my butt. It was a cop. Betty was fifty yards away. We couldn't run.

"What are y'all doin' out here?" came the voice of a campus police officer. He moved closer, and my heart beat faster. Exactly how much trouble could we get into for being on the soccer field under the sprinklers, making out but mostly clothed, in the middle of the night? I wasn't sure if we were trespassing. I did not know what would happen to me if campus police busted me for the second time that year.

Then the officer recognized James, and I knew we were off the hook. Everyone on campus, including the cops, knew and loved the men's basketball players.

"You know you can't be on this field right now," the officer said. "And anyway, the sprinklers are on! Y'all gonna mess up the grass. Go home."

"Yes, sir," James said.

"Yes, sir," I said, glancing back and forth between the two of them. Such large men, and so at ease with each other.

"All right," the officer said sternly, but looking like he wanted to smile. "Get outta here, you two." He turned around, got back in his car, and pulled away. James and I looked at each other and shrugged. The mood wasn't the same. So I put Betty back on, we walked back toward the party and said good night, and I went home to bed by myself. I couldn't wait to tell my team about it over Commons brunch the next morning.

A few weeks later, most of my teammates, and some girls from my hall, came to watch the FreeWord slam poetry spring show. When the emcee called me to the stage to perform my poem, my team went crazy. That was one of the most beautiful things about Davidson to me: the jocks supported the poets because the jocks were friends with the poets, and sometimes the jocks were the poets.

The spring semester ended, and we took our finals, went to the beach, said teary good-byes for now to the seniors, and scattered for the summer. Still no word from the Athletic Department about a new coach.

A few more weeks went by. Finally, on May 27, Jim and Katy emailed the team, including the recent graduates, with a message marked CONFIDENTIAL. Jim thanked us for our help and patience in the process and said they had decided to hire Teresa Harris. Davidson would officially announce this the next day at a press conference, which we were invited to if we were in town.

My dad, as usual, did more research on Coach Harris than I did. He wrote me an email and explained he had read that Harris's players loved her and that she had a "knack and a way with people." That was an important quality for this job. A big chunk of it was public relations—getting people excited about a women's sports team.

"Two of the UMass coaches who are no longer at UMass were on the staff at Northwestern when Harris played there," my dad added. "(The head coach, Gina something, and her associate head coach, Pam Egan. Remember them? . . .) I wouldn't be surprised if one of them comes on as an assistant."

Within a few weeks of Coach Harris's hiring, Coach Katz had gotten a new Division I head-coaching job, at Jacksonville State University in Alabama. Her former Davidson players kept tabs on her over the next few seasons.

I did not hear a word from Coach Harris or any of her new staff for two months after the announcement, not even a quick, "Hey, y'all, I'm excited to be your coach." It was the end of July before we learned of the assistants Coach Harris had picked: Heather Montgomery, Trish McDermott, and—my dad was right—Pam Egan. Four women, two black, two white.

Pam was the one who had chatted with us more than anyone at UMass, the one who told my parents and me that the UMass coaches would try to be as honest as possible during the recruiting process, but that they were looking at other people for my position. Hers was rare recruiting honesty that I appreciated.

I would be coached by someone who had recruited me, after all—not only someone who had recruited me, but someone who had also coached my new head coach. I didn't know anything about Heather or Trish, but I was excited that Coach Harris had hired Pam. Maybe I would see some playing time under this staff.

Dozens of coaches switch schools right after the Final Four in April, but that process tends to happen pretty fast. May 27 seemed to us a late date for a head-coaching hire. It looked like Coach Harris had to scramble for a staff and ended up hiring two people she didn't really know and who didn't know Davidson.

Trish was in her midtwenties, fresh from a master's degree and looking for a Division I women's basketball coaching job, any Division I women's basketball coaching job. It was so hard to get a foot in the door, especially as a woman in a field that had previously been women dominated but was increasingly hiring men as well, that Trish would have said yes to almost any school. She had played high school basketball with a woman who later played under Coach Harris at Tulane. That teammate put Trish and Coach Harris in touch, knowing that Harris was looking for an assistant. Trish knew almost nothing about Davidson or Coach Harris or our team, but she wanted to coach. So she said yes to the job almost overnight, moved to North Carolina, and immediately was on the road to Orlando, recruiting with Heather, her brand-new colleague.

A few days into my junior year I stopped in the office to meet the new coaches. We had not heard much from them, but I figured it would be a good idea, especially because I was a junior now, an upperclassman, a leader. Emma had already been to the office and warned me that these new women had barely looked up from their computers. I had put it off for so long in part to avoid this impending awkwardness.

I wandered in, gazing around at the changes they'd made in the office. "Hi," I said. I should be more assertive this year, I thought.

Terry, our administrative assistant—she'd stayed on through the transition—looked up. "Hey, sweetie," she said to me. We chatted about our summers. The men's basketball program could afford, in addition to a secretary, a director of basketball operations, a kind of extra assistant coach who helped organize travel and recruiting logistics and could lend an extra hand on and off the court. The women's program didn't have one, so Terry and our coaches were stretched thin.

Emma was right—no one else looked up from her computer for several seconds. Finally, Pam scooted backward on her wheelie chair in the back office and frowned out at me over the tops of her red-framed glasses.

"Hey, Amanda," she said. "What took you so long?"

"It's, um, been a crazy beginning of the year," I explained. "It's good to see you again, Coach. We met when you were at UMass." We shook hands.

"I'm Amanda, but everyone calls me Otto," I said, waving to Trish and Heather, and I shook their hands too. Coach Harris came out of her office, and we exchanged pleasantries. After a few minutes I excused myself and left. Year three.

10 Our Bodies, Everyone's Business

It was like we were all freshmen again. Having a whole new coaching staff on campus meant that that year's preseason was more than the usual display of our trying to prove how hard we had worked that summer. We were making first impressions, all of us, coaches and players. The upperclassmen tried to show our new coaches not only that we deserved playing time, but also that we could help them lead the team. Since Coach Harris had not recruited us, anything we had done on the court in the past few years—good or bad—didn't matter anymore. The sophomores and freshmen showed off, begging to be noticed.

Coach Pam Egan, the one who had recruited me at UMass, threw herself into the Davidson community and quickly established herself as the team chatterbox. She had a million questions for everybody about everything. How were our classes? Which professor was the toughest? Did we have any tests coming up? Had we finished that paper that was due this week? How about that event on campus last weekend—did we go? What did we think about it? What about that new dish they were serving in Commons? We were unaccustomed to this level of cheerful interrogation and regarded Pam with wary, baffled curiosity.

The coaches typically came to observe our weight workouts but didn't lead them, since that was Coach Swieton's job. Pam and Trish both used our lifting sessions as their own workout time, riding the elliptical in the corner and keeping one eye on us as Coach Swieton guided us through squats, bench presses, hang cleans, yoga-ball push-ups, ladder agilities, and exercises with weighted medicine balls.

"So Pam's ellipticizin', just pedaling away in that corner by Swieton's office, and she just stops," Amber said dramatically one morning at Commons breakfast after a preseason team weights session, brushing a few long braids off her shoulder and taking a sip of her teal sports drink.

Amber was a sophomore Coach Katz had brought to campus the year before as an "invited walk-on"—meaning she did not yet have a scholarship but had come with the expectation, unlike Coop, that she would earn one within a year or two. But with the coaching change, Amber had to prove herself all over again. Coach Harris gave her one that year, conditionally, and Amber would have to fight to keep it. In pursuit of this goal she was aggressive, sometimes frustratingly so. She was fun and quick to laughter, though, and good at making us laugh, too. She was loud and radiant, one of the best storytellers on the team.

"And because of my back, it's hard for me to do a lot of weight with that exercise, so my medicine ball was probably eight pounds. But I hadn't explained that to Pam because she'd just ask a zillion questions," Amber said. "And Leah's next to me doing, like, twenty pounds, 'cause Leah's a beast. So Pam peers over at me, like over her glasses, and she's frozen on her elliptical, like this—"

Amber struck a pose, arm flung out over her tray of cheesy eggs, one knee hoisted up, like someone stopped in the middle of an elliptical pedal, and peered down her nose at us.

"And she goes . . . ," Amber giggled and continued in a prim, mock-casual tone, like a lady commenting on the calorie count of a tea-party dessert: "'So, Amber, I couldn't help but *notice* that, uh, your ball is significantly *smaller* than everyone else's.'"

We burst out laughing, imitating Amber's imitation of Pam. Jokes about balls never got old. "So I, uh, couldn't help but *notice* . . ."

One of the coaches' favorite preseason workouts that fall was swimming, which helped preserve our joints and which they probably also found personally amusing. Some players liked swim workouts. Some hated them. Early in the morning, before class, we swam laps in breaststroke and backstroke, paddled with kickboards, treaded water in place, did defensive slides on the pool bottom, played monkey-in-the-middle, and practiced leaping out of the water like mermaids to catch balls tossed at us from poolside. One time we played water polo, but the coaches nixed that after we tried to drown each other for possession of the ball. Throwing a dozen large, highly competitive, athletic women who play a land sport into a pool with one ball and a loosely defined set of rules is a bad plan.

Freshman Sam hated both pool workouts and mornings. It was a rough combination. She had almost been late to our first morning weight workout that year because she slept through her alarm. When Rory, who lived on the first floor of their freshman dorm, went up to the third floor to grab Sam so they could walk together, the door was locked. No one came when she knocked. Rory assumed Sam had already left and walked to weights alone.

The coaches had a rule: "Early is on time, and on time is late." Fortunately, Marie arrived to weights early enough that day that she managed to run to Sam's dorm, bang on the door hard enough to wake her up, and hustle her over to the weight room, just in time. Sam did not get in trouble, but she knew it had been a close call. The night before our first swim workout, she slept in her swimsuit.

We didn't have team swimsuits, so most of us swam in our team sports bras and Spandex bottoms. One-piece suits were also permitted. Sam said she had an old one-piece she wanted to wear. That morning she rolled out of bed, wrapped herself in a towel, and stumbled to the pool.

When it was time for all of us to drop our towels and get in the water that first day, Sam stripped down to her one-piece. It was zebra striped, with many suggestive cutouts. We about fell into the pool laughing. Sam stood stock-still on the deck, arms at her sides, blinking blearily, scowling around at us, her bed head frizzing wildly around her face like a mane.

Coach Harris walked in to watch the workout and looked her up and down. "Girl, you tryin' out for *The Lion King* or something?" she said dryly, and we lost it.

We also did yoga about once a week. It was usually our last workout of the day. We'd crash into the dark physical education classroom in our sock feet, sleeveless workout shirts, and baggy shorts, sweaty and stinky from pickup or a small-group workout, ready to relax, not wanting to be challenged.

Our instructor, Nolan, was a textbook bona fide yogi with a soft and gentle voice, a heap of curly hair, and an admirable amount of Zen-like patience for our sarcasm, our goofing off, and our heinous yoga skills. There are all kinds of athletic women, and Nolan was one. She wasn't the kind of athlete we were used to, though—any teammate probably could have thrown her across the room—and many of us didn't take her seriously.

One day in the locker room during her freshman year, Marie, who had slept just two hours the night before because of homework, experienced a mild crisis familiar to us all. "But when do we sleep?" she had groaned, aghast, to no one in particular.

We still repeated that line with gusto, like some student-athlete motto. Marie eventually figured out when to sleep—lying flat on her back in yoga class, doing the "Christ pose."

It was a good preseason, much better than the previous year's. We knew we were deep enough and talented enough for a conference championship and a trip to the NCAAs that year, perhaps better equipped than ever for a long postseason. Two of our leading scorers, Alanna and Emma, were back. We had Rory, the sensational freshman. Taylor would probably start regularly this year, although I was fighting for that spot, too. Leah was coming into her own at point guard, and Ashley would, hopefully, have finally found her stride. Olivia was a question mark in her ability both to compete again and to stay healthy.

We were going to have to spend the season without Mac, though. She was a senior now, applying to graduate programs to become a physician assistant (PA). Between that and a whole new coaching staff who probably wouldn't understand her unique situation as injured former player/student assistant coach/captain/manager/hospital bed-side buddy/team mom, she didn't have the heart to work out a new role on the team. She didn't want a repeat of the previous year, when she'd cried every day. She didn't have the time or energy for that kind of emotional investment in her last year of college. She had talked to Beth and Jim Murphy and, with their support, decided that she would earn her scholarship that year by working in the training room instead. That way she could also get clinical hours for her PA school applications. We would still get to see her, just not on the court.

Our daily routines—workouts, food, and school—remained the same through the coaching change, but our team dynamics began to reconstruct themselves that fall. On the drive home from a team ropes course in September, for example, one of our gay teammates had a long, honest conversation with the coaches about sexuality. From that moment on we were all immensely more open in our discussions about it. We talked about lesbian sex in the locker room for the first time. The entire culture of the team shifted.

Other big changes came, too. Coach Harris switched our home bench so that we now sat under our own pep band, opposite the dimples Coach Katz's high heels had left in the floor on the other side. We were not allowed to wear any of the Davidson gear we had been issued by Katz's staff. Makeup and nail polish were strongly discouraged, long ponytails banned. This was a new era.

Our new head coach, we were learning, was the polar opposite of the previous one in many ways. Harris was quiet and introverted with a wry, deceptive sense of humor. She was black, progressive, midwestern, and businesslike; did not wear makeup; and had been a post player in college. She shied away from the spotlight. She used only as many words as were absolutely necessary. She seemed guarded. But we had big expectations for ourselves that year, and we expected a bold, fearless leader to take us there. We did not have time for a learning curve.

Coach Harris remained introverted. She was so obviously a minority in the Davidson community. Nonminorities could and did offer support, but very few people on campus could fully understand her position. At the time there were no other black head coaches or athletic administrators at Davidson, men or women. People of color, particularly black women, were also—as they are at many private liberal-arts schools—poorly represented among the students and faculty. That year 72 percent of Davidson students identified as white, just 6.5 percent as black or African American. More than twice as many men as women were full-time professors, and of all 167 full-time faculty members, just 23 identified as minorities. There were still just 4 African American full-time professors.

As a Presbyterian school in the conservative American South, Davidson grappled constantly with the gap between its more than century-long history as an expensive, exclusive college for mostly white men and as a place that now genuinely seemed to want to encourage diversity, but made slow progress.

White women's basketball players slightly outnumbered black players in the Southern Conference. But in all of Division I women's basketball the previous year, 51 percent of players were black and 40 percent white. Some teams were almost all black, others almost all white, others half and half. Those numbers were not reflected when it came to the race of players' head coaches—black women held just over 11 percent of Division I women's basketball head-coaching jobs.

Basketball culture for players of all races and genders, though, borrowed heavily from aspects of black culture. In high school I could quote most of the movie *Love and Basketball*, wore my shorts long, got my hair cornrowed, and blasted DMX out of our family minivan. Beyoncé was on the warm-up CD of nearly every school we played against that year, representing not just woman power, but black woman power.

We flew to Little Rock, Arkansas, for two games in mid-November, early in the season. The University of Arkansas–Little Rock (UALR) destroyed us, 76–51. Olivia was back on the court, but she didn't look like herself. Liv had once been a bruiser, but she spent her eleven minutes that day looking timid and scared. She took one shot, grabbed one rebound, made three free throws.

The next day, a Saturday, we practiced at the University of Arkansas in Fayetteville, where we had a Sunday game. After the UALR game, we had kept up with the weird Katz-era tradition of showering in our sports bras and Spandex shorts, maneuvering our loofahs awkwardly to scrub at the skin underneath. But today Olivia had had enough.

"This is bullshit," she announced. She dramatically peeled off her red team sports bra and flung it behind her, where it crumpled on the locker-room floor. We watched the tanned, rounded muscles on her broad back and wide shoulders ripple as she strode toward the showers. She kept going, pausing briefly to wiggle out of her Spandex shorts, and tossed them behind her, too.

Olivia and I lived in an off-campus apartment together, and she didn't have any trouble walking around naked there. But for a team so accustomed to modesty, here in an open locker room, it was a radical move.

I was already in the shower, wearing my sports bra and Spandex. I considered Liv for a second. "Yeah," I said loudly, putting down my bottle of shampoo and following suit, throwing my dripping under-garments on the floor. Then a few others got naked, too. Then a few more. Within the next half hour most of us—not quite everyone, but most of us—had just showered totally naked together for the first time.

The last two years of awkward tiptoeing around my best friends, of being self-conscious about my body around some of the people who knew it best, were over. No more dripping plastic bags in our luggage. We were all women. We all had powerful bodies that we'd worked hard for. There should be no shame in that.

We lost to Southeast Conference team Arkansas the next day by just thirteen. The SEC was one of the best conferences in the country. We were only down seven at halftime but couldn't figure out their press and had thirty-three turnovers for the game. Olivia played six minutes; I played eight. Afterward, we showered naked.

College-age women think about their bodies a lot. As women's college basketball players, we thought about ours perhaps more than most. On the court and in the weight room, it felt good to have a big body;

we were proud to be strong and powerful, proud of the work we'd done to make ourselves that way. There were few things more satisfying than successfully bench-pressing or hang-cleaning a new, heavier amount of weight.

"When you can feel yourself being stronger, when you can move another person who's strong as well, that's a positive feeling," as Allie put it. But it also meant that we often felt most secure about our bodies when we were together. If we went to the lake in Davidson, we wanted to go with a teammate, somebody who looked similarly jacked in a bikini.

Not quite two weeks after Arkansas, on Thanksgiving Day, we left campus at five in the morning to fly to San Antonio, Texas, where Ashley's family lived, for a two-game Thanksgiving tournament. We spent Thanksgiving at Ashley's house. Her family fed all of us. My freshman year we had eaten Thanksgiving dinner in the athletes' cafeteria at Vanderbilt University in Nashville. Sophomore year we ate in a roadside barbecue restaurant with checkered tablecloths on our way to Wilmington, North Carolina. This wasn't quite the same as being home, but being in somebody's house with somebody's family felt right.

The day after Thanksgiving we rocked the University of North Texas, 70–55, qualifying for the championship game against the University of Texas at San Antonio. The scouting report, which we went over in the hotel, listed UTSA's team stats, top offensive rebounders, best three-point shooters, worst foul shooters, and their injured players. Our three assistant coaches took turns watching game films of our opponents, putting these reports together, and presenting them to us, just as Coach Katz's assistant coaches had.

Bullet points describing UTSA's offensive tendencies said things like, "Will use the high ball screen similar to Winthrop—ball handler is looking to get to the basket." That meant that if my player was near the three-point line with the ball, I should be ready for one of her teammates to try to set a screen on me. I had to remember how we were handling screens on this particular player based on her personal strengths and weaknesses. Maybe I was supposed to trap her with one of my teammates. Maybe my teammate was supposed to "hedge"—

jump out in front of my player to slow her down while I made my way around the screen. Maybe I was supposed to slip underneath the screen and meet my player on the other side. In the moment, in the game, we would have no more than a second to remember, so mental preparation was crucial. My problem was that I could rarely remember details like this on the court, whether I studied or not.

"Four out one in will look to penetrate and kick" meant that when UTSA was on offense, four of their players stood around the three-point line with their biggest player on the block near the basket. One of the outside players would dribble toward the hoop, try to draw the defense close to her, and then quickly pass the ball back to someone on the outside. We had to make sure the dribbler didn't get the whole way to the basket while also being ready to run out and guard whom-ever she passed to.

We learned UTSA did not press much, but when they did they ran a press similar to ours. They would probably start the game in a tight, aggressive man-to-man defense, which meant we would have oppor-tunities to make backdoor cuts—quick, slanted sprints toward the basket behind our overplaying defenders.

We read a few bullet points on each of their players. Number 10, for example, was a "quick point guard who will take it 94' [the full length of the floor] in transition—slow her down but don't foul her—very good FT shooter/shoots a lot of 3s so be ready to extend out on her."

There were two keys to our winning, according to the coaches: "Execute our offense if they are in player to player defense—they will over play so take advantage," and, "UTSA is a very good rebound-ing team—we need to win this battle—#22 and #40 are relentless on the offensive boards—get a body on them and match their physical play."

I appreciated the political correctness of saying "player-to-player" defense instead of "man-to-man," but I preferred to call it "man" myself. "Player-to-player" or "woman-to-woman" had too many syllables and took too many precious seconds to say during time-outs or on the court.

We begged Coach Harris to let us see the Alamo while we were in town. We often visited cool or historic cities on road trips—Nashville,

Asheville, Charleston, Birmingham, Little Rock—but we usually saw nothing but the arena, the hotel, a few restaurants, and whatever we could spot out the bus windows. Most of us had grown up on the East Coast and had never seen San Antonio before.

"If y'all win this tournament," Coach Harris said, grinning in spite of herself, "we can see the Alamo."

Our schedule for the next day looked similar to the schedule for any other game day on the road. We had learned to do our homework in the fractions of hours between activities.

9:00 a.m.—Breakfast at the hotel
10:45 a.m.—Depart for shoot around (dressed and taped) (black travel sweats)
11:00–12:00 p.m.—Shoot around @ UTSA Convocation Center
1:00 p.m.—Pregame meal @ EZ's Brick Oven & Grill, San Antonio
3:20 p.m.—Depart for the Stephens Ctr (dressed and taped)
5:00 p.m.—DC vs. UTSA
ASAP—Depart for Austin TX (black travel sweats, grey long sleeve T-shirt)
ASAP—Dinner @ Pappadeaux's, Austin TX
TBA—Check into hotel (Holiday Inn, Austin TX)

We won, beating the University of Texas at San Antonio 69–60. Coach Harris kept her promise, and on our way to dinner in Austin, where our flight would depart the next morning, our driver steered the bus through downtown San Antonio. When we reached the beginning of the street the Alamo was on, we hit heavy traffic. The driver flung open the door of the bus, and we raced out, single file, in our matching black tracksuits and sneakers. Gavin followed us at a jog, clutching a camera, the coaches and Brian right behind him. The bus driver shut the door and continued to inch through the traffic. We gathered hurriedly in front of the limestone building, posed for a few photos for the school athletics website, and then sprinted back to the bus at the other end of the street. Breathless, flushed, and giggling, we piled back on. Tourism, check.

We ate dinner at a swanky Cajun and creole seafood restaurant. I glanced at the prices on the menu and felt a rush of gratitude for my scholarship. This was a luxury. Somebody even ordered fried alligator as an appetizer, just so we could all try it. When we lost we got McDonald's or nothing at all. When we won we got freshly caught seafood and fried alligator. Maybe this was the trick to winning—to bribe us with food.

Our team had an obsessive relationship with food. We loved eating it. We loved thinking about it. We loved talking about it. We loved watching other people eat it. We usually wanted to help other people eat it.

We felt we had to stick together on this. Davidson was a place where the women who were not athletes—"nonners"—seemed to be unusually small. Outsiders frequently remarked on how thin the women were on campus. We were a school full of competitive, type-A academics—perfectionists, controllers, and disordered eaters. Many of us knew someone personally who struggled with her weight. Our team was not immune to disordered eating, either. At one point two players were eating little more than cereal and vegetables in Commons; a coach had told one of them she had a "beer gut." One teammate—unbeknownst to the rest of us at the time—was making herself throw up in the team shower.

The school nutritionist Coach Katz had us meet with at the beginning of my sophomore season had told us all that we needed to be eating about four thousand calories a day, about two times what a regular human should eat. We believed her, and for the most part we tried to. Most of us did not use food to fuel our bodies so much as for fun and to find another way to compete. We just shoveled in as many calories as we could, no matter what form they took. We ate a lot of barbecue, a lot of pasta, and a lot of bread.

In what was perhaps our own personal counter to the eating issues we saw on campus and to the fact that the coaches had so much control over our bodies, many of us were aggressive about what we ate and how much of it there was. We were also constantly hungry. We continued to overeat even when we found out the nutritionist had grossly overestimated the number of calories we needed in order to function. It was as if we wanted to prove to the world that we were healthy. When she arrived at Davidson, our one European player, Marie, ate two plates of food for dinner at Commons and was baffled that her classmate Amber could demolish six. Within two months Marie had six plates, too.

Our sport demanded not just agility and speed but strength and power and solidness. We loved food, and we wanted everyone to know it.

On the bus ride back to the hotel after our seafood dinner, I lay sideways in my seat, holding my stomach in a contented carb coma. I heard someone talking excitedly.

"And I had scallops wrapped in bacon—yes. Wrapped. In. Bacon. They were *wrapped in bacon*, Mom! And they were grilled, like char-grilled, and just, the bacon, oh my gosh. And there was cheese in there, too; they put some kind of cheese in there with the bacon. And dirty rice, which was delicious, and I ordered lemonade—like, we were allowed to order drinks besides water for once, and we ate fried alligator. Fried alligator! As an appetizer! It was so crazy."

It was Allie, on the phone with her mom, telling her every detail of the meal we had just eaten. I started giggling to myself. But she wasn't done yet.

"Well, the alligator was all right," she continued. "It was, like, a little chewy? But it tasted like fried anything basically, like chicken nuggets. Dad. Dad, listen to this. Listen to this meal we just had. I had scallops wrapped in bacon. With cheese. I know! They were wrapped in bacon!"

I sat up, my mouth buried in the sleeve of my team jacket to muffle my laughter, trying to determine in the dark whether anyone else was listening. I made eye contact with Amber, who was struggling to keep a straight face, tears leaking from both eyes. I looked up and down the aisle and saw shoulders shaking with held-in laughter.

"Is anyone else listening to this?" I texted to everyone except Allie.

Before long half the team was in tears in our separate seats, hysterical with silent giggles. Allie was still going.

"I'm telling you, it was wrapped in bacon. It was just—I can't. I can't even do it justice. The bacon and the cheese, and the scallops. I know. We should win tournaments like this all the time. It was so good. That bacon. Scallops wrapped in bacon. Who even thinks of that? We should just wrap everything in bacon."

She finally hung up the phone, and we all burst out laughing.

"You liked that bacon, huh, Al?" I smirked.

She flushed a little but grinned. "It was so good!" she exclaimed.

It was good. It was all good.

Fall-semester finals rolled around a few weeks later. Because our scholarships covered the full cost of living and the off-campus apartment we shared was cheaper than one on campus, Olivia and I each pocketed a few hundred dollars a semester. It had been a weird fall between the two of us. Olivia slept constantly. She was grouchy and combative, and I swiped right back at her. She barely came out of her room. She had been dating a football player since her early concussion days, and he was over a lot, using our hot water and our electricity. That bothered me, and Liv and I fought about it.

Olivia spent most of her time in the apartment, feeling too sick to do much, but it looked like laziness to me. She wanted cable. I didn't want to pay for it. She angrily footed the bill and threatened that she better not see me ever watching the TV in the living room.

Olivia and Hope had gotten into a fight at the end of the previous spring when Hope was moving out of their room, and Hope, who was supposed to live in the apartment with us, had backed out over the summer. Olivia was turning into a different person now than the woman I knew. She grew more selfish, more demanding, more unpleasant and rude. I missed my old best friend, the preconcussion Liv, the fun, outgoing, loving one, my late-night milkshake and dorm-room karaoke buddy, my wingwoman, my girl.

One afternoon in December, Mary Marshall, a soccer player and also an English major, and I sat at my kitchen table in sweatpants with notebooks and novels strewn all around us. Olivia was in her room with the door shut. She spent a lot of time in her room with the door shut.

Mary Marshall and I were studying for our world-literatures final. Our professor was a novelist and poet who didn't treat Mary Marshall and me any differently because we were athletes but also acknowledged that we were, asking us informed questions about our teams and seasons. He particularly liked basketball and played pickup in Belk Arena sometimes during lunch. If a student's phone rang in class, he picked it up and had a conversation with the person on the other end. We read Gabriela Mistral, Franz Kafka, Kōbō Abe, Italo Calvino, Nadine Gordimer.

Mary Marshall read a few lines of poetry dramatically out loud, gesturing with one freckled, manicured hand, a book open on the table. The piece, by Chilean poet Gabriela Mistral, contained not-so-subtle vagina innuendo, and the two of us dissolved into giggles.

Mary Marshall had an incredible laugh, like no laugh I'd ever heard, light and downy and joyful, choky and wheezing because of her asthma.

"Shh-hhh-hhh," I gasped. I didn't want Olivia to come out of her room and yell at us for being too loud.

"Okay," Mary Marshall said once we had calmed down. She took a breath. "Okay. What's the title of that one?"

"The Fig."

"Who wrote it?"

"Mistral." She was one of my favorites.

I still couldn't talk about vaginas without snickering, but I was beginning to finally understand their magic.

"Women have vaginas that can speak to each other," wrote another of my favorite poets, Dominique Christina. Ours certainly did, in the women's basketball locker room. Every month there were a few rough days where most of us, both coaches and players, were grouchy and short-tempered.

My mid-December birthday fell a few days later. Every year it came inconveniently during both the middle of dry season and finals week.

But this year, Coach Harris's first year as head coach, we didn't have a dry season. At least we didn't think we did.

Coach Harris herself did not drink much and didn't see why we needed to. Her philosophy was that if we couldn't go five months without a drink, we should be in rehab.

"Well," she had said at the beginning of the year, "I don't think y'all need to be gettin' drunk every night." And that was the phrase our seniors and captains, Emma and Ashley, used to determine that we would have a "be-smart" rule like the men's team had, meaning no alcohol twenty-four hours before a practice or forty-eight hours before a game. We were all a little confused about the parameters and about whether this was what Coach Harris had actually meant, but if it meant we could drink in season without getting in trouble, I certainly wasn't going to question it. Discussion over.

Years later, Trish told me that she thought dry season led to bingeing. "You're supposed to do it [drinking] in moderation," she said, "but I don't know if eighteen- to twenty-two-year-olds know what moderation is."

These lax new rules, this accidental non-dry season, meant that I could have a drink on my twenty-first birthday. To my shock Olivia and Mary Marshall worked together to throw me a surprise party in our living room. Olivia and I were still mostly avoiding each other in the apartment, but she was so excited to be involved in a social event that she went all out, spent money on it, bought me a T-shirt from Urban Outfitters that screamed "IT'S MY BIRTHDAY, BITCHES!" above a rainbow-colored checklist of five different kinds of alcohol—just the kind of thing I didn't know I would love until I shared it with her. I promptly pulled it on.

A few girls on the team had a drink, but everybody took it easy. Clutching my coconut-rum and pink-lemonade Crystal Light mixed drink—a favorite of ours—I plopped down beside Olivia on our living room floor.

"Thank you for this," I said, and I meant it. I put my drink down and stretched slowly, grabbing a foot with each hand, and winced.

"Of course, Otto," she said. "I've missed you."

"I've missed you, too. Fucking RDLs," I said, still stretching my hamstrings. RDLs were Romanian dead lifts, a hamstring-strengthening exercise that made everyone sore for days afterward.

Liv glanced down. "I hope this is okay," she said. She was talking about the party. "I wasn't really sure who to invite. Like, I don't know your friends anymore."

I looked around the room. She was right. Most of our close mutual friends were teammates. As Olivia and I drifted apart, I had started hanging out more with Mary Marshall and her volleyball-playing roommate, Madison, meeting people through them. I spent time with my FreeWord friends and my English-major friends, finding community outside of basketball to temper the pain of sitting on the bench so much. Olivia was hanging out with her boyfriend, tempering the pain of not playing at all. I was barely in the apartment these days. Olivia was always there.

"That's weird," I said to Olivia. We'd always had the same friends.

"Yeah."

Because of finals we hadn't seen our practice players much on the court lately. But they had been coming pretty regularly all fall, and although unlike us they would go home for a full winter break, they would join us again in January.

Male students and sometimes even professors had practiced with us occasionally under Coach Katz, but Coach Harris's staff wanted to cultivate a dedicated group of guys for us to play against regularly. That fall Trish printed out flyers and hung them around campus. A regular bunch started showing up, a motley crew of shaggy-haired Davidson dudes eager to relive their high school and YMCA glory days. They were not promised gear or food or much in the way of reward, the way some wealthier programs could do for their practice squads. They came because they wanted to.

We all pleasantly surprised each other. The guys were surprised that we usually beat them and that we were as tough as, if not tougher than, they were. We were surprised this ragtag band of showboating misfits could legitimately challenge us. We quickly found mutual respect, and we genuinely enjoyed their company, particularly because having them there meant some of us got to sit out when we scrimmaged.

Their presence, by default, lightened the mood at practice. The coaches didn't yell quite as much when the guys were there, and we spent less time being annoyed with each other. The practice players did silly things, like blocking a shot into the stands and screaming in our faces, and instead of sulking or getting pissed off—like we might have if a teammate blocked us—we just laughed. Instead of beating up only on each other at practice, we could now take out our daily aggression and competitiveness on a different group of people.

"Are the boys coming?" was usually our first question when we banged into the locker room before practice. They considered themselves a part of the team in many ways, and we agreed.

Sometimes, during boxing out or posting up, there would be awkward moments where someone grabbed body parts they did not mean to grab or when somebody didn't realize his or her own strength and knocked a player of the opposite gender down hard. But the guys took our practices seriously, playing their butts off, listening to the scout coach, and asking her questions as she taught them our next opponent's offenses so we could practice defending them. Our practice players gamely let us call them by our opponents' first names—Ali, Tonia, Anna, Paige, Latisha. They came and they cared, and they wanted to make us better.

There was Mike, whom we called "Kobe" because he was from LA and always wore Lakers gear, sometimes head to toe. There was Craig, a lurpy, mop-headed post player. Brandon was solid as a tank; if he drove at someone toward the hoop, it was in her best interest to get out of the way rather than take a charge, because she might break a rib. In high school I had chipped my collarbone when I made the mistake of taking a charge on my large male English teacher during a students-versus-teachers charity game. There was Allen, a men's soccer player trying to stay in shape out of season, who was athletic and easygoing and passed out compliments on the court like Skittles. And there was David.

David was a tall and lanky freshman, a handsome blond with quick hands, a high basketball IQ, and a deadly jumper. He was the most skilled of the practice players and usually pretended to be our opponent's best player, regardless of her position, when we went over the scout. He could play all the positions. He was Rory and Sam's age, and he and I had an English class together.

"He's really cute!" we said. "Someone should date him."

Sam was already after a different guy, whom she also dragged to some of our practices, and Rory was the only freshman left. She and David would make a cute couple. We started to push for it, tease Rory about him.

"Hurry, David's here," Sam would tell Rory in the locker room before practice. Or if they were in Sam's dorm room, watching people walk home from class—"Come, look. David's wearing a cute scarf!"

Yeah, Rory thought, he is pretty cute. She and Sam started hanging out on David's hall. They became close friends and Rory's crush grew, and although her teammates and coaches teased her at practice and made her face go redder than her jersey, we knew her feelings were serious. David had a girlfriend, though, someone from home, and so that was that. He and Rory were just buddies.

One day Rory and Sam were walking on campus, up the stairs past the Wildcat statue, when Rory got a text from David.

"What are you doing tonight?" he asked. He just wanted to hang out with them on the hall, but Rory and Sam both squealed with excitement.

"In two years you guys are gonna start dating," exclaimed Sam, dramatic as ever, "and in ten years you're gonna get married!"

Rory laughed. "Yeah, right!"

11 Students or Athletes?

Olivia played in just four games that year. Every time she got jostled on the court, she felt her symptoms trickle back, and she grew timid. When Olivia was healthy, she played dirty. She usually pissed us off by throwing elbows or shoving too much in practice. But she wasn't pissing anybody off anymore.

"You can't play like you're afraid," her Pittsburgh concussion doctor, Micky Collins, told her.

"I don't feel right," Liv said.

Dr. Collins did a few more tests on her and sent her to vestibular therapy. The vestibular system controls the body's balance and vision, so when it is damaged, as it can be by a concussion and as Olivia's was, it can wreak havoc on a person's ability to function normally. Often the patient's vision is affected, and she has trouble shifting focus on objects different distances away from her eyes, like the steering wheel up close and a stop sign thirty feet away. She might feel dizzy or nauseated when she tries to read, because of the back-and-forth movement reading requires of the eyeballs. She might not be able to balance on one foot.

A few days into the official season that year, scrappy, high-scoring freshman Sam, who had been dominant during preseason, had also joined our college concussion club. During a full-court drill, Rory and Sam were supposed to sprint down opposite sides of the court, pass each other under the basket, and run back on the other side. But instead of running past each other, they collided head-on.

A heavy handful of injuries occurred either at the beginning or end of preseason or at the beginning of official practice. Maybe we really did work harder during those times, trying to make good impressions on the coaches. Maybe the pressure to impress got us so wound up that we didn't control our bodies as well as we could. When freshmen came to college out of shape—and they always did, because you could not understand what "in shape" meant for college players until you were one—their bodies tended to be extra vulnerable due to the new strains they put on them.

This collision was like something out of a cartoon. Rory and Sam crashed into each other and fell straight backward. We cracked up as they staggered to their feet, blinking hard.

"Y'all good?" Coach Harris asked them, raising her eyebrows, like, *Seriously, this is what I'm dealing with?* She hadn't recruited any of us. She had inherited us.

"Yeah," said Rory.

"Yeah," said Sam, shaking her head like a dog in a bathtub. But she wasn't the same after that. She felt foggy, and her head wouldn't stop hurting.

Sam's usual playing style was chicken-with-head-cut-off. It was stressful to even watch her run around the court looking confused and panicked and lost, as she often did. Somehow it worked for her; she had talent. But after the collision with Rory, she looked even more lost than usual. She took the computerized concussion test and failed.

The Davidson athletic training room used a controversial but popular computer test to help athletic trainers diagnose and treat concussions. Dr. Collins, Olivia's doctor, part-owned the testing company and did a lot of its research. At the beginning of every school year, each Davidson athlete had to sit in a quiet room and take the test to get our baseline score. If at any point in the year an athletic trainer suspected an athlete was concussed, the athlete took the same test again, and the trainer compared her new score with her baseline.

This test was a difficult, high-pressure exam even for someone with a perfectly healthy brain. Try to memorize these shapes as they flash on the screen. Remember these squiggles. Remember these words. Is this one of the shapes you saw earlier? Is this one of the squiggles you saw earlier? Is it exactly the same squiggle, or is it facing the opposite direction? Is this one of the words you saw earlier, like *salt*, or is it a word in the same category, like *pepper*? Find and click on randomly ordered tiles labeled from 25 to 1, in reverse order, before time runs out. How are you feeling? Are you tired? Does your head hurt? Are you feeling sensitive to light or sound? How many hours of sleep did you get last night?

We hated it. And this testing system was far from perfect. One *ESPN: The Magazine* reporter wrote in 2012 that the false-positive rate could be up to 30 or 40 percent. But it was all we had. The idea was that the athletes were supposed to trust their trainers enough to be truthful with them and go to them with symptoms, that human interaction always outweighed a test on a computer.

After Sam failed the computerized test, Brian examined her and diagnosed a concussion. Sam and Olivia were in the club together.

Month after month and year after year, the training room was our sanctuary, a safe, mostly stable space amid the constant changes on the court and with the coaching staff and the college itself. Its employees were full-time athletic trainers and our unofficial part-time therapists. Beth, the head athletic trainer, was so loved that years later she was a greeter at Mac's wedding.

We knew that if there was a two-hour practice on the schedule, we could expect to be in Baker for about four hours—an hour early to get ready, followed by practice, film, then showers, then ice. Then dinner and debriefing. We spent about a quarter of that time every day in the training room.

The trainers were kind, gentle, and steady. They, not the coaches, were our parents away from home. They taped our hairy ankles and ground the knots out of our backs and shoved cotton up our bloody noses. They wrapped ice on our sweaty joints, examined our smelly feet, and held us when we cried. They told us what to do when we had a fever, or were throwing up, or were pooping blood because we took painkillers to play through a chronic injury and those painkillers gave us stomach ulcers.

In the training room we bonded with athletes from other teams who came in to do their rehab at the same time. We fell asleep or did our reading for class on the training tables or the couches, gossiped or did our reading for class in the ice bath or hot tub in the back, and begged Brian to show us the practice schedule while he taped our ankles so we could see how much we would have to run that day and then whine about it accordingly. Even players who weren't injured sometimes found the training room a more welcoming atmosphere than the locker room. They found reasons to come hang out—"I need ice for my water bottle." "I need a Band-Aid." "I need to use some pre-wrap as a headband."

The training room was one of the safest spaces we knew on campus, partly because the coaches didn't often walk in there. The athletic trainers did not dictate our playing time, so we could complain to them when we needed to complain, which was often. As our careers went on, most of us slowly learned, with their help, what kind of pain we could play through and what kind of pain was stupid to play through. We could show weakness when we needed to, break down and cry, tell them we were hurting. We could not always trust that they wouldn't pass the information along to the coaches, and there were times where we were not totally honest with them, but we generally assumed the athletic trainers were on our side.

Sam sat out for a few weeks after the collision with Rory. When she came back she worked frantically at practice, trying to make up for the time she had lost. Sam had grown up around people who verbally abused her if she played poorly, made her feel like she was nobody. She was rabid on the court, a manic, athletic bulldozer of a player with exceptional instincts and a scorer's knack for finding the hoop. She scored more than two thousand points in high school. She felt like she had to. She was obsessed with basketball because it was how she determined her self-worth. It was the only thing in her life at the time that made her feel important and worthy. She could not be hurt again.

At one practice just days after Brian cleared her to play, Sam and I crashed the paint hard for a rebound, both of us flailing for the ball. She was a guard, two inches shorter than me. My elbow collided with her forehead, splitting it open.

Sam clutched her head and moaned, blood spurting through her fingers in alarming quantities. She tried to sit down but instead collapsed rather dramatically near the foul line like an actress in a bad horror movie. Brian was not in that day, so Olivia ran from her spot on the sidelines to the training room to grab whoever was free. The women's volleyball trainer was eating a sandwich at his desk.

"Bill! Someone's bleeding on the basketball court," Olivia announced breathlessly.

"Okay," Bill said, as if someone was always bleeding on the basketball court.

"Um," said Olivia. "So, can you come up?"

"Yeah," said Bill. The rest of us trooped to the other end of the court to continue the drill as Bill, Pam, and Trish mopped up the blood.

Our coaches, for their part, were suspicious—sometimes even disdainful—of concussions. They were not the only ones. The science on this injury, and on the dangers of coming back to the court too soon, was still new.

Research was gathering steam. Scientists said sports-related concussions were "on the rise" in young athletes, and some doctors wanted new guidelines for athletes with suspected head injuries. They told the media that, contrary to the accepted beliefs of the past, concussions were not actually something to shake off.

All these warnings, though, even as they intensified in force and frequency, were still far from causing a sea change among the people whose livelihoods depended on our remaining healthy. Our new coaches had little patience for Olivia. Their collective attitude, like that of so many coaches, seemed to be that invisible injuries did not exist. If a player busted her ankle badly enough, it bruised. That was clearly an injury. If she tore her ACL, her knee swelled, and she had to wear a brace while it healed. She got surgery to fix it, and then she had a scar. But stress fractures and concussions, two of the most common injuries for women's basketball players, were nearly impossible to see. Concussion symptoms in particular—headache, irritability, fatigue, confusion—could be explained away by any number of other ailments, including, in women, premenstrual syndrome. A "concussion" was basically a headache. You could play through a headache, unless you were a wimp. Were you a wimp?

Brian was supposed to be our champion when it came to injuries. It was his job to convince and placate the coaches when we were genuinely hurt and to come up with a treatment plan that everyone could live with. But he couldn't do that if we didn't trust him. Sam was a strong-willed, stubborn eighteen-year-old who had a complicated relationship with basketball, and she and Brian did not yet know each other very well. He had already diagnosed her with one concussion. He could only take her off the court. He didn't control her playing time on it; the coaches did. So they had the power.

"Why don't you just cheat on it?" Sam remembers one of the coaches asking her one day in the office, referring to the concussion test. (Years later, the coach said she didn't remember saying that at all, although multiple players confirmed Sam's story.)

Sam wasn't sure if the coach was joking, but it was all the encouragement and approval she needed. She wanted to play and was letting herself down by sitting out. The coaches also wanted her to play, and she was letting them down, too, she thought. She sat alone behind a closed door, in the athletic training room of a school famous for its strict Honor Code, and wrote down the test's vocabulary words and drew the shapes as they appeared on the screen so she could "remember" them when it prompted her to later.

We knew something was still wrong when Sam came back to the court. We were practically professionals at recognizing concussion symptoms at this point, and she had obviously reverted to her space-cadet-concussed mode. But Sam's teammates took her cue, and we didn't say anything. Coach Heather noticed Sam's confusion and went down to the training room to tell Beth and Brian. Beth gave Sam a talk about the Honor Code, and Sam found herself back on the sideline. She got two more concussions that season and ended up sitting out until the following fall.

After she threw me my surprise birthday party, Olivia spent winter break at home in Pennsylvania instead of in Davidson with us, trying to get her body to cooperate with her. It would be possible—but painful—to train it to function properly again. She sat on a table in a small room three times a week with her vestibular therapist, a perfectly friendly person whom Liv hated because the exercises made her sick. Liv was no longer puking in a courtside trash can after running too many sprints. Now, the mere act of sitting down and focusing her eyes on a moving target was enough to make her vomit.

After all the work with her vestibular therapist, Olivia came back to the practice court and promptly got hit in the head again. Again, a teammate was responsible. The coaches had designed a rebounding drill where we all had to straighten our arms above our heads, lock our elbows, and stretch a small towel taut between our hands. All elbows were thus at face height. A coach or manager would take a shot, and with our arms occupied holding up the towels, we had to use our legs and butts to box each other out so that the ball came off the rim and bounced on the ground before anyone could go after it. We were running that drill—scuttling around the half court with our hands in the air, smacking our butts into each other—when Allie clocked Olivia in the head. Just like that, Olivia was back on the sideline. I joined her there when I accidentally ran into Sam at practice and sustained a mild concussion of my own, my second.

Then Taylor, the third junior, got hurt, too. During our breast cancer awareness home game against Western Carolina at the beginning of February, she was leading a breakaway when Leah tossed a long pass a little too far out in front of her. Taylor sprinted to chase down the ball and dove for it, colliding directly with the wide, padded pole that held up the basket.

"Oooof," she grunted loudly. The bench players doubled over laughing. Taylor heard something crack. That night she couldn't lift her arm.

The training room staff cleared her, and she played the rest of the season, icing her shoulder after games, toughing it out. She spent the next month instructing us not to pass the ball to her, saying she couldn't catch it. And she couldn't. The coaches nicknamed her "Paddles."

We won the Western game the day Taylor got hurt and then promptly lost four in a row. That was kind of how the season went. For every small winning streak, there was a losing streak to drown it out. We had a good group of players that year, so to Ashley, a senior, every loss felt like a disappointment.

We won our first game in the conference tournament, something we had not done in several years, but got eliminated the next day. We ended the season with a 12-19 record. It was a gross underachievement, considering the talent we had, but since it was Coach Harris's first year, everyone except us cut us some slack.

We'd had much higher expectations than this. But Ashley had been dragged through so much for so long that she did not want to do it anymore. She and Emma had had eleven different coaches, three coaching changes, and two head-coaching changes in their four years. There was no continuity, no stability. Our team didn't have any ground to build on. It was hard to take steps forward when we were still figuring out how to stand.

Even though she took two weeks completely off when the season ended, Taylor's shoulder did not heal. An MRI showed she had torn her labrum. She scheduled the surgery for the beginning of the summer.

Olivia, also out of commission, flew back to Pittsburgh that spring for another check-in with Dr. Collins. Her mom went with her.

We understand the human brain perhaps less than we do the vast belly of outer space and the depths of the ocean. When it is injured—when the body's very command center is impaired—consequences span from chronic headaches to mental health issues to dysfunctional taste buds to relationship woes, the injury's impact like twisted lines of dominoes sent reeling by the tap of a finger. The pain is vast and varied and often unpredictable. Olivia's symptoms were classic of concussion patients, but they were all over the map: depression, debilitating headaches, nausea, irritability, vision problems, overwhelming fatigue.

Over the time since the day she had first hit her head, the constant pain and the chemical changes in her brain had turned Olivia into a different person. But she kept coming back to basketball. She had taken the rest time. She had done the therapy. Her brain should have healed itself by now.

Dr. Collins was a tall, trim man with bright-blue eyes and a small gap between his front teeth. About three and a half years later, he would become my concussion doctor as well. He had a calm, confident, businesslike air about him, a valuable quality in the field of neuropsychology, a must for a man who spent his career telling people with mild traumatic brain injuries that the everyday realities of their lives were no longer the same and might never be the same again. He didn't patronize his patients, whether they were National Hockey League stars or teenage girls. He was not excessively gentle. He was frank and clear and honest. Olivia's medical problems were backed by hard science, by things he had studied, by long words and physics and chemical reactions. But they were also complicated—no one fully understood what was going on in Olivia's brain—and she needed someone to explain them in a way she and her mother could understand. A former collegiate athlete himself, the doctor had played in the NCAA Division III Baseball Championship the year Olivia was born. He had to know the gravity of what he was about to say.

"Look, Olivia," Dr. Collins began. "If you're any normal person and you injure your ankle or twist your knee, that is forever gonna be your weak spot. It's the same with a brain injury. It's forever gonna be your weak spot."

Finally, after a year and a half of fog and pain and confusion, Olivia realized that her brain would never be the same again. The horror of this truth began to flood her. But Dr. Collins wasn't finished.

"You are never playing basketball again," he said firmly. "I am not taking that risk."

Olivia was twenty-one years old. That silly towel box-out drill had been the last time she would ever lace up as a college player.

"You are free to go get a second opinion," Liv told me Dr. Collins continued, "but I promise you that they're gonna call me. And I'm gonna say no. And therefore, they're gonna say no."

Olivia leaned forward and put her forehead on the conference-room table. The sobs came hard and fast, wracked her over and over and over. Deep down she was also relieved.

We all understood, on some level at least, the ephemerality of college athletics. Olivia always knew it would end someday, that she would not play basketball forever or even professionally after college. But she had not anticipated these last four years being cut short, having the thing she loved to do most ripped out from under her with no warning, for no reason she could fathom. She had dreamed of senior night in Belk Arena with Taylor and me, of her homecoming game in Pittsburgh, of bringing her college teammates to her hometown, to her parents' house, showing us where she came from. They had the food spread all planned: they would order Italian, Syrian, and Lebanese, to show us all the diversity of the immigrant population in her town. She wouldn't have any of that now. She didn't even know if she would be invited to our weddings anymore. She felt robbed.

She quit the team, realizing, as Mac had, that this new coaching staff did not know her whole story and probably wouldn't be able to treat her with the patience she needed. Also like Mac, she kept her full scholarship, but would have to continue to work for it. She didn't want to be a manager because she felt so separated from the coaches and us. Instead, Olivia took a part-time internship in the sports information office. The coaches changed the locker-room code and told the rest of us not to share it with anyone who wasn't on the team.

Taylor got surgery to fix her labrum right after school let out for the summer. A few weeks later, in mid-June, two years after their graduation from Davidson, Erin married the quarterback of the football team she had been dating on my recruiting visit. Almost every Wildcat women's basketball teammate she invited to the wedding showed up, a testament to how dearly she was loved. They held the ceremony on campus.

Since most of us were naturally tall, we often refrained from wearing high heels on special occasions, opting for flats so as not to tower over our companions more than we already did. But when we were all together, a pack of broad-shouldered, long-legged Amazons, we felt a special freedom. When all of us were three inches taller, we were simply a gaggle of six-foot-three women instead of a gaggle of six-foot women.

"This is the largest group of tall women I've ever seen," remarked another wedding guest, gaping at us as we stood in the buffet line. We smiled. We had heard that one before. I was proud of it that day, because it meant we had an obvious connection to the bride.

In a glorious, too short reunion, Lyss, Whitney, Jenni, Ashley, Olivia, Taylor, and I all sat at the same table, along with Jenni's boyfriend. We spent most of cocktail hour shuffling back and forth from the bar, double-fisting drinks and depositing them on the table, stocking up for the rest of the night. Since we had been freshmen when Erin was a senior, Taylor, Olivia, and I were the youngest players at the wedding. Taylor and I had to go straight from the reception to the dorm for the first night of Davidson summer basketball camp, where we were counselors.

Later on the dance floor, the team—bride, bridesmaids, and guests— gravitated into a tight circle. We rocked there together, seven generations of Davidson women's basketball, currents of strength and joy and pain and nostalgia running through the channels of strong arms, of hands on waists, hands on broad shoulders, the deep bonds that linked us made briefly visible. We put our fists in the air, and Erin in her wedding dress counted down, "One, two, three—"

"Cats!" we shouted. We looked cheesy and we didn't care. The wedding photographer flitted around us, snapping photos.

A few hours later, Taylor and I headed for the dorms to begin our last year as Wildcat basketball camp counselors.

North Carolina summers are oppressively, suffocatingly hot, the air swampy and thick, slow, sticky months when even the cockroaches scramble inside for shelter. At camp a few years earlier, I'd been the lone counselor in the basement when it was overrun with the critters. They scuttled across our dorm floors and under the bathroom stalls and out of the closets, sending teenage girls by the handful screaming down the hall to my room, where I cowered on my bed, terrified to even put my feet on the ground. By the end of the week those same girls were sitting calmly on the floor in the hallway where we gathered every morning to walk to breakfast, dumping cockroaches out of their gym bags and basketball shoes and stomping them unceremoniously to crunchy piles of twitching legs and mush.

This year a group of older campers, in their early to midteens, started gathering in one of their rooms late at night to eat candy from the camp store and braid each other's hair and giggle. It was harmless fun, but it was against Trish's camp rules. They broke curfew every night.

"They remind me of us," I said fondly over lunch one day. "We were that age once. Remember that? It was fun. Basketball was so much fun then. No bullshit, you know? Just ball and your girls."

No coaches running my entire life, telling me what to wear and when to eat and what time I had to go to bed. No horrible early-morning conditioning tests that kept me up all night beforehand, dizzy with fear that I would oversleep my alarm. No all-nighters finishing papers I hadn't had time for. No hours in the training room doing rehab. We had been so healthy and carefree once. Now we were creaky and jaded and awash in nostalgia. One last year, I thought. And if we could win the conference and make the NCAA Tournament, it would all be worth it.

It took a long time to get all the campers settled for the night. Someone was usually homesick and crying, which meant patient chats and gentle calls to parents. Once we lost a camper. It turned out she had called her parents and gotten picked up without telling any of us. When all the kids were in their rooms for lights-out, we could finally relax or just fall asleep.

One night during this last summer, purely for our own amusement, we decided to give the curfew-breaking rebels a little scare. An hour after curfew freshman Lindsay joined Sam, Rory, Allie, Leah, and me as we tiptoed down the hallway to the dorm room we knew they gathered in, right across from the one I shared with Lindsay. We could hear their low, eager voices, the sound of them shushing each other and trying to stifle their giggles. We smiled softly, remembering the joys of being fourteen at basketball camp with our friends.

Leah grinned at us and then banged on the door. "Hey," she said in her most intimidating voice. "It's Trish. Open up!"

We smothered our laughter as we heard their gasps, the sounds of chairs being shoved around, the shuffling of frantic feet. They flicked the light off.

"Y'all!" Leah growled. "Open the door."

A squeal came from inside. Leah hammered on the door with the side of her fist.

It opened, and a small white face peered up at us out of the darkness. The six of us puffed out our chests, crossed our arms, and swaggered toward the teenage camper, making mighty efforts to keep our faces straight, trying to look as intimidating as possible.

"Who else is in there with you?" Leah demanded.

"Just—just my roommate," the girl said. "We're in bed."

Leah craned her neck, trying to see over the camper into the room. "We're coming in," Leah said.

The camper looked terrified.

"Let us in. What's your name again? Rachel? Let us in, Rachel."

Rachel stepped back, and we strode past her into the room. Sam flicked the light on, and we all started yelling in the scariest voices we could muster, like cops in a movie. "The jig is up, y'all!" we shouted. "Everybody out. Now. *Now!* Get out here!"

They started appearing within seconds, a shocking number of them, like clowns out of a car. They came slinking out from the closets, from behind the door, from under the desks and the covers on the beds. Above our heads, near the ceiling, two campers crawled out of the storage spaces over the closets and hung there like monkeys before dropping several feet to the ground. They gathered in the middle of the room, at least ten of them, looking nervous.

"It's past curfew, you guys. You broke the rules," Rory said.

"We know," a couple of them mumbled. "We're sorry."

"We're not gonna tell Trish," we told them. They looked up at us, big-eyed, relieved.

"But as a punishment," Leah announced grandly, "you must now put the title 'Queen' before all of our names. So I am, what? What do you call me?"

"Um," the girls said timidly. A few of them giggled. "Queen Leah?"

"*What's so funny?*" Leah thundered. "You think this is *funny*?"

The giggling stopped. Leah gestured at Allie. "And who's this?"

"Queen Allie."

"And this?"

"Queen Otto."

Leah continued down the line until the campers had called us all queens.

"That's what I thought. You will not address us by any other names. If you do, we'll tell Trish y'all broke curfew."

We saw real fear in their faces.

"Just call me Queen," said Leah, "and we won't have any more problems."

A few months later, that August, Davidson hired a new college president, Carol Quillen. For a school that had not opened to female students until the early 1970s, bringing a woman to the helm was a huge and important step.

President Quillen grew up attending Quaker schools in Delaware, followed by the University of Chicago and Princeton. A measured and graceful public speaker, she emanated a quiet, modest brilliance. I liked her immediately because she was a woman, she was smart and tall, and she liked sports. Any time a person in a position of authority at Davidson liked sports, it was a good thing for all of us athletes.

Early that fall we hosted two of our top recruits, and the coaches planned an elaborate photo scavenger hunt for us around town. We didn't always buy into the cheesy things the coaches had us do, but we bought into this. Rory, freshman Natalie, Amber, and I called our team the "Three Bs: Keepin' Undercover." It was a play on something

Coach Harris liked to say, that we should at all times keep our "three Bs"—boobs, belly, and butt—covered up.

We figured we would get extra points for a photo with the president and decided that the "take a picture of running water" requirement was our best option. We knocked on the front door of President Quillen's big, white, classic southern on-campus house. We had no idea if she would be there, but she came to the door in workout gear, her thick brown hair swept into what we later learned was her signature ponytail.

"Hey, guys," she said, gracefully recovering from any surprise she may have felt. Four sweaty young women had just appeared on her front porch on a sunny Saturday morning, clad in raggedy headbands and cut-off white T-shirts we'd scribbled on with pink marker, our arm and leg muscles bulging from preseason workouts. Rory wore neon-pink shorts with zebra stripes.

"Can I help you?" President Quillen asked. For a moment, we panicked.

"Well, um, we're on the women's basketball team," we stammered. "We, ah, have recruits this weekend and we're doing a scavenger hunt and we're supposed to take a picture of running water, so we're wondering if you could, uh, turn on your sink really quick?"

President Quillen invited us inside. It was clear she had just moved in. The house felt oddly empty. As she led us to the kitchen she asked our names and about our majors and how we thought the team would be that season. We told her we figured we were going to be pretty good. Then Carol Quillen, Princeton PhD, Fulbright scholar, Harvard research-grant recipient, author of two books on Petrarch, the first female president of Davidson College, a month into the job, turned on her kitchen sink and grinned with Natalie as Rory snapped a photo.

"Can I do anything else for you ladies?" she asked.

"That's all," we said. "Thank you so much." We scampered out.

That summer the coaches had sent out an email, including to the incoming freshmen, asking us not to schedule Tuesday–Thursday morning classes so they could hold practices during those times.

The problem was that their request was against Davidson Athletic Department rules. "Division of the Day" was designed to protect the distinction between academics and athletics at this highly ranked institution whose sports teams also competed at the Division I level. Division of the Day meant that professors owned student-athletes from 8:30 a.m. (8:15 on Tuesdays and Thursdays) to 4:20 p.m. every weekday. Coaches could have their athletes anytime outside of those hours but weren't supposed to hold mandatory full-team practices between them, although we often lifted in small groups between classes. The rule, rare at the Division I level, drove our coaches crazy.

Commons, the only cafeteria on campus, closed at 7:15 every night, which meant that when we had late practices, we had to eat dinner in the student union. That food was greasier, more expensive, and served in smaller portions, often à la carte. Division of the Day ended at 4:20. So if a coach wanted her team to eat dinner in Commons, there was only one window between 4:20 and 7:00 for practice each day. Because at the time we shared a court with the men's basketball team—and at the beginning of our season the volleyball team as well—only one team per day could fit a full practice in that window. This was at least part of the impetus for our coaches' plan to schedule morning practices.

But I also figured our new coaches still didn't quite understand just how important school was to people at Davidson. At many Division I schools their demand would fly, no problem. Hell, we learned later that while we were in college, employees at the University of North Carolina were running GPA-boosting blow-off "paper classes" whose students were mostly athletes. At Davidson, where the athletic stakes were lower, the academic stakes were higher. The class-scheduling issue was already causing resentment on our team.

After one preseason workout early that fall, I peeled off my practice jersey and shorts and tossed them into the laundry bin. I wrapped my long white sweaty socks on my laundry loop and pulled the cord around them to tighten it, listening to my teammates discussing the problem: that some people had dropped classes when the coaches asked us to, and some had refused.

Allie pulled her shampoo out of her locker. She was in a Tuesday–Thursday-morning psychology-methods class, a necessary credit for her major and a hard course to get into. "I'm not dropping it," she said. "We have Division of the Day, guys. This is a rule at Davidson. The coaches know that. It's a rule for a reason, because this isn't, like, UConn. Here we're always supposed to be students first. I'm not gonna be playing basketball forever. After next year I'm done for good, and I want to be able to do other things with my life. Like get a job. I love you guys, but I have to get this class."

Our coaches could not believe that some of the biggest drama they had with us was that we always wanted to get home to our books. Academics were a relief for us. They were the time where we got to go sit down. On the other hand, going to practice was often a refreshing break from studying. There were days when that balance felt healthy.

Once, the year before, Trish walked into the locker room for our pregame speech and saw Emma sitting with a book as thick as the foul line in her lap. Another time, while we were getting dressed for a game at Wofford, Ashley walked up to the whiteboard with her warm-up jersey on and her game shoes untied and started doing chemistry equations next to the scouting report.

Our coaches' job was not to help us get As and Bs. Yes, they had to make sure we stayed eligible to play, but we worked hard in school and could mostly take care of that on our own. The minimum GPA to be eligible was low.

Our coaches' job was to win. Their careers—their *livelihoods*—literally depended on a bunch of eighteen- to twenty-two-year-olds winning basketball games. Their livelihoods did not depend on our impressing our professors, having things to say during class discussions, getting summer internships like our nonner classmates did, or finding jobs when we graduated. They didn't have time to worry about stuff like that.

Likewise, our professors' job was not to help us win basketball games. Every day we went back and forth between our vastly different groups of grown-ups and tried to keep everyone happy.

I was at a point in my career where I'd had enough of basketball dominating every facet of my existence. I didn't like that our new coaches had just parachuted in and started changing things. I was a senior, and I didn't want my younger teammates missing out on classes they wanted or needed. Because my dad held the position at Saint Francis, I knew that "faculty athletics representative" was a position mandated for each school by the NCAA, so although I had never met ours, I looked him up. The FAR is supposed to be a professor who liaises between student-athletes, their coaches, and their professors. I wrote to Dr. Fred Smith and explained the circumstances.

Dr. Smith thanked me for letting him know, assured me that I was right to alert him to the situation, told me that I should tell Allie to keep her class, and said I should come talk to him in his office as soon as I could get there that day. "I know, and have known for some time, that the dining hall situation is causing problems for student athletes," he wrote. The trustees were aware of the issue, too, he added. "This may be just the thing to finally allow us to make some meaningful changes on this front."

Dr. Smith promised to try to keep me anonymous so the coaches didn't get mad at me for telling him what was going on. He told my teammates to try to get their classes back. As many as six had arranged their schedules specifically around the Tuesday–Thursday practice time. Dr. Smith talked to athletic director Jim Murphy and met with our coaches to discuss the situation. He said Pam and Trish told him they wanted to learn WebTree, our complex class-scheduling system, which he took as a gesture of genuine, if misguided, goodwill.

Most people got back the classes they had dropped, but the coaches scheduled morning practices anyway, Tuesdays and Thursdays, from 7:00 to 9:00. Allie and Marie, who saw significant playing time, both had to rush to class at 8:30, so they missed almost half of each practice on those days. The message that athletics always came second to school did not seem to have totally gotten through to our coaching staff.

Incidents like this often came up when a new coach had not herself attended or coached at Davidson or a school like it.

"When you hire coaches really interested in turning something around quickly, who want to change the culture, the success of the team on the field, that's where you can see these boundaries getting pushed," Dr. Smith told me several years later. It seemed like that was what Coach Harris was trying to do. Our team had so much talent, but had underperformed on the court for years. She wanted to fix that.

One of the great parts about Davidson, and one of the biggest reasons many of my teammates had chosen it, was its academic reputation. School was hard, though, and we didn't get much special treatment or extra support as student-athletes. We didn't have team study hall, although the men's team did, but we didn't want it anyway. Tutors were rare. If we had a question, we went to office hours like everyone else, if we could get there around our workout schedule. Our assignment due dates were the same, even if we were traveling. Instead of taking tests late when we were out of town, we sometimes had to take them early. We received the same assignments and had the same workload as every other student at the school, except that we worked thirty-hour weeks on top of it, plus the travel, physical exhaustion, and emotional workload it took to be on a team. Our coaches expected us to perform well on the court no matter how late we had been up doing our homework, and our professors expected us to perform well in the classroom no matter how late the coaches ran practice the night before.

Most of our Davidson classmates were incredibly supportive of the athletes who made up 25 percent of the student body. Others implied, or said outright, that we did not deserve to be there or that we didn't have to work as hard in school as they did.

Many of us had heard offhand comments along the lines of, "Oh, you got an extension on that paper/test/lab? It must be because you're an athlete." Little jabs like that added up. We knew that thought came from somewhere. Athletes, especially the full-scholarship ones, constantly battled the stereotype that we didn't fit in academically, that we weren't as smart as nonathletes.

There were pockets of legitimacy in that argument—the Admissions Department reserves "admitted" spots for athletes every year at the expense of other students who might be more qualified academically.

It's part of the school's attempt to create a well-rounded student body. It also holds spots for musicians, international students, and so on.

"I'm not convinced I would have gotten into Davidson if I didn't play basketball," I once said to an admissions officer.

He looked me in the eyes and shrugged a little. "You might not have," he said.

As if to demonstrate this, two of my younger brothers, neither a recruited athlete but both with better high school grades and more extracurricular activities, were turned down by Davidson after I got in.

The first word in a student-athlete's title, that pesky word *student*, can sometimes rather notoriously take a backseat to *athlete* in the NCAA. But especially at smaller schools like ours and particularly among women, where chances of having a comfortable, sustainable living as a professional athlete are slim to none, plenty of student-athletes do take their studies seriously. We certainly did. Only a few of us were even considering going pro. It was rare for any player, female or male, from the Southern Conference to go that far. The NBA superstardom of Stephen Curry was an almost inconceivable exception.

12 FTP

Aside from the year we got punished for letting a recruit get drunk, this final fall was the hardest preseason I had experienced. And I wasn't having the toughest time of it. Olivia had officially left the team. Taylor's body was not cooperating with her. After her labrum surgery at the beginning of the summer, she'd had to take eight weeks completely off to let her shoulder heal, and after that it was a while before she was even allowed to start running again. She couldn't do the summer sprint workouts the coaches had designed to help get us ready for their fall conditioning tests, which they told us we had to pass before we would see any playing time.

Coach Katz had designed some pretty brutal sprint drills, but Coach Harris's were worse. We ran each test once a week. The guards were required to meet a time a few seconds faster than the forwards. If we didn't pass, we had to run it again the next week until we did.

For "110s" we all lined up at one end zone of the football field and at the whistle ran the length of the field, all the way through the opposite end zone, 110 yards in either seventeen seconds for the guards or nineteen seconds for the posts. We got the remainder of the minute to rest and then had to run another sprint. We did this a total of sixteen times.

The first few weren't hard. The sprints were actually fun at the beginning, letting our legs loose with all that open field ahead, watching our feet eat up the turf in long, smooth gulps, feeling how strong and fit we were, our lungs opening deep to let in the clean Carolina air. It was a delicious feeling.

By the eighth sprint we would start to struggle, taking hard breaths and planting our hands on our hips to hold ourselves up afterward. By twelve we hunched in the end zone between sprints, waiting until the last possible second to toe the line for the next one. If someone put her hands on her knees, a coach barked at her to stand up straight. But there was a careful kind of slouching we could do that helped a little, an arching forward of the upper back and a tight gripping of the front of the shirt with both hands to hold the weight of the upper body. By sprint fourteen, we were gasping. Fifteen and sixteen were a half-stagger as we started to lose control of our muscles, our legs no longer flying straight forward but a little sideways, too, like wobbly wheels.

I thought the shuttle-run "300s" were worse than 110s. We had to sprint 300 meters on the court, running back and forth from one baseline to a hash mark a few feet past the opposite foul line, twelve times in sixty-five (guards) or sixty-eight (posts) seconds. That meant we had to get up and down the court in less than six seconds each time. After two minutes of rest, we did it again. We got two more minutes of rest and then did the sprint set one last time.

The slowest part was changing direction. Coach Bailey had once taught us the quickest way to change direction on the court: by keeping the core low and tight and dropping the hips, doing the work with the hamstrings and butt instead of bending at the waist. That was also the most effective way to play defense. It helped, but changing direction was still difficult and it took time, and in this drill we had to do it eleven times.

We did the conditioning tests early in the morning, before Division of the Day started. In some ways that timing was good because it meant we didn't spend the whole day dreading them. We spent the whole night dreading them instead.

"I could not sleep last night, you guys," Taylor said as we put-tered blearily around the court during warm-ups on the first day of 300s testing.

"Me either," Rory exclaimed. "I was waking up like every hour."

"Me too," said Sam. "Nobody is gonna pass this shit."

"I seriously practiced these all summer," I said, "like I timed myself and everything, and I had so much trouble passing. I think I legiti-mately passed like twice."

We were walking slowly up the court, kicking up one leg at a time and touching our toes with our fingers to stretch our hamstrings. I glanced over at Taylor.

"Just think, Tay," I said, grunting a little as I swung a leg up. "Once we pass these, we literally never have to do another conditioning test in our lives. Once we finish this, we are done *forever*."

"Oh, God," Taylor said. "No more conditioning tests ever again? I can't even imagine. What will we do with ourselves?"

I shrugged. "Sleep in. Sit around. Watch *Sex and the City* marathons. Drink margaritas. It's gonna be terrible."

"Ugh, I'm so jealous," Sam groaned. "I'm quitting. I can't do this."

"We just gotta get through these ten minutes," Rory said as we lunged sideways, stretching our groins. "Then we're done. Just ten minutes of terribleness, and then it's all over."

Every year I convinced myself that if I ran the fastest in presea-son, or at least close to the fastest, or lifted the most weight, or at least close to the most weight, I would impress the coaches enough to get more playing time once the season came. Every year I realized it didn't work like that. If the coaches didn't want to play me, they wouldn't play me, no matter how well I performed in preseason. Every year I tried again.

In a similar mind-set, a few weeks earlier, one of our five fresh-men had pushed herself too hard in the Cake Race, a fall tradition for Davidson first-years. They ran a two-mile course around campus and got to pick a cake made by a townie when they finished. The Cake Race was supposed to be a fun thing Davidson students did with their hall or their friends, but because coaches and older teammates watched, for freshman athletes it was just another thing to compete in and be evaluated on. The cross-country team took it especially seriously, body paint and all. Kelsey, one of our basketball freshies, ran too fast in that year's Cake Race and tore her hip flexor. In mid-October doctors diagnosed her with a much bigger issue, laid bare by the injury: Kelsey had bilateral hip dysplasia, a misalignment or deformation of both hip joints that would require two surgeries, one on each hip, each with a six-month recovery period. Doctors would essentially have to break her hips and reset them.

"You know what happens to dogs with hip dysplasia?" Kelsey told us one of the coaches said to her when Kelsey got back from the doctor's office that day and broke the news to them. "They take 'em behind the shed and shoot 'em!" (Years later, that coach told me she would not have said such a thing.)

"So basically you're telling me," another coach remarked, "that I purchased broken merchandise." (Years later, she told me she couldn't remember saying that.)

Multiple teammates confirmed Kelsey's version of the coaches' comments.

We were frustrated when we got hurt, of course. The coaches were, too. Our bodies were obviously crucial to the job they had "hired" us to do. They made these jokes to their injured player, presumably without meaning to hurt her feelings, but she was in her first three months of college and their comments made her feel like a racehorse.

"We were employees doing a job," Kelsey said to me a few years later. "It wasn't us that were being sold for the scholarship; it was our skill set. I needed someone to be like, 'Oh, I'm really sorry about that. I hope that we can see you again soon,' not 'Wow, this really sucks for me because I made a bad purchase.'"

Back on the court for our first day of 300s testing, we finished stretching. The coaches counted us off into two groups.

"Group one, on the line," Coach Harris said, in that flat, vaguely amused voice coaches use when they know they're about to almost kill you.

Half the team toed the baseline, eyes on the ground, bodies tense, weight balanced, hearts pounding. The whistle blew.

Amber led the pack, her form perfect, her long, toned legs gobbling up space, arms pumping, head high. Taylor and Allie as well as Natalie and Kaylee—both freshmen—lagged far behind.

"Atta girl, Amber," Pam said.

"You got this, Kaylee!" Rory shouted. "You got this!"

"Come on, Allie! I see you, Al! You're almost done, girl. Finish strong."

"Group two, get ready," came Coach Harris's command less than a minute later. Group two stepped to the line, hearts beating fast with anticipation and dread. Group one finished twelve up-and-backs and careened over the finish line, swerving around the members of group two and slamming into the padded wall behind the basket. The whistle blew again, and group two took off. Group one immediately put their hands on their heads and started walking around, shaking out their legs, using whatever breath they could summon in their delicious two minutes of rest to cheer on group two.

We did that three times. By the third set we gasped raggedly in the cool gym air, our heads down as if we could somehow boost our momentum by dipping our necks, our mouths stretched and teeth bared like skeletons'. Our arms pumped harder as our legs faltered, on fire with a surreal combination of needle pricks, cramping, and heaviness. We lurched over the finish line, some of us collapsing on the ground, lying on our backs and propping our feet on the wall to feel what the coaches told us was lactic acid trickle hotly back up our legs.

Amber was the only one who passed. Several people had not even come close. In a few days we would have to do it all over again. Once we managed to stand up, it was time for showers and a slow walk to class and then more workouts.

The NCAA Division I women's basketball season began that year at the beginning of October. We were allowed to have thirty practices in the next forty days, before we ever had a game. Games were the fun part. Without them it was easy to forget what we were practicing for. Practice dragged on with little to look forward to, just hours and hours of full-court drills and defense and learning plays and trying to impress the coaches, overanalyzing the teams they assigned us to— first string, second string, third string. Fifteen minutes into the first day of official practice, Kaylee, a freshman, broke her hand. Now two of the five newcomers were out with injuries.

We finally started the season with a close loss at ACC school Clemson, followed by a win, a loss, and another win, all out-of-conference games. In our loss to High Point I played just six minutes. In a blowout win over Gardner-Webb three days later, I played one minute, less than anyone else on the team, including walk-on Lindsay. I was furious. I was a senior. I was a scholarship player. I had done my time on the bench—three years of it. I was not injured, nothing more than my usual chronic aches. I had passed the conditioning tests. The team was definitely not worse when I was on the floor, and I felt like I contributed for the better. I didn't know what was going on.

Then it was time for Taylor's and my homecoming trips. We had Thanksgiving dinner at Taylor's parents' house the day before we lost at Princeton by nine. I played three minutes. The next day we drove west across Pennsylvania en route to play Duquesne in Pittsburgh. We stopped halfway there, in my hometown, to visit my parents' house and spend the night in a hotel down the street before finishing the trip the next day.

My mom and dad had a sign made that read "WELCOME TO HOLLIDAYSBURG, WILDCATS" and stretched it across the front-porch railings. They paid for a catered dinner and invited relatives and family friends, and my mom spent hours baking desserts. Excited and nervous, I directed the bus driver over the railroad tracks at the bottom of my neighborhood, explaining fondly that those trains used to make me late for school in the mornings. We chugged up the winding hill that made the family cars fishtail in the snow, around the roundabout, and back down the hill toward the house where my family had lived for eight years. Our mammoth team charter bus was quite a sight in this rolling little neighborhood in my pint-size town.

My youngest brother, Casey, eleven at the time, was young enough to unabashedly adore our team, and my teammates adored him right back.

He was the baby of the family, sweet and affectionate, and he and I were close buddies. For three years he had watched me come home and cry because I wasn't getting playing time and had so much trouble remembering our slew of half-court plays, sideline and baseline out-of-bounds plays, defensive formations, and press breaks. College basketball just wasn't turning out for me how I had imagined it. So my junior year for Christmas, Casey gave me a shoe box. He had gone to the Davidson athletics website and printed out, in color, every teammate's photo from the waist up, so I could see the face and jersey number. He cut out the photos and laminated them and then attached them to Popsicle sticks and taped each stick to a Lego so they stood up like little paper dolls. I could move the figures around, Casey explained, and practice the plays.

Casey was a strategy kid, also a master chess player. At our house that day he challenged Rory to a game, then Sam, then Lindsay. He played the piano for us. A few of my high school friends, home from college for Thanksgiving, showed up to say hello. My beloved aunt Julie, my dad's sister, had driven down from Buffalo with my cousin Annie. Despite our loss to Princeton the day before, the atmosphere was warm and joyful as people I loved from one of my worlds met people I loved from another of my worlds. Coach Harris, for whom social interaction was still not a strong suit, lay down on the family-room couch with her head on two pillows, covered her face with her arms, and barely talked to anyone.

The next day, after stopping back at my house for a leisurely brunch homemade by my mom, we drove two and a half hours to Pittsburgh. One day later, Duquesne destroyed us, 84–53, the worst loss the Davidson women had suffered since our 82–50 loss to Vanderbilt, which had been ranked seventeenth in the nation at the time, during my freshman year.

I played eight minutes in my homecoming game at Duquesne, in front of friends and family, against the girls their head coach had chosen to give scholarships to instead of me all those years ago.

"I think the Duquesne coach said more words to me in a few minutes before the game today than Coach Harris did the entire time she was at our house," my dad remarked thoughtfully afterward.

I sat in the stands in Belk Arena a few days after the Duquesne game, sprawled in Section 5 with my computer in my lap, working on an essay assignment for my creative-nonfiction class with Dr. Lewis. I wrote about what it was like to play basketball at this level. I wrote how frustrating and sad it was to see this sport I loved reduced to a string of numbers and tired limbs and chilly bus rides. How my teammates and I and our love helped each other through.

Coach Harris walked past. "Why you sittin' in here, Otto? Is this . . . ," she paused doubtfully, looking out at the glossy, expectant, well-loved court, "inspiring you or something?"

I nodded and smiled. Sure is, Coach.

The coaches had instilled a points system to get us to work harder in practice, outside of practice, and in games. We were each assigned a different color marble. For every so many points we scored, or rebounds we got, or charges we took, or shots we put up outside official practice times, we got a marble. We lost marbles if we made mistakes, like having too many turnovers. Every so often we'd all pour our individual marbles into a big jar, where the color distribution became clear.

The marble system quickly became a point of contention. Because the marbles were a physical indication of coaches' approval, some players felt like their teammates sometimes played more for marbles than for the good of the team. I was stubborn and skeptical and had learned long ago to make my trust of authority figures, particularly coaches, hard-won. Off-court conversations with them about playing time had never worked. I had always felt that Coach Katz told me what I wanted to hear and then did whatever she wanted. Coach Harris simply did not have answers for me about why I didn't play.

I finally gave up asking. College basketball had taught me a tough lesson: sometimes hard work does not pay off. So I stopped going to the gym when I didn't have to, preferring to spend my time writing or on schoolwork. I cared about basketball and about my teammates, but I didn't care about marbles. I didn't see the point anymore.

Many of the players who chafed at the play-for-marbles tactic—including me—belonged to a team clique Heather had nicknamed "Fuck the Police." The name as we interpreted it meant that we did not suck up to the coaches like we felt some of our teammates did. Some of us, like Kelsey, had had their feelings hurt by the coaches. As the coaches interpreted it, the group didn't respect their authority.

We decided we liked the name Heather had christened us with and shortened it to FTP. Some of FTP, like Sam and me, gave the coaches attitude outright. I didn't feel respected by them, so I didn't show them respect in return. FTP was cliquish, but we didn't have a vendetta. We simply didn't trust the coaches, who in turn did not trust us.

Sam felt she'd done what Coach Harris had asked her to do in order to get playing time: score, hustle, and get rebounds. She still wasn't getting off the bench much. She finally went to Coach Harris's office, frustrated.

"You must be out of your damn mind if you don't think I'm doing everything you asked me to do!" Sam shouted at her.

Coach Harris suspended Sam and never said a word to the team about it. We heard the news from Sam.

Sam, Lindsay, and Natalie—three members of FTP—had gotten so used to sitting at the end of the bench that they actually started to look forward to that time together, which they spent making fun of various fans, players, and coaches; giggling; and generally not paying much attention to the game. If they watched too closely, they might remember how much it hurt not to play.

"You peer at a bench, and you can see a team's soul," Marc Skelton, high school boys' basketball coach of the Fannie Lou Hamer Freedom High School Panthers, told the *New York Times* in 2015. Our team soul overflowed with dancing, crude jokes, sass, and laughter.

We had a running joke about the Spandex shorts we had been issued that year, because they looked like they were made for men. They had an unnecessarily spacious crotch area. We called them our "mandex"—no longer our "spandy-panties"—and frequently discussed the wide range of items for which we could use the extra storage space.

"No more room in my duffel bag; guess I'll just stick my [shower shoes, shampoo bottle, textbooks, hair straightener, game socks] in my mandex!" we announced before road trips.

"You guys hungry?" Lindsay asked Sam and Natalie that day as the second half got under way and they settled back into their soft seats at the end of the bench. Nobody paid attention to them down there. I often sat there with them.

"Duh," said Sam.

"Always," said Natalie.

Lindsay pretended to reach a hand down her shorts.

"Here, I brought some snacks," she cracked. "They're just down here in my mandex." Natalie let out her wonderful loud burst of a laugh. Sam and Lindsay always made Natalie laugh.

Those of us who wore mouth guards really did tuck them into one thigh of our mandex for safekeeping when we came off the floor. The combination of leg sweat and old spit was something we tried not to think about too hard when we shoved them back in our mouths.

Sam spent so much time on the bench that she had taught herself one of the dances the cheerleaders did, a combination of foot stomping, knee slapping, and hand clapping. When she got especially bored at home games, she would make eye contact with one of the cheerleaders and start doing the dance on the bench. They would catch on and join in. She, Lindsay, and Natalie had also invented a game where one person gave the others three letters—for example, *T, G, O*—and they would have to figure out what adjectives those letters stood for by scanning the crowd for people who might match those adjectives. For example *T, G, O* might stand for *tall, girl, orange* and indicate a tall female wearing an orange shirt or with orange hair.

To my surprise and delight, after the Duquesne game I suddenly started to get more and more playing time, leaving my buddies on the end of the bench for sometimes up to half the game. I made baskets and took charges and grabbed rebounds. The less I decided I cared, the better I played. During our last game before the Christmas break, at Radford, I scored eighteen points in twenty minutes. Finally, after three and a half years of college, I was starting to feel like the player I'd been in high school again. And we were winning.

The Radford game was our eleventh of the season and our seventh win, our fifth win in a row. We got a few days off at home with our families around Christmas. Rory and David had had a long talk and decided they wanted to take their friendship to the boyfriend-girlfriend level. Nobody was surprised. His girlfriend from home was long gone. He was still one of our best practice players and most loyal fans. He was gentle and kind and a baller. He was worthy of our Rory.

After Christmas we lived in the hotel again, spending about six hours a day at the gym. The men's team was doing the same thing from a different hotel just across the highway. We were so bored that one night we decided to kill time at a back-road red light by seeing how many rotations we could sit through before another car showed up behind us.

I shared a hotel room with freshman Brittany. All of us had different strengths on the court—defense, rebounding, hustle plays. Britt was a scorer. She'd had a breakout exhibition game, scoring twenty-three points, including a stretch of eleven straight. But her production dropped off dramatically once the regular season started in November. She was young, and freshmen are notoriously inconsistent. The pressure to re-prove herself was tremendous.

Three games into the season, at a practice in mid-November, Brittany had the ball on the right wing in a half-court shell drill. She swept the ball across her body, drove left hard to the hoop toward a crowd of people, and went down. As soon as we heard her scream, we knew what had happened. There was no sound in women's basketball like an ACL scream. It was chilling and unmistakable.

Brittany's parents—her dad was a pastor, and her mom did not work at the time—had health insurance, but she told me they still dropped $5,940 out of pocket for her knee surgery. While they were grateful for Brittany's full scholarship, they spent years paying off this extra medical expense. Eighteen-year-old Britt didn't think to tell the college or the coaches her family was financially strapped to see if they could help, and because we already had full scholarships, we didn't fill out government financial-aid forms. A lack of communication on both sides meant Davidson may not have known that the medical bills gave her family trouble.

Instead of going to practice every morning over break, Brittany went straight to the training room. Although she had the other injured freshmen for support—by now three of the five of them had sustained a serious injury—she felt separated from the team. Like Olivia, like Lyss, like Ashley, like Erin, like every player before her who had a long-term injury, Britt felt that because she missed practices, she missed the most important bonding time we had. At team meals we usually talked about practice, about what the coaches did or said. The players in the training room could not contribute to these conversations. They were lonely.

A typical day for me over winter break—with minor variations—looked like this:

8:30 a.m.—Wake up with alarm. Make sure Britt is awake. Brush teeth. Grab room key, phone, and car keys with paisley zippered wallet attached; head downstairs in the team sweats I've been wearing more days and nights in a row than I care to count. I feel confident and sexy in sweats, though. They're the clothing of my people. Gobble yogurt, green banana, and dry cereal from breakfast bar. I know this is the last food I'll have until midafternoon, but if I eat more now, I'll feel sick at practice. Carpool to gym with any teammates who want to arrive at a similar time. Try to avoid morning traffic on the highway. Sit in morning traffic anyway.

9:00 a.m.—Arrive at gym. Wait outside, make phone calls, and stomp around in the cold for approximately twenty minutes, since even though we spend six hours a day in there, we do not have card or key access because apparently the people who run the building do not agree that student-athletes should have it, and the coaches don't arrive this early just so players can get our creaky bodies ready for practice. Finally, teammates and I bang on the door and wave frantically as we spot a custodian walking past; he lets us in.

9:20 a.m.—Throw on practice gear and a pair of socks, plus a long-sleeved shirt since they don't tend to turn on the heat much in the gym over break. It's a big building, probably expensive to heat, and our team and the men's basketball team are the only ones around.

9:22 a.m.—Grab shoes and ankle braces from the bottom of my locker. Pad down the hall to the training room, twenty-two minutes late for daily prepractice rehab and treatment.

9:25 a.m.—Halfheartedly, and in a hurry, perform rehab exercises for ankles and Achilles tendons. While browsing a year-and-a-half-old copy of *National Geographic*, soak legs in a hot whirlpool from the shins down for ten minutes so joints warm up enough to move. Don't submerge knees in the warm water, though, because they will swell up like balloons. Crawl out of the hot tub and dry off. Lie on stomach on the training table for therapeutic ultrasound treatment on both Achilles tendons, performed by Brian, who squirts gel on the tender spot above each heel and massages a warm metal rod with a flat tip over the gel in small circles. Babble to Brian about the article I just read about the secrets of human sleep. The ultrasound is supposed to reduce the chronic, painful inflammation of my Achilles, which eventually gets so bad that I have to wear a boot off the court. This treatment deep-heats the tissue and stimulates blood flow. It also feels really good. Doze off.

9:45 a.m.—Get one ankle taped, by Brian again, who's really earning his salary with me; I sprained it recently, and knowing I have the extra protection of tape underneath a lace-up ankle brace is reassuring. Strap on ankle braces and shoes. Wind prewrap around chronically swollen knees to keep pressure on the joints and ease the constant pain there. Fill up water bottle with ice and water from the training-room sink.

9:51 a.m.—Six minutes late for prepractice stretching, hustle up to the chilly gym. Attempt to warm up muscles at least a little bit.

10:00 a.m.–12:40 p.m.—Practice. Run and run and run.

12:40 p.m.—Practice over, late. Head to locker room, change shirt and shoes, walk with team outside to weight room.

12:45 p.m.—Late, as usual, to weights session. Do the workout, but not with too much weight since I don't want to be sore for the next week, and we have games.

1:30 p.m.—Walk back to locker room and adjacent film room for film session. Scour the locker room for food. Find only the two-year-old chocolate-flavored protein bars (one year past their expiration date) that have been sitting on top of the empty refrigerator for as long as I can remember. Choke down half of one. One day our strength coach gets so tired of our complaining about how hungry we are when we see him that he buys us bagels, peanut butter, chocolate milk, and fruit, and we have a picnic right there on the grimy weight-room floor.

1:45 p.m.—Watch film of next opponent with coaches and team in near silence, in the dark. Recall the time Coop fell asleep during film and giggle to myself. Try to stay awake and think about things other than my growling stomach.

2:30 p.m.—Film session adjourns. Snap to consciousness. Collect per diem meal cash ($20) from Coach Heather.

2:32 p.m.—In a daze remove practice gear, throw it into the laundry bin, and stagger to the shower. Don't shave legs. Someone blasts the music. Sing along with Chris Brown and Usher and that awful Big Sean song Sam likes to blare from the stereo on a loop while she and Lindsay practice twerking in their sweaty mandex, the one with the chorus that repeats the word *ass* a dozen times. Black teammates teaching their white teammates how to dance was a frequent occurrence on this team: in the locker room, in hotels, at parties on campus.

2:45 p.m.—Clean, wet-haired, and dressed once more in the same sweats, galumph down the dark hallway back to the training room. Ladle ice into four bags and suck the air out. Have Brian secure them onto both knees and both Achilles tendons with the plastic wrap.

3:00 p.m.—Waddle stiff-legged back to the locker room. Perch on stool with legs sticking straight out like the Tin Man and argue with team about where to eat—Lunch? Dinner? Argue about whether to call it "dunch" or "linner." Three of the four ice bags start to leak down legs and into socks.

ALTERNATIVELY: Take an ice bath in the training room after practice. Wearing Spandex and a sports bra with a towel over head and shoulders and thick booties on my toes to keep me warm, lower body waist-deep into a tub of water that hovers around fifty degrees. For a few seconds the cold is an utter, stabbing, throbbing shock, and sometimes I can't help myself and yelp a little. But I go numb quickly. Ten to fifteen minutes later, hop out, legs purplish-red and somehow feeling five times better. This is addictive.

3:15 p.m.—Team inevitably decides to split up, just like every other day. Carpool to restaurant of my group's choice.

3:30 p.m.—Collapse around a table and inhale our food. Often we are at some fast-casual chain where we wolf down loaded nachos and burritos and other synthetic items. The eating process lasts approximately four minutes. There is no talking during this period.

3:34 p.m.—Commence discussion about coaches and the day's work and about how badly we need an off day. NCAA rules require coaches to schedule off days only when student-athletes are in class. Per the rules we must get one day off every seven days during the season, although coaches could put our "on" weeks back to back and make us play thirteen days straight if they wanted to. When we're out of school, though, no off days are required. Some years over winter break we have not had a single off day upon returning to campus after Christmas. This year, miraculously, we have two.

4:30 p.m.—Drive back to hotel. Convene in one or two rooms, pull the shades, and pop in the next DVD of whatever TV show we're watching. Sprawl three or four to a bed. Check Twitter and Facebook. Doze off.

6:30 p.m.—It's dinnertime, but since we just ate dunch/linner, no one is hungry. Plus, we want to save our per diem money for shopping later, and we are too tired to move.

7:00 p.m.—Sneak down to lobby and steal fruit and oatmeal from cupboards under the breakfast bar. Flirt with cutish guy at hotel front desk in the hope that he'll make us another batch of cookies. Once these few weeks of break are over, I'll find I have lost seven pounds from running so much and eating so irregularly.

7:30 p.m.—Get bored. Also, now we're hungry again. Whine about being bored, sore, tired, and hungry.

8:00 p.m.—Try to figure out something to do to alleviate the boredom.

8:45 p.m.—Got nothin'.

9:00 p.m.—Watch more TV.

10:30 p.m.–midnight—Go back to own room and fall asleep for the
night. Wake up and repeat.

One of our boredom-busting activities that Christmas break was to sit
in a hotel bathroom and bleach and dye streaks of each other's hair in
bright colors—red, purple, blue. Before that Sam and Rory had been
ballroom dancing around the room in their sweatpants along with a
public-access special, and we were teasing Rory about her new boyfriend, our practice player David.

Later, Leah, Rory, Sam, and I, with our brightly colored hair, lay
listlessly on the beds in Leah's room, gazing at the ceiling, bored out
of our brains and whining about how bored out of our brains we were.

"Well, we could count the dots on the ceiling," I said dryly.

Not picking up on my sarcasm, Leah the math major sat up. "Yeah!"
she said enthusiastically. "If we section them off it'll be easier."

It was in that moment we realized we had to get out of the hotel. We
piled into the car and drove to Petco, which was inexplicably a place we
had found ourselves more than once when we were bored over break.

"You know what we should do?" Sam said as we wandered through
the aisles, scrunching up our noses at the smell. "Buy some goldfish."

"Uh."

"Why?"

"Because," she said, "we should use them to prank the men."

For years we had been in the midst of an unofficial and mostly unac-
knowledged prank war with the men's basketball team. The prank I
admired most so far was one pulled by Jenni, Whitney, and Lyss during
my freshman year, their junior year. The men were on a trip to an away
game, and a group of them, who shared an apartment, had left one
of their CatCards with our juniors so they could get in and play video
games. Our juniors promptly bought handfuls of door alarms and
cheap alarm clocks and scattered them all over the boys' apartment—
door alarms on the front door, a kitchen cabinet, the guys' individual bedroom doors. They hid an alarm clock in everybody's bedroom
except Bryant's, because he had been smart enough to lock his door.
Lyss, Whitney, and Jenni set the alarms to go off at ungodly hours of

the night. The guys managed to get rid of the door alarms, which they could see, but they weren't expecting the alarm clocks.

Over the next few years no women's basketball player had come close to topping the famous alarm-clock prank. Live goldfish, we thought, had potential.

For a couple of cents each, using our per diem money, we bought two gray goldfish and two orange ones, since two of us were black and two of us were white. We promptly named them after ourselves—Rory Fish, Leah Fish, Sam Fish, and Otto Fish—and then went to Target, where we purchased a Barbie-pink bucket to put them in.

"So, where to?" I asked as we clambered back in the car.

"The men's hotel," Sam said.

We pulled into the parking lot with the headlights off, parked, and crept out of the car. Through the hotel's front windows we could see some of the guys playing cards in the lobby.

The four of us crept up the hotel's outdoor staircase, gingerly holding the bags of goldfish.

"If we get split up," Sam hissed, "meet in the parking lot by Otto's car."

We reached the hallway where Sam and Rory's good friend Ryan, a team manager, was staying. We deposited the fish bags on the floor outside his hotel room door, Sam knocked on it hard, and we fled, banging on every door as we went, giggling wildly, down the hall and back down the stairs. We sprinted to our getaway car and squealed out of the parking lot with the headlights off.

Safely back at the hotel, Sam got a call from Ryan. "What just happened?" he asked. "What did you just do? Did you guys seriously just leave live goldfish outside my door?"

"What?" said Sam indignantly. "No! Why would we do that?"

"Samantha," Ryan said. "Seriously. I know you did it."

"Absolutely not," Sam replied. "Talk to you later, Ryan. 'Bye."

Then Billy called. Billy was the on the staff of the men's team and had been one of the two coaches to lead us through our postseason workouts the year Coach Katz resigned. He had been a student manager for several years, including during the Elite Eight run, and then graduated and got hired for real. Bob McKillop was good about hiring people who were loyal to him and about giving scholarships to walk-ons. The guys were dedicated right back. A bunch of them got tattoos of their permanent team slogan, "TCC," or "Trust, Commitment, Care." Our team slogan that year was "It's on Me," meant to encourage individual accountability. None of us got tattoos of it. As soon as women's players graduated, I watched most of them get as far away from the program as they could.

"Sam," Billy exclaimed. "Hello. I'm calling because we've apparently got some, ah, fishy activities going on over at the hotel this evening."

"What are you talking about, Billy?" Sam said flatly. On the other bed Rory and I pulled our knees to our chests and giggled silently.

"Have a great night," Sam continued. "'Bye!"

Later I felt deeply guilty, because by buying the fish and leaving them on the ground outside somebody's hotel room, we had probably sentenced them to a worse death than they would have suffered at Petco or in some little kid's bedroom. We were so excited, and desperate for activity, in the moment that we hadn't stopped to consider that our prank was neither humane nor particularly creative. The alarm clocks still held the top spot.

At that point we were having our best season in several years. The men were doing well, too. We were undefeated in the Southern Conference, and so were they. We had all spent New Year's Eve together, playing poker and having a dance-off. Off-the-court antics were so much more fun when things on the court were going well.

13 The Popularity Contest

January hit us like an unexpected screen from a 230-pound center. Classes started again. Our bodies felt old and tired and were starting to fall apart. We played eight games in those thirty-one days, five at home and three on the road, all of them high-stakes conference matchups.

When we got back to Baker Sports Complex on January 9 after a shocking four-point loss at Wofford, picked last in the league—our first league loss of the season—a handful of FTP dumped our laundry in the bin, stuffed everything else into our lockers, and collapsed on the squashy black couch in the team room with snacks we'd hoarded from the bus. I had stolen an extra strawberry-kiwi Gatorade from the Wofford locker room, which housed a well-stocked refrigerator. We lounged on the couch in our sweats, eating fruit snacks by the fistful and venting furiously about what had gone wrong that day.

We traced most of our problems to fatigue. We had been doing so well around Christmastime, but Wofford was our third game in six days and the coaches were running us ragged at practice and shootarounds. Rory's back was killing her. My Achilles tendons were swollen and sore from overuse. The inflammation, which had once just surrounded the tendons, had spread over the top of the right tendon itself, which made

Brian worry the Achilles might snap under the pressure. He put me in a walking boot when I wasn't playing.

We were talented but frustrated. The coaches favored and relied on Alanna heavily even when she wasn't playing well, and Rory, our leading scorer, ended up having to work too hard to get clear shots off. Alanna and Rory were both outstanding players, preseason all-conference picks, and their skill was partly why we had been winning so much. But every other team in the SoCon knew about Alanna and Rory, too. Playing those teams the first time around was the easy part. During the latter half of the season, when we faced each of them a second time, they would know what to expect, scout the crap out of us, and possibly figure out how to shut down our top two scorers. We needed backup plans.

Plenty of us, including me, were also on short leashes, getting yanked after one or two mistakes. This coaching technique, as always, made us play with debilitating hesitance. I'd had a few good games in a row at the end of December, and then my confidence and playing time faltered again.

We struggled with Coach Harris's triangle offense because it did not really work a lot of the time. It was predictable and didn't give us much room to be creative. The majority of our plays started with a pass into a post player, usually Alanna, followed by the guards cutting, at which point the offense could begin, depending on how the guards cut and where they went. Any team that scouted us knew everything ran through Alanna, and since she was also the preseason conference player of the year, she was always heavily guarded. When our guards couldn't get the ball inside—and often they could not, since other teams knew the key to stalling our whole offense was cutting off that one pass—we got stuck, and nothing flowed naturally.

The offense wasn't all bad. We were winning games, after all. But we felt we were winning on skill, not strategy, and we needed both. Many of us these days didn't fully trust our offense or, by extension, Coach Harris's game-coaching or play-calling ability. This was only her second year ever as a head coach. We were intensely aware that she was learning as she went.

It was a Monday night in Baker Sports Complex when we got back from the Wofford game, and no one was around. As we talked we grew more and more frustrated. We started alternately yelling and shushing each other, in case anybody walked down the hall past our team room. Around ten we decided to go to Waffle House. It would be a safer space for venting and, plus, waffles. We were also currently breaking one of the rules in our team handbook: "Players should not be in the arena or the locker room at night alone."

"Also, what the fuck is with this home-game curfew?" I asked as we gathered our keys and slipped back into our sneakers. "We have to be in our rooms by eleven the night before a home game? Do they not understand how much homework we have? What if we're in a group meeting or study session? Literally, the other night I was at this meeting for FreeWord in the union, and I had to leave early and Skype in from my apartment because of curfew. Like, I am the vice president of that organization, and I had to go home to bed like a small child. It's bad enough we're out of town half the time. How is anybody supposed to take us seriously?"

"I really don't think the coaches understand."

"You know what else pisses me off? When they make us stay like an *hour* after practice for film when they haven't put it on the schedule." We also sometimes had to meet in small groups of teammates to watch game film on our own time. I was extra annoyed by that time commitment.

"You put it on the schedule, fine. But I'm busy. I plan out my days. I make other commitments. What if I have to meet a study group or a professor or something? Like, basketball is not the only thing I'm doing here."

"What if I need to print something out after eleven, and I'm not allowed to leave my room because of curfew? Eleven is two hours before the library even closes. Eleven is, like, early evening, Davidson time. *Nobody* here goes to bed at eleven."

"Trish literally has to drive around campus and knock on our doors randomly to make sure we're in there."

"Actually, that totally sucks for Trish. I wouldn't want to be the one with that job," said Lindsay.

Lindsay, a walk-on, still hardly played. Her teammates loved her for her easygoing nature and her quick, dry wit—she was one of the funniest people I had ever met. But she wasn't really on the coaches' radar. Like Coach Katz with Coop, Coach Harris barely communicated with her.

"I would just go to practice some days and feel like a ghost," Lindsay told me years later. She did not feel valued. "I would go, do the drills, burn my calories, and be out of there without ever having interacted with her."

Lindsay barely got playing time even in games we were winning by thirty. FTP thought she deserved to play—she practiced just as hard as the rest of us, and she was smart, in good shape, and had a nice jump shot. Bucknell had once recruited her. But this wasn't high school anymore. Division I coaches handpicked their teams and didn't have any obligations to play their bench. Although the coaches fielded calls from parents all the time, the parents had much less power now. I thought the right thing to do would have been to put Lindsay in more, but I was not in charge, and basketball at this level wasn't about "doing the right thing." The part of Lindsay that was a perfectionist actually didn't mind riding the pine, either.

They're gonna yell at me if I go in the game, she thought. *At least here on the bench they're not gonna bother me.*

"I am so over all this bullshit," I said as we banged out the locker-room door. "I am so ready to be a nonner."

I knew with more certainty than any other year that we could win the SoCon. We were that good. But I was ready to be done. I was a senior, so I should have been acting like a leader, but I was pissed off and tired. I had been slowly checking out for years.

My teammates and I all understood that college basketball was in many ways a business deal for us.

"I appreciate that sports is a business," our early walk-on Coop told me years later, "but like any business, it drives on the emotion and willpower of its employees."

My emotions about basketball were complicated. Sometimes I remembered that I loved it, but by junior year I had developed the mind-set that instead of practice or a game, I was just going to work every day. My willpower came from the court being my office. My teammates were coworkers. The coaches were our bosses. Plenty of kids got jobs to pay their way through college. This was mine.

We were genuinely thankful for our full rides—I would not have been anywhere near Davidson, financially or academically, without mine, and I was starting to understand the exceptional quality of the education I was getting there. But it is an odd feeling when the thing you love to do most becomes your full-time job and then when that job begins to dictate most aspects of your life and identity. We had drinking rules, curfew, a meal plan, and workouts. We had to eat, sleep, drink, lift, travel, and run when we were told to and study when we could. No matter how much we loved our sport and appreciated our free education, we hated that we couldn't make decisions for ourselves. I resented basketball even more in the days and months and years I spent on the bench watching us lose, the times it was easy to forget I loved it, this exhausting, time-sucking, pain-inducing creature that ruled almost every part of my life.

I had decided early in college that I was already too burned-out and my body hurt too much to pursue a professional career overseas. Now, as my career wound down and as my brothers grew older and more independent, my parents tried to come to as many games as they could. It still proved a challenge, since three boys lived at home and all three of them were in basketball season, too. But my dad drove almost seven hours from Pennsylvania for our 2:00 p.m. tip-off at Wake Forest on New Year's Eve. For one of the first times in my career I got significant playing time—almost thirty minutes—and scored fifteen points, and he was so proud that he and my mom bought an action photo of me in that game, got it framed, and hung it in the house. I was proud to have played well for once in front of him. My college career had been disappointing for both of us.

It tends to be much harder for players' families to attend a college game in person than it is a high school game, so it becomes a treat to play in front of your parents. As a child and teenager, I hated—*hated*—playing in front of my dad. I told him not to come or asked my mom to have him sit where I couldn't see him. But then I grew up and moved away, and now I found it comforting to spot him in the crowd.

Whomever's parents came to games, especially home games, became everybody's temporary family, handing out homemade goodies for the locker room, sometimes taking a group of us out for dinner, giving hugs to all the girls who wished their mom or dad could be there that day, too. Other families paid $200 a year to watch the fuzzy, choppy live stream online from home and listen to commentary by our radio guy, Derek Smith, who'd been the voice behind the broadcast of every Davidson women's basketball home game since 2003.

But our parents were supposed to love watching us play. That had been their job since we picked up our first ball. We had a few other devoted supporters; women's basketball fans might have been sparse, but they were loyal. The Pines retirement home still bused residents to every one of our home games.

Nyra Brannan was the Pines' unofficial leader. She was tall—as tall as many of us—and sturdy and red-lipsticked and loud as hell, the kind of woman who probably would have made quite a baller herself once. Nyra loved attention and she loved us. These two great loves of hers came together at our games, where she could be heard throughout the entire arena hollering, "*Get the ball!*" at the top of her voice at somewhat random intervals. It was the only thing she ever yelled, regardless of whether our team already had the ball. Whenever she yelled it, we knew she was there.

For their home games at Belk Arena, the men's team ran up the stairs from the locker room to the court to roars from several thousand enthusiastic mouths and Guns N' Roses' "Welcome to the Jungle" blaring from the loudspeakers. Sitting in the stands watching this spectacle, I always got chills. The dramatic jog out in front of the crowd to warm up, game faces set hard, competitive springs coiled tight, had been one of the most exciting parts of the game for me since junior high school.

Before our home games, on the other hand, we trotted up the stairs and onto the court from the locker room to a tinny recording of the school's fight song, in front of a few hundred fans and a smattering of applause. Once a women's player had to turn on Davidson's own warm-up clock because there was no one at the scorers' table to do it. Little slights like this added up. We understood that even though people cared about us, we were not a priority for them.

But one day in mid-January of my senior year, just a few days after the disastrous loss at Wofford, we ran out to the biggest crowd I had ever seen for a women's basketball home game, more than a thousand people. It was a Friday at noon, and the bottom bowl of the arena was almost entirely full, mostly with children under the age of twelve. We didn't care how old our fans were, though. If they wanted to watch us and they were having fun, we would happily take them. They wore brightly colored T-shirts, held posters, and jumped up and down in their seats when they saw us. We felt like bona fide celebrities.

It was Education Day, when students from local schools got free admission to one of our games so they could see a college campus and hang out with some college students as a field trip. I loved that Education Day, a tradition carried out by programs around the country, was built around women's basketball games, so that kids of all genders would have female athletes to look up to.

"There's always little eyes and ears on you," Coach Katz used to say.

That morning the kids had a geography lesson with our hometowns. They figured out who on our team had come the farthest to college and who was closest to home. Coach Harris welcomed them personally to the gym. Then it was time for the best part—the game itself.

The kids were a raucous crowd with posters and pom-poms. Some of the boys had even taken off their shirts and painted their prepubescent chests. They knew when to cheer, and they cheered loudly. We felt like celebrities.

"Here we go, Wildcats, here we go!" the kids chanted from their seats. They danced to LMFAO's "Sexy and I Know It," which the media table played during time-outs and which included lyrics my parents would not have let me dance to when I was twelve. The year Britney

Spears's song about threesomes came out, the media table had blasted that over the loudspeaker, too. At men's games they played an excerpt of LMFAO and Lil Jon's "Shots" when one of our guys went to the foul line. Kids in the crowd bounced with the Phi Delts, chanting, "Shots!" along with the song, despite the fact that it was clearly not about foul shots. I spent four years of men's and women's time-outs utterly baffled by these song choices, feeling like somebody's grandma for wondering whatever happened to "Space Jam."

That day we played the Western Carolina University Catamounts, another SoCon team. We had been picked fifth in the league at the beginning of that season, but exceeding all expectations except our own, we were undefeated at home and, despite the loss at Wofford, tied for second in the conference.

It was a scrappy, heady game, a particularly fun one, full of dirty hip checks and thrown elbows and grunts and heavy falls. Sam almost got into a fight. When we scored or got a steal the crowd went wild, bringing back memories of my high school days when we packed our small, creaky gym for rivalry games.

After the thirteen-point win we jogged up and down through the stands, high-fiving every eager hand we could reach, and then sat behind the press table to sign autographs on posters and T-shirts. We signed so many I stopped writing my full name and just wrote "Otto #33" with a smiley face, because it was quicker—the sign of a rare good autograph session.

"Hey, how are you?" we said with a smile to every kid, holding our Sharpies at the ready.

"Good," the kid said, usually swaying shyly back and forth, handing us a poster.

"Did you have fun today?" We would sign the poster by the picture of our face with the swish of a pen. We ribbed each other if someone signed too close to someone else's face. Sometimes we signed on each other's faces as a joke.

"Yes."

"Awesome. Me, too. You wanna come to another game sometime?"

"Yes."

"Good answer. Here ya go!"

Outside of two special occasions—Education Day and one double-header with the men's team—we averaged about five hundred fans at our home games that year. The men averaged almost four thousand. Our records were similar; by that point in mid-January, we were 6-1 in the conference and 10-6 overall, and they were 6-0 in the conference and 12-4 overall. (We would finish that season at 22-10, the men at 25-8—two solid records. They would go 13-2 at home in Belk Arena that year; we would go 12-1 there.)

We loved the guys dearly, and we were proud of them. But it was frustrating to play in their long, deep, history-laden shadow. We worked just as hard and were just as sore and tired. We spent the same amount of mandatory time in the gym and the film, training, and weight rooms. We were winning almost the same number of games that year as they were, having one of our best seasons in program history. But the attendance numbers said that the support the community showed the men was consistently eight times the support it showed us.

In some ways it made sense. Davidson men's basketball had a legacy program. They had made the NCAA Tournament ten times. They'd had All-Americans on their team. Several Davidson men's basketball players went to the NBA, and Stephen Curry was practically getting more famous by the minute, making his college program ever more visible. We had none of those things. But maybe once Davidson's women's basketball program was 105 years old, we would have thousands of fans, too. Maybe we just needed time to catch up.

As far as I could tell, much of a team's cycle of success stemmed from the coaches the school hired. Davidson men's basketball had been around for fifty-three years before Lefty Driesell came along. Once a team had an outstanding coach, he or she could recruit great players, build a program, get exposure, and then recruit even better players. Then more good coaches would follow. It was like what Pat Summitt had built at Tennessee. People came out in droves to watch the Tennessee women play; they averaged more than fourteen thousand fans a game that year.

Tragically, Summitt had announced the previous August that she had been diagnosed with early-onset dementia, Alzheimer's type, the same disease that doctors diagnosed my grandmother with when my mom was just a sophomore in college. Summitt planned to continue her head-coaching duties with the help of her assistants, but nobody knew how long she would be able to work. The loss of her brilliant mind would be a devastating one for both the men's and the women's college basketball communities.

Pat Summitt led in an era where women made incredible strides in athletics, probably the most progressive few decades in the history of women's sports. But we still had so far to go. My teammates and I came to college with preconceived ideas about the range of ways in which female athletes are still objectified, and we were mostly proven correct. It was the twenty-first century and we were four decades into Title IX, but the way straight men looked—or didn't look—at women still mattered.

Basketball, we always joked, was not a "sexy" women's sport like soccer or tennis or lacrosse. If women athletes were pretty and lean, we knew straight men sometimes wanted to watch them play. That fact was both empowering and degrading. We both cared about whom men watched and knew we shouldn't.

Women's basketball hit a popular streak in the 1990s with the rise of stars like Sheryl Swoopes and Lisa Leslie, the U.S. women's basketball team's Olympic gold-medal win in 1996, and the first WNBA game in 1997. I was seven years old then, so when I was old enough to fall in love with basketball, the sport was just settling into its new high. I had so many role models.

As a player there's a lot to be said for a full arena, no matter who fills it—parents, twelve-year-olds, horny college guys. Few women's basketball teams ever fill up their arenas, though. Despite early enthusiasm for the WNBA, over and over for the next fifteen years, empty stadiums and arenas and countless sports columns around the country reinforced the message that women's sports were not as exciting to watch as men's.

Hundreds of thousands of women, like men, played college sports. People simply didn't turn out to watch us in similar numbers. Our game was undeniably slower and more fundamental than men's basketball. We didn't jump as high or run quite as fast. Mac once described women's basketball as "men's basketball in two feet of water." We were tall, sturdy women who wore big, baggy shorts and clunky shoes, same as the men. We spent a lot of time shoving other women around and grunting. We were not conventionally sexy females.

The women's hoops boost of the '90s did not last long enough or reach quite far enough for small, mediocre programs like Davidson's to attract large or even medium-size crowds. Our sports marketing department tried. We had Education Day and Girl Scout Day. Marketing staff offered giveaways to students, who already got free admission and simply had to be bribed away from their studies or social lives. Other schools have promised free kale salads, free bacon, and raffle drawings for iPads and TVs and gift cards to students who showed up in support of women's basketball. Nobody seemed to have a long-term answer.

But fans or no fans or few fans, after the Wofford setback and despite our fatigue and widespread irritation, we kept winning.

After the embarrassment at Wofford we plowed through our opponents in January and February, losing just two games in the rest of the regular season—to Samford at home, 73–65, and to Chatt on the road, 55–48. We always lost at Chattanooga, but it was a fun place to play. They had active fan turnout at their women's games, and getting heckled was, for some of us, more fun than a silent or nonexistent crowd.

We played at UNC-Greensboro (UNCG) on Valentine's Day. Our coaches had started a pregame tradition where they bought silly children's toys from an Oriental Trading catalog and made up a related corny joke about each opponent. With the water guns, for example, we were supposed to "put out the fire of the Elon Phoenix." At Appalachian State we had little gooey men that stuck to the wall to inspire us to "climb the mountain." We were not quite sure what to make of any of it.

UNCG was the Spartans, so we were supposed to "play them away." This game's toy was a brightly colored plastic harmonica. If we won, we each got a harmonica of our own. If we lost, nobody got a harmonica.

We had just gone over the scout one last time and were sitting in rows on the benches in the locker room, wearing our full warm-ups, our shoes tied and retied, strips of prewrap wound around our knees and used as headbands, earrings out and necklaces off, braids and buns tightened. Coach Harris had made a rule—one of many I chafed at—that we weren't allowed to wear our hair in regular long ponytails.

We looked up at her expectantly, faces set and ready, waiting for her last words, our final, focused moments before we would stand up, break the huddle, and jog coolly onto the court to the ESPN3 cameras (which broadcast only to an online stream) and boos from the home crowd.

"All right, Trish," Coach Harris said. "Hit it."

Trish, holding her phone, pressed play. The tinny sounds of Stevie Wonder's "Isn't She Lovely" filled the locker room. Instead of giving us a motivational speech, Coach Harris held the toy harmonica to her lips and pretended to play.

We stared at our head coach, mouths slightly open, bewildered. No doubt the ancient enemies of the Spartans had intimidated them into surrender with a rousing rendition of this Stevie Wonder hit about his newborn baby girl. We could not look at each other for fear we'd start laughing, so we just watched Coach Harris, who was grinning cheesily from ear to ear, bouncing a little off the beat, the cheap plastic toy held to her lips. It was awkward. It was excruciating. We couldn't look away.

Amber was the first to giggle. She let out a snort and buried her face in the collar of her warm-up to muffle her laughter. More people started to snicker, but guiltily. Coach Harris was serious. She was trying. She wasn't kidding.

The coaches clearly meant well. They had obviously gone to some effort for this, to think up the puns, buy the toys, and carry them along to road games with us. But we didn't have a good-enough relationship with them to know how much of a joke this was supposed to be. Because we didn't know what result they expected from it, we didn't know how to react. We didn't know if we were allowed to laugh or whether we were supposed to laugh or hop around and grunt and chest-bump each other like a football team. And what was up with the song choice?

Years later, Trish said the song choice was probably because "Isn't She Lovely" had a harmonica section. She explained that the toys, which were meant to inspire us, also helped give Coach Harris something to focus on during her pregame speeches, something to ground herself with. But we didn't understand that at the time.

"When you're a leader of twenty-year-old women," Lindsay pointed out, "you need to communicate, because we're not on the same page as you."

We won the game by nine points and collected our harmonicas.

Senior Night, our last home game of the season and the last of Taylor's and my career, fell against Wofford in late February. We were ready for them this time. We had a 15-2 record in the conference, and we were in a fight with App and Chatt for the top of the league standings, having the best season we'd had in four years. My parents and youngest brother, Casey, drove down to celebrate. Taylor's family came down too.

It was tradition to put the seniors in the starting lineup on Senior Night, no matter how little they played in every other game. Every coach I'd ever had in high school and college had done it every year. It was a way to honor the seniors and their years of commitment to the team. Taylor was a regular starter. I was not, but I was contributing regularly, usually getting about half a game of playing time. I was looking forward to hearing my name announced as a starter that day, for only the second time in my career. The first time was a fluke my freshman year, when Coach Katz started Olivia and me as a way to motivate the upperclassmen whose spots we took.

So when Coach Harris gathered us in the locker room for the last-minute scout preparations and the pregame pep talk and she acted like nothing was out of the ordinary, giving Alanna, a junior, and Taylor their starting defensive assignments, I sat up a little straighter and stared at her.

I was not particularly surprised—Coach Harris had never seemed to like me much—but I felt hurt, angry, and deeply disrespected.

It was true that Coach Harris and I did not get along. By the time Coach Katz left, I had developed some serious trust issues with authority figures, a general wariness of basketball and its institutions, and a tendency to back-talk. But I still played hard, and this slight felt personal.

Years later, I called Coach Harris and asked her why she did it. After a long silence, she said, "I really don't know, Otto, and it was probably just bad on my part."

Even then, nearly five years after that day, I felt the anger blaze back up.

"When you're eighteen to twenty-two, every little thing that your coach does impacts you," Troy once told me. He was right. I'm not sure any coach of ours was aware how deeply their young players internalized their actions, praise, and criticism.

That night I snorted loudly, raised my eyebrows at Coach Harris, dropped my head, and stopped listening, clenching my hands together to keep them from shaking.

We won the game by twenty-four points. I played eighteen minutes off the bench, scored seven points, and had two assists and three turnovers. At the party afterward our underclassmen showered Taylor and me with gifts and cake and group hugs. My parents and Casey proudly showed me the signs they'd held. My roommates, Mary Marshall, Madison, and Hope—wearing my practice gear, which Sam had managed to sneak to them from the locker room—had painted "OTTO #33" on their cheeks. If they stood in the wrong order, their faces spelled "TOOT." These people loved me whether I started or not.

I didn't know it at the time, but Olivia was at home in her room that night, crying. She couldn't bear to come to the game, couldn't stand to see Taylor and me walk out arm in arm with our parents, holding bouquets of flowers, to our fans and teammates and friends standing and clapping. She could not listen while our game announcer, Leslie Urban, read our biographies over the loudspeaker, told the crowd what our majors were, who we hoped to be someday. Olivia was supposed to be there with her family, too, but none of us had so much as told her we wanted her in the stands. If that horrible October night two years earlier had never happened, she would have been in a uniform that day.

A week later, the day before our last game of the regular season at Samford, we were practicing in their gym in Birmingham, going over the scouting report. Samford ran a complicated offense, the Princeton.

The Princeton offense is perhaps most famously associated with Princeton University men's coach Pete Carril. He worked to perfect the system while he was at the school from 1967 to 1996, in an effort to set up his players for the best, most open shots they could possibly take. Dozens of NBA, college, and high school teams, both men's and women's, have used the offense with various tweaks. It is an intricate combination of backdoor cuts, on-and-off-ball screens, and, most important, nonstop motion. It's tricky to learn, tiring to run, and tough to guard—but it's fun as hell. The Princeton is an offense that breathes, a scaffolding of moves that allow smart players to react instinctively to a defense rather than being tasked, as our team often was, with running a specific play exactly as it's drawn up.

That day at practice we were working on how to defend it. I always had trouble remembering how we were supposed to guard screens on this one. Depending on our opponent and which of our players and their players were on the floor, we played screens differently.

If the player I was guarding set a screen on one of my teammates—standing still and making contact with her body to block my teammate's path—I was supposed to let my teammate know as soon as I saw it happening by yelling, "Screen left!" or, "Screen right!" If I didn't yell in time and my teammate got hit by the screen, she would be slowed down, our defense would be one man short until she recovered, or, worse, she could get hurt.

We played screens in a couple of ways:

Getting Through: If someone set a screen on me and I was guarding a slow player and someone had yelled out a warning in time, I could chase her around a screen that her teammate set on me without running into it.

Trapping: If a player was a poor ball handler or if we needed to force turnovers to make a quick comeback, we trapped the screens people set for her. The defender of the girl setting the screen popped out at a ninety-degree angle to guard the dribbler, and the dribbler's original defender blocked her path to the basket in a right-angled double-team. Everyone else on defense took a few steps away from their players to cover more space, since two of our defenders were now occupied with one of their players.

Hedging: Probably most often, we "hedged," which meant the player defending the screener popped out in front of the dribbler for only a second or two, just long enough to get in her way and slow her down while her defender caught up. Then the hedger darted back to her own player.

Switching: Sometimes, if the players were quick or good shooters, we switched altogether—the girl guarding the screener started guarding the ball handler instead, and the girl who'd been guarding the ball handler took the screener. This was logistically the easiest option, but only if we communicated about it.

It was all complicated, especially given that in a game scenario we had to make decisions and act on them within a fraction of a second. Obviously, the other three defenders on the floor had to literally be on their toes, ready to move. Good defense required constant vigilance and communication. When it worked right, when we all talked well and read the court and each other's movements, this kind of man-to-man defense was pure magic. It was like all five of us were attached to one string, and when one of us moved, the others shifted in turn to protect her, to have her back. There was no feeling in the world like a successful defensive rotation, a flawless display of the hard, gorgeous intricacies of teamwork.

Defense was difficult, though, on both the body and the mind. Often the way we played a screen depended on the exact player we were defending. So, for example, we would switch anytime number 25 came off a screen because she was a good shooter. We'd trap number 3 and number 5 and hedge everyone else.

I was having more trouble than usual today remembering the specifics and flailed around the court, looking lost.

Lindsay dribbled the ball toward me, guarded by Rory, and I couldn't remember which of Samford's players she was supposed to be. I was guarding Taylor, who prepared to set a screen on Rory.

Do I hedge on this one or trap it? I wondered frantically. By the time I decided to hedge, I was late, and Lindsay dribbled right around me while Rory stumbled over Taylor's screen. I screwed up the play in this manner several times in a row.

Coach Heather stopped the practice. "Otto," she hollered, "you have got to get it together!"

She reamed me out while I stood still at the foul line, staring blankly at her. Whatever.

Heather stormed toward the bleachers, grabbed her purse, and left the gym. Sam started laughing.

After practice we took the bus back to the hotel to shower.

"Thanks, Steve," I said to the driver, climbing down the stairs with my team backpack slung over my shoulder and nearly running headlong into Heather.

"Otto, lemme talk to you for a minute," she said.

"Yeah, sure." I waited.

"I'm pullin' real hard for you to start tomorrow," she told me. "I think we're better right now with you on the court, and I've been trying to convince Coach Harris of that. So when you pull shit like you did today, I lose credibility. Does that make sense? But you're starting over Taylor tomorrow, Otto. Prove me right, okay?"

My heart pounded. I was starting? After four years I was finally starting. I had earned my very own starting spot, just two games after they were supposed to have gifted me one for senior night. Now I had one for real.

"Yes, ma'am," I said, immediately feeling guilty for brushing her off at practice. "Thank you, Heather."

Because we had lost to Chattanooga two days earlier, we were in a tight race with their team and with Appalachian State for the regular-season conference championship. We had beaten App twice and split with Chatt. Those two teams were playing each other the same night of our Samford game. If Chatt won, we would win the regular-season championship. (Officially, we would tie with App and be cochampions, but since we had beaten them twice head-to-head, we considered ourselves the winners.) If App won, they would take the regular-season championship by themselves. We obviously wanted Chatt to win.

I started the game against Samford, like Heather said I would. I played well. We were tied at halftime. When the second half opened, we went on a 22–5 run and never looked back. As the clock ticked down, Trish kept checking her phone for the Chatt-App score. They were playing in Tennessee on eastern time, and we were in the central time zone, so their game was scheduled to finish before ours.

Finally, with just a few seconds left in our game, we had it well in hand. Trish came down the bench. "We won," she said, her face working furiously to hold back a smile until our buzzer went off. "Chatt beat App! By nine! We won!" We screamed.

The regular-season championship technically didn't mean much. Mostly it was for bragging rights and for the top seed in the conference tournament. If we didn't win the tournament, we still wouldn't go to the NCAAs. We would go to the Women's National Invitation Tournament (WNIT), the second-tier tournament to which we now had an automatic bid. But no Davidson women's team had ever won the regular season before. Our seventeen league wins were a school record. We would get a trophy for this. It was a big deal to us. So when the buzzer went off at Samford, we flew off the bench into each other's arms.

The coaches had brought confetti in case of a win, and we threw it all over the locker room. We took our showers, spent twenty minutes cleaning up our own confetti, strapped on our ice bags, and loaded up the bus.

The Samford trip was always a rough one. We didn't get out of their gym until ten thirty at night, eastern time. The men's team could afford to fly to their games at Chatt and Samford. But we took a bus and drove all night so we wouldn't miss class the next day. Every year a bunch of us crawled off the bus in Davidson at five or six in the morning, stopped at our dorm rooms for a quick nap, and headed to early classes, still in the rumpled team sweats we had worn all night. We started buying Tylenol PM at the rest stop where we changed drivers, putting our blankets and pillows on the floor, and stretching out there so we could get a few hours of sleep.

Tonight, though, we were so full of joy that we didn't care we had an all-night bus ride ahead of us. We updated our Facebook statuses with news of the championship and had a competition to see who could get the most likes. We giggled and sang and wolfed down our boxed dinners. We were allowed to watch actual TV, not game film, on the bus screens.

So this was what a championship felt like. One down, one to go.

14 The Dream

Coach Harris had no voice. She exhibited symptoms of laryngitis a few times every year, and they materialized again right before the eleven-team Southern Conference Tournament. Because we had won the regular season and earned an automatic bid to the Women's National Invitation Tournament, our season wouldn't end if we lost in Asheville—but we were gunning hard for more than that. To snag our conference's single bid to the Big Dance, we would have to win here first.

For the first time in program history, the Davidson College women's basketball team had received the top seed in the postseason conference tournament. We were getting votes in the midmajor Top 25 poll. After coming into the preseason ranked just fifth in the league, we were now expected to win it all. The coaches had put together a video for us called *Oh, the Places You'll Go!* made of clips of people who loved us—folks on campus, practice players, recruits, graduated players—offering encouragement for the tournament. We were ready.

Thanks to the laryngitis, normally soft-spoken Coach Harris, who had just been named the Southern Conference Coach of the Year, was this week even quieter than usual. "You might have to get a little bit closer," she'd croaked at the reporters who crowded around her in a hallway after our satisfying quarterfinal win over Wofford twenty-two hours earlier. Our January loss in their gym was an embarrassment that still stung, especially because our coaches had spent the previous two months reminding us of it as motivation, but we had finally done them in for good.

Now, in this big, creaky, old arena before our semifinal game against Samford, we watched Harris's lips. When they mouthed, "One, two, three—" we dutifully responded, "'Cats!" The huddle broke, and our five starters walked slowly to midcourt for tip-off. Marie shoved in her mouth guard. I licked my fingers, reached back, and wiped the bottoms of my shoes with them and then wiped my hands on my white shorts. Rory adjusted her headband. We settled ourselves around the circle and waited for Samford's starting five to join us.

Neither team had had even twenty-four hours to rest between the quarterfinal games and our semifinal matchup. Such was the rigor, and the strange beauty, of the playoffs. We were all equally exhausted by the schedule and energized by the atmosphere.

During warm-ups our team doctor, Dr. D, had administered powerful painkillers to Alanna and me in a quiet room down a long hallway under the bleachers. The injections, stuck into our bare butts, kicked in fast, numbing the accumulated pain of a long season, an even longer career. Sitting on the bench during introductions, I could, fascinated by this new trick, use my fingertips to push around the thick, gelatinous fluid in my swollen knees without flinching. A bruise I didn't remember getting covered my entire right elbow. The ankle I had sprained in the Wofford game was as fat and juicy as a ripe peach but no longer painful. Brian had wrapped it more tightly and with heavier tape than usual under my black lace-up ankle brace, hoping to keep me from rolling it two days in a row—more of a risk now that my body was almost completely numb. And he kept a close eye on me from the bench, worried that since I couldn't feel the usual warning pain and my legs were already tired, this could be the game when one of my Achilles tendons, swollen and still under pressure from the season-long bout of tendinitis, finally snapped.

The ball went up. Samford's center won the tip over Alanna. A Samford guard flew left-handed down the court for an easy layup, and within the first four seconds of the contest we were losing.

The night before the Samford semifinal, Lindsay and I lay in our beds at the hotel, both of us reading quietly. My pain shot from that day's quarterfinal game against Wofford, which we had won 69–58, had worn off, and my freshly sprained ankle swelled and throbbed hotly, shooting pain up my leg. I'd wrapped it firmly in an Ace bandage and propped it up on a few extra pillows. I swallowed some ibuprofen with water from the bathroom sink.

The television was off, all was quiet, and we were both snuggled under the covers. We didn't get a chance to read for pleasure very often, so Lindsay and I were totally content. It was spring break for Davidson students, but as basketball players at playoff time this was the closest we had come to a "real" spring break so far.

I was utterly absorbed in the first book of the *Hunger Games* trilogy, which I was reading on my phone. It was my first time ever reading a book on a mobile device, and it was weird and difficult, but I was so into the story I didn't care that I had to hold the screen four inches from my face.

At nine there was a knock on the door, jarring us out of our respective reveries. Linds and I lowered our reading material and glanced at each other irritably.

"Oh, come on."

"She's early!"

"Do we have to let her in?"

"She's not supposed to be here until ten."

"I'm just using this to read my book, and I'm at a really good part. What if I promise her I'm only gonna read my book and not text any boys? Not that I actually do that anyway."

"Why is she so early?"

Lindsay shuffled to the door in her oversize T-shirt and shorts and opened it. Trish stood in the hallway with one hip jutted, chomping her gum, holding out an ice bucket in which a colorful array of smart-phones lay like a seashell collection.

"Phones, guys," she said. It was our nightly pregame ritual on the road. Having us leave our phones on the bus during team meals was one thing, but FTP thought the nighttime confiscation was a patron-izing and unnecessary display of power. Our team, however, did not really operate as a democracy.

The lack of phones also meant that we depended on hotel alarm clocks and wake-up calls, and twice that season our hotel wake-up call never came, we set the alarm wrong, and my roommate and I accidentally overslept. At Appalachian State Brittany and I had woken up on game day to our room phone ringing and Heather on the other end, demanding to know why we weren't on the team bus, which was about to leave for shootaround. Brittany had a torn ACL, but I spent a good chunk of shootaround that day running sprints as punishment.

I pushed my covers back and limped over to the doorway to join Lindsay. "Do we have to?" I whined, holding up my phone to show her the screen. "I'm just reading a book on mine. It's helping me focus. I won't text anybody, I promise."

Trish shrugged. "Sorry, Otto."

I pouted, turned off my phone, and dropped it in the bucket with the others. Lindsay did the same.

"Why are you taking them so early tonight?" I asked.

"'Cause shootaround is so early," Trish said. Our game against Samford was at noon the next day, and we had a busy morning ahead of us. We had to get dressed and taped, ride the team bus to the U.S. Cellular Center Arena for shootaround, pull the rest of our gear on, warm up and stretch, practice for an hour, go back to the hotel, shower, wolf down a pregame meal, repack our duffel bags, get taped again, and arrive back at the arena no later than 10:30 a.m. to get regeared, restretched, rewarmed, and ready for the game.

"Okay," Lindsay and I sighed. "Night, Trish." She reminded us what time the bus left in the morning and moved down the hallway to the next team door.

On game day Samford was supposed to have the morning shootaround slot directly before ours, but their team was nowhere to be seen when we arrived at the arena. Because we were the higher seed, we got the later shootaround time. They must have skipped theirs, choosing sleep over scouting.

A smart move on their part, I thought grumpily, wincing as I rolled out my sore ankle on the sideline. In my opinion, we didn't need any extra time on our feet either, but the coaches wanted us to get our blood flowing and run through the scout again. We laced up our shoes, shook the sleep out of our eyes, and staggered onto the hardwood.

It would have been one thing if game-day shootarounds consisted only of walking through the scout and a few of our own plays. On our team, though, under both Coach Katz and Coach Savage, we treated them essentially like miniature practices, running full-court drills and competing five-on-five in the half court. After an hour of shootaround, we went back to the hotel and showered. Then we ate our pregame meal on white tablecloths in a private meeting room. The coaches could not resist running through the scout one more time, quizzing us on Samford's top players' statistics, strengths and weaknesses, their team out-of-bounds plays and preferred defensive sets. By the time we loaded up the bus to head back to the arena, we did not think we could be any more prepared.

As always my teammates and I communicated with our hands as we passed each other during warm-ups: a soft touch on the lower back, a playful pat on the head, a firm low-five. We were tired and wary, but confident. Only six days earlier, we'd beaten Samford by thirteen at their gym in Birmingham to clinch the regular-season title.

Covered in goose bumps, I scanned the faces of the Davidson crowd behind our bench. I saw my parents and brothers and my brother's girlfriend, all decked out in Wildcat gear. Luke watched the live stream from Australia, where he was studying abroad. I felt that old dream of playing in the NCAA Tournament leap deep in my stomach. Two more wins and we would be there. I had dreamed endlessly of this day during the long, sweltering summer afternoons of my teenage years, shooting hundreds of free throws in the old YMCA gym in my hometown.

All that time, I thought, feeling strangely like I was outside my body watching it have this experience, came down to this.

The first half of our semifinal game against Samford was an ugly slog, a defensive tug-of-war. Women's basketball games are often like this, intricate and technical, well-scouted defensive battles, not offensive circuses. We relied on solid teamwork, communication, and fundamentals like boxing out and setting screens rather than pure athleticism. John Wooden, famed men's coach of the University of California at Los Angeles and perhaps one of the best of all time, once said, "The best pure basketball that I see today . . . is among the better women's teams."

Samford's starting point guard went to the bench early with two fouls, which was excellent news for us. Their coach replaced her with sophomore Shelby Campbell, a tanned, ponytailed role player, a mere blip on our scouting report. We paid little mind to her entrance.

We could barely hear anything Coach Harris was saying. From the court we relied on hand signals and the assistants to translate, which slowed us down. But there were deeper communication issues as well—many of us still disliked our own triangle offense, and Samford had scouted us impeccably. When our offense didn't work, we tended to play one of two ways: either we relied on good defense and fast breaks so that we didn't really need plays, or we clammed up. Today, well scouted and tightly guarded, we were clamming.

As in all our games, there were media time-outs every four minutes of play so the radio and television stations broadcasting the contest could go to commercial. I always counted down to these guaranteed rest times. During the second break I tuned out Coach Harris altogether and gazed around the dim arena, something I did often, to her constant exasperation.

The second level of the arena was almost entirely empty, but we were accustomed to this. The night before, as we filed into much fuller stands before the start of the Davidson men's game, Wildcat fans all over the arena had stood up and beamed at us, clapping enthusiastically. Totally surprised by and unused to such a lather of attention, we waved and grinned awkwardly in our matching black tracksuits. This was probably what the men's team felt like all the time, I mused as we settled in to watch them. I wondered how many of these other people would show up at our game the next day. It seemed like many of them had not. Two arena employees and a security guard hunkered behind our bench, looking bored.

In the middle of the first half Samford went on a 24–6 run with Shelby Campbell, the little sub nobody had heard of, pouring in buckets from all over: three-pointers, drives in the paint, free throws. She would finish the half with fifteen points. We couldn't seem to figure out what to do with her. That season, overwhelmed by thick, complex playbooks and detailed scouting reports, I felt we had lost much of our ability to improvise, react, and play with the good instincts we had spent our lives developing.

Campbell wasn't on the scout! we exclaimed to ourselves over and over. So how were we supposed to know how to guard her? Because we had not seen in writing what she could do, we were paralyzed when it came to stopping her in person.

"Feeling a little bit of panic from Davidson," remarked one of the ESPN3 announcers with a minute and thirty seconds left in the first half. She was right.

With less than a minute until halftime, down 34–15, I ended up with the ball at the top of the key. Later, I would remember this moment more than any other from that game: the hot blaze of panic, the hard flash of my career through my exhausted brain, the recognition that my childhood dream of making the NCAA Tournament might very well die here today on this dingy old court in Asheville, a slow, twitching, tortured death broadcast live on ESPN3. In that burst of wild anxiety I put my head down and drove right hard.

But I had forgotten that as part of the play, Taylor was already cutting across the key toward the right block off a screen from Marie. She couldn't get out of my way in time.

"Taylor, move!" I grunted at her, losing control of the ball as we collided. Somehow it bounced into her hands. Taylor kicked it out to Rory, and I dashed across the key, out of the way. Rory drove baseline and got fouled. Two shots. Somehow we had stumbled our way out of disaster.

"Otto, you need to calm down," Taylor told me firmly as we set up for the free throws. "Run the play."

"No!" I wailed, close to tears, wiping my mouth on my jersey. "You need to get out of my way."

But I understood, slamming my hands onto my hips, that she was right. Blind, selfish hysteria was not going to get us anywhere.

When the halftime buzzer sounded the score was 36–16, and Samford held its largest lead of the game, having just kicked in a 10–1 run to end the period. Incredibly, they had shot almost 50 percent from the floor. We had connected on only 22 percent.

A few of our cheerleaders sat in the bleachers. They had double duty this tournament, cheering at both Davidson men's and women's games. Our pep band burst into song. I couldn't keep from crying.

It was not often that the team sat in dejected silence of its own accord before the coaches even entered the locker room at halftime, but that day was one of those days. Even rarer were the times that silence was broken by a player with something to say, someone who felt her thoughts were worthy of cutting into the heavy, hallowed air. But today, revved up on adrenaline and panic and painkiller, I had something to say.

We had started the season ranked fifth, but now we were the top seed in our conference and two wins away from a guaranteed spot in the NCAA Tournament for a goddamn reason. We had surprised everyone before, and we could do it again. "This game is not over, guys," I told my teammates firmly. "It's not fuckin' over. We can do this."

The room echoed with the sounds of labored breathing, thick snuffles, some coughs. There were a few small murmurs of assent. I stood up and walked slowly toward the bathroom, untucking my jersey as I went. As I peed I dropped my face into my hands and took a deep breath. I felt sick to my stomach. I stumbled back to my seat and stared at my shoes. Despite what I had said out loud, I knew my dream of making the NCAA Tournament would probably be dead within the hour.

The locker room door opened, and the coaches filed in. I swiped at my tears with the neckline of my jersey and glared at them. Coach Harris's bowed head and hunched shoulders told us all we needed to know. Our head coach, quiet and often seemingly apathetic, was acting even more so than usual. She spoke in the strained whisper she'd been using all week, but also in the tone of voice she usually reserved for the ends of games we had already lost. It seemed like she had given up on us.

We stood up for the huddle and gathered our fists in the air, hands resting weightily on each other's backs and shoulders.

"Let's go, y'all," I said, shaking a little.

"One, two, three, 'Cats," we intoned.

We jogged back onto the court to an enthusiastic greeting from our crowd, pep band, and cheerleaders. Even if they didn't believe in us, they were at least pretending to. There was a sense of harnessed urgency in our layup-line high-fives. My panic had melted a little, morphing into a kind of wobbly determination.

Per orders from Coach Harris in our courtside huddle to start the half, we ramped up our defense in a stifling full-court trapping press Samford wasn't ready for. We got all over them. Quickly, we cut their lead to fifteen, 38–23.

Samford called time-out. We trotted to our bench as our crowd roared, half our fans on their feet. Three male Davidson students, friends of my teammates, were jumping up and down in the front row. I had chills.

"You knew this run was coming from the Wildcats," said the TV announcer, raising her voice over the crowd. "You don't get the top seed in the Southern Conference by falling apart for too long."

For the first time in my college career I stopped thinking, stopped analyzing, stopped caring, and just played basketball. My mind was blissfully blank, but I was focused. My body was drained, but I could will it to move. We made our comeback on steals and fast breaks and perfect passes, on the heady, primal leaps of joy borne of throwing aside the playbook and running on pure hustle and instinct. Forget Coach Harris and her negativity. We could do this.

We kept chipping away. Marie forced a Samford player to miss a shot in the paint and dove on the floor for the rebound. Lying on her stomach, she managed to roll the ball toward Leah, who took off and dumped it inside to Alanna, who put in the layup. The whistle blew. She'd get a foul shot, too. 38–30.

Our bench and fans were beside themselves. We held each other back on the sideline, but barely. Sam, who had been standing up off the bench and leaning forward anxiously for the entire play, flew forward like a rabbit onto the court, and I reached over Taylor to corral her with my left arm. Kaylee, on my other side, threw one long, skinny arm across all three of us.

Six Davidson players stood in a row on our feet, all leaning forward and yelling, some wearing our red long-sleeved warm-up shirts and some in our white jerseys. Six strong, tense pairs of legs, muscles bulging under six pairs of baggy shorts; twelve black ankle braces; twelve red socks. An ebullient red-and-black-clad crowd had risen to its feet behind us. Taylor's father stood sporting a Davidson sweatshirt and ball cap, a proud, close-lipped Dad grin on his face as he clapped. A man near him leaned back at the waist with his hands palms up in the air and his mouth wide open like he was at church praising Jesus.

Alanna hit the free throw to make the score 38–31. We were on a 15–2 run. Our crowd and cheerleaders and pep band started a "De-fense! De-fense!" chant, and the bench joined in, shouting and stomping our feet along with everyone else.

Fewer than thirty seconds later, Shelby Campbell drained an open three-pointer, Samford's first field goal of the half. Our fans quieted; our bench sat back down. Samford's lead rose back to ten, and now it was their crowd leading the "De-fense!" chant.

We were drained, and it began to show. Our defensive rotation moved just a beat too slowly. We gave their shooters too much space because we couldn't get a hand up in time. We missed putbacks we should have made. Samford's lead crept back up, first to twelve, then fifteen on another Campbell three-pointer.

Leah had a solid drive and got fouled, and we were so glad for the break in action that we could barely summon the energy to congratu-

late her, lurching in her direction for limp high-fives and then trudg-
ing to the bench for a time-out. Exhaustion clouded Leah's eyes as she
stepped to the free-throw line.

Then Rory got a steal but accidentally staggered sideways into someone. They barely made contact, but she couldn't keep her feet under her,
collapsing while she dribbled. The jump ball went to Samford. She got
up slowly. Four and a half minutes to go. The score was 49–39, Samford.

We never got any closer than eight points the rest of the game.

With thirty-four seconds left, I fouled out. Kaylee and our manager,
Charlie, each placed a gentle hand on my back as I watched the car-
nage through tears from the bench. Rory air-balled a three-pointer.
Taylor saved the ball from going out-of-bounds only to throw it into
the hands of two Samford players. Alanna air-balled another three as
the buzzer sounded. Final score: Samford 62, Davidson 51.

I was self-aware enough to know what a cliché I looked like, the devastated senior with her face contorted and tears pouring untouched
down her cheeks, as we plodded through the line to shake hands with
the Samford players and their coaches. I thought of our season-ending
losses the previous three years and how much I had pitied my seniors
after those games. Now I was just another senior to be pitied. The
Samford coach grasped my hand tightly and gave me a little hug when
I reached him, showing me in that moment more genuine affection
and respect, I thought angrily, than my own coaches had in my career.

"Good game, three-three," he murmured. "Good season."

In the locker room afterward, Coach Harris reminded us that we'd
had a good regular season, better than last year's. Most of the team—
everyone but Taylor and me—would be back next year, so they would
probably be even better. *Gee, thanks*, I thought.

We would find out the location and date of our first-round WNIT game
after the NCAA Tournament pairings were announced in a week. The
season was not over yet, added Alanna. I wished it was. I felt like it was.

Slowly and silently, we unlaced our shoes and ankle braces. A handful
of us trudged to the showers in our flip-flops, carrying our shampoo
and soap, stuffing our stripped-off uniforms into the laundry bag, loos-
ening up braids and buns with our fingers as we went. The rest, mostly

underclassmen, waited for their turn without a word. Coach Harris summoned a red-eyed Rory out to the postgame press conference.

Rory came back into the locker room as most of us were packing up. I touched her sweaty head and walked out alone, wandering through the emptying stands of the arena with my duffel bag strapped across my chest, hands shoved in my pockets, hair dripping from the shower, feeling raw and empty and fragile. My chin trembled. A few people tried to talk to me, but I gave them close-lipped smiles and ducked my head away. I couldn't find my parents, and I needed them. I needed someone to pity me lavishly, to hold me as my heart fell to pieces.

Eventually, after calling her cell phone several times in increasing levels of distress, I found my mom sitting on the second level behind the basket. I sat down next to her.

"I'm so sad," I told her.

"Oh, honey," she said.

The tears came again, slow and hard and wracking. My mother and I rarely hugged, but she hugged me then and held on.

We were allowed a few hours for family time that afternoon. We would leave Asheville for Davidson the next morning. To my surprise Trish was patrolling the hallway when I arrived back at the hotel room I shared with Lindsay, who had headed home to Charlotte with her family. I let myself into the room, threw my bag down on a bed, pocketed my phone and key, and headed back out. I knocked on Allie's door.

"Hey, Trish," I called down the hallway, hoping that by acknowledging her presence I would appear less suspicious. She lifted her chin at me, the sole of one sneakered foot propped up on the wall behind her. They had never kept such a close eye on us in the hotel before.

Sam let me in and made sure the door closed tight.

"What are y'all doing in here?" I asked.

"Gettin' in trouble," Allie announced conspiratorially, indicating the open Facebook chat on her computer. "You in?"

FTP had had a group text message going around for much of the afternoon. Caroline, one of Allie's nonner friends from Davidson, had come to Asheville for spring break to watch the games. She'd offered to run to the Walmart and secretly bring us some beer and wine. It looked like she was the key to making our spring break a little more like spring break was supposed to be.

We had spent the past five months in full dry season; Coach Harris finally realized that she needed to clarify team rules about alcohol, so we couldn't get away with drinking on a technicality like we had the year before. From the day of our first practice at the beginning of October until the night our last game ended, it would be against team rules for any of us to have even a sip of alcohol. By this point in the season, though, many of us were ready to be normal college kids again, even if it meant shattering the rules.

We were also irritated with the coaches, whom we blamed for our loss that day. This was the perfect way for us to conduct a secret revolt, to challenge their authority right under their noses, and to reassert our free will as humans, not just athletes, and have fun doing it.

"Hell, yeah, I'm in," I said. "Who else knows?"

"Kelsey and Leah," said Sam.

"Okay. How's she gonna get it in here? Did y'all see Trish just chillin' in the hallway? So weird. Like, what is she doing?"

"I can go meet Caroline upstairs with my backpack, and we can do a transfer in the bathroom."

"Too risky. The bottles will clank."

"They must suspect something. We're all in here."

"So what? Maybe we're talking about the game."

And we did. While we waited to hear back from Caroline on the status of our contraband delivery, we draped ourselves around the room with a *Law & Order* marathon on in the background and hashed out that day's game and the season. We came back to the same issues over and over: Why hadn't Shelby Campbell been on the scout, and when she started hitting, why hadn't we been able to stop her? Why did we always force the ball inside even when teams doubled down on Alanna? We shouldn't have been so tired. We were all so tired. We could have pulled off the comeback if we'd had our legs under us. But we shouldn't have had to make a comeback in the first place.

My pain shot was wearing off again. I wanted this numbing medicine in my body every day, all the time. I wanted a shot for my brain. One for my soul. I lay flat on the floor on my back in our black team sweats, taking deep breaths, my bad ankle propped on Allie's bed. Loud and violent things were happening on the television. My heart broke the way a heart breaks in unrequited love, a slow, throbbing reel. I wallowed deep, letting the pain roll me up. The sun slumped behind the mountains.

"Do y'all smell that?" Leah said suddenly, sitting up on the bed.

"What?"

"Somebody's smoking."

"Where?"

"Smoking what?"

"Outside?"

"In the hallway?"

"Oh, God, Trish is in the hallway."

Sam got up, pulled back the blinds, and opened the sliding door. We crowded around her. The rich, warm smell of pot mixed with the night air. Two people on the grounds moved quickly into the shadows of the building.

"Hey," whisper-yelled Sam. "Hey. We're not gonna get you in trouble, I promise. Can you come here for a sec?"

One of the hooded figures moved cautiously a few steps toward us.

"Can you guys do that somewhere else?" Sam asked, all business. "We're on a basketball team and our coach is right there in the hallway, and we don't want to get in trouble and we don't want you to get in trouble."

"Yeah, okay, yeah," a male voice grunted. They walked away.

"Dumbasses," Sam muttered. "Trish must have smelled it, too." None of us had ever been drug-tested, but technically under NCAA rules any of us could be, randomly and without much warning. At the time, if an NCAA drug test came back positive for marijuana, the athlete would be suspended for a full season.

"If they get us in trouble before Caroline can bring the stuff . . . ," I began. "Shut the door, quick, so the smell doesn't get in."

A few minutes later, I poked my head out into the hallway. Trish was, astonishingly, still there. She looked bored.

"Hey, Trish," I called cheerily. *(Look at me, Trish! Look at how sober I am!)* I asked her what time the bus left in the morning.

"She's still there," I hissed once I'd shut the door. "What the fuck?"

"Caroline can't bring us stuff anyway," Allie sighed hugely from her bed. "It's Sunday. She can't find anything open."

"Fuck Sunday," we grumbled. The hotel bar was out—too risky. There were no stores within walking distance. We couldn't exactly wake up our bus driver for a booze run. But we could not give up. We were exhausted and sore and sad, and we didn't want to feel anything anymore. Plus, we weren't quitters.

Finally, we came up with a plan. Leah would sneak into her parents' room and swipe the keys to their rental car while they dozed, and we would go for a little drive.

Trish had finally surrendered her post in the hallway. When Leah returned with the keys, the five of us tiptoed out the back door and piled into the rental car. We crept out of the parking lot with our headlights off and hit the highway, unfolding all sweet and empty ahead of us.

I rode shotgun and played deejay. We rolled down the windows and breathed deep and whooped into the clean mountain air, reveling in our escape and this new freedom. Spring was coming. We were all going to be okay.

"So, where to?" asked Leah. We didn't really know. The liquor stores would be closed. So we sped aimlessly down dark, quiet roads, singing and chatting and dancing in our seats, not really caring that we didn't have a destination pinned down. The adrenaline rush of this ultimate act of rebellion, of sneaking out of the hotel right under our coaches' noses and "borrowing" a rental car to buy ourselves some booze, made this a joyride of unparalleled proportions. Leah relaxed at the wheel. We laughed harder than we had laughed in days.

Eventually, we tracked down a twenty-four-hour gas station that sold alcohol. When Leah pulled into the parking lot, a hush fell over the car. We turned the music down and rolled our windows up.

"Park over there, Leah," I said, pointing to a shadowy corner. Leah did, peering carefully over the wheel of the rental car. She turned the lights off but left it running.

"And Otto and Allie," somebody piped up from the back, "y'all better turn your sweats inside out."

We had only packed team clothes for the Asheville trip, so we were all sporting our baggy black sweat suits emblazoned with WILDCATS on the left breast and DAVIDSON on the right thigh above our jersey numbers. The NCAA Division I Southern Conference men's and women's basketball tournaments were a big economic opportunity for this scenic North Carolina city, so people—especially, probably, salespeople—knew a bunch of college basketball players were in town. The least we could do, given the risk we were about to take, was disguise our school name.

"Hurry," Leah breathed, glancing around nervously.

As Allie and I entered the near-empty convenience store, a bell dinged over the door, announcing our presence, and we squinted under the grayish fluorescent lights. Both about six feet tall and solidly built, we were dressed in the exact same outfit and had them on inside out. We were, I imagine, pretty hard to miss.

Trying to act casual, Allie and I inspected the cases of beer—not strong enough, we decided, and too unwieldy to carry. We needed the smallest containers that would pack the biggest punch. Presently, we came upon the garish, shiny shelves of Four Loko, a potent alcohol-and-caffeine-combination drink. Perfect.

I hugged the cold, slippery Four Loko cans to my chest, and Allie held open the refrigerator door with her butt as we peered at bottles of wine. We grabbed one and headed toward the register, hearts beating fast.

"Wait." I'd realized something. "Is that a screw-top bottle?"

Allie glanced down. "No. Shit."

Anxiety levels rising, we searched in vain for a corkscrew for several minutes before sheepishly asking the cashier if he could help us. He surveyed us disinterestedly and informed us the store didn't carry them. We needed to find a screw-top wine bottle.

We did. It was called Thunderbird, and it had nearly 20 percent alcohol content.

I started to pull my ID and debit card out of my wallet, but Allie growled and shoved my hand down. "No cards," she hissed. "I have cash."

It took me a second to figure out why she was so adamant about this, but then I realized: leave no trace.

"*Right*," I whispered, pocketing the card. "Duh. I'll pay you back." The cashier checked both of our IDs while we stared around nervously, and then he rang us up.

Allie handed him some bills, waited impatiently for change, and snatched up the clanking plastic bag. The bell dinged again as we walked out.

"What took you guys so long?" our teammates squealed as we hopped back into the car. Leah locked the doors, we rolled down the windows, and, giddy with joy over the success of the first phase of our plan, we peeled off again into the cool night.

When we arrived back at the hotel, Leah turned off the headlights and pulled into the spot we were pretty sure we had vacated earlier. After a brief scuffle over which can to open first, we popped one of the Four Lokos and began passing it around, carefully monitoring the size of each other's sips. We had decided it would be much more fun, and would make for a much better story, to sneak back in a little buzzed.

I took my first pull of the cranberry lemonade–flavored drink and held it sizzling on my tongue. Four Loko was sickly sweet, like Hawaiian Punch, but it also had a urine-like sourness to it, like an energy drink. The bubbles tickled. Delicious warmth trickled down my whole body as I swallowed, and one thought occupied my whole brain: *We did it. We just broke dry season.* I waited for the guilt to rush in. I was joyful, proud, content, full of love, terrified we'd get caught. But guilt never came, that night or ever.

It was the contagious, innocent, dreamy kind of drunk where you're mostly convincing yourself that you're drunk because everybody around you is acting drunk, but probably nobody is actually that drunk. Whether as a real result of the alcohol or because we were so pleased with ourselves and our plan and overcome by the freedom we'd just experienced, all five of us were giddy and giggling within minutes. We tipped back the can for the last drops and placed it carefully back inside the plastic bag, arranging the cans and the wine bottle gently inside Kelsey's team-issued backpack, packing them in with a T-shirt to help muffle any clanking. We took deep breaths. It was time to sneak back in.

"Come on," we teased Kelsey, who was wearing the backpack, as she struggled, limping heavily, to keep up with us through the parking lot. "Why so slow?" She had been walking without crutches for only a couple of weeks.

As we got closer to the front doors of the hotel we had a clear view into the brightly lit bar next to the lobby. We realized with horror that Trish, Pam, and Heather sat inside the bar, no doubt debriefing over drinks. Just like us.

There was no way we could go through the main entrance now. We would have to sneak around to the back door. One at a time we held our breath, ducked, and sprinted at a crouch beneath the windows that lined the front of the hotel. As I passed the bar I raised my head slightly and sneaked a peek inside. My breath caught in my throat again at the sight of our assistants.

It was Leah's turn to cross. She doubled back to check out the coaches and then all of a sudden started sprinting toward us, wild-eyed.

"Heather turned around," she whispered. We took off, completely forgetting Kelsey hobbling along in back. We turned around and crouched at the corner of the building to urge her on. She was still wearing the backpack—not a single able-bodied teammate had thought to take it from her—and unlike the rest of us she couldn't bend at the waist, duck, or hustle. Thanks to adrenaline and delirious exhaustion and Four Loko, we found the whole thing infinitely hilarious.

"Kelsey, hurry—hurry up. Why are you so slow? Come on!" we whisper-screamed at her, giggling, hands on our knees, all energy flowing outward, a crazy echo of our fervent bench during that afternoon's game. Kelsey lurched, clanking, past the bar windows, standing almost straight up, backpack of booze perched high on her shoulders, staggering along as fast as she could go. What a superstar.

I could see from the glow of the bar light inside that Kelsey was grinning but in a crazed, panicked kind of way, a dear-God-I'm-only-a-freshman-what-did-these-upperclassmen-get-me-into-holy-shit-what-if-I-actually-get-kicked-off-the-team kind of way. As she inched closer with excruciating slowness I ran over disastrous scenarios in my head. Wow, we were dumb. As the only senior on this mission I felt responsible for what happened to the others. I didn't care about anything the staff could do to me, but everyone else had to come back next year, and if we got caught and punished and then the coaches held this against my underclassmen as a grudge, I would never forgive myself.

After a million heart-pounding years, Kelsey reached us. We whisked her around the corner and in through an unlocked back door and piled inside, all breath and titter.

Someone checked to make sure the coast was clear, and then we hurried down the hallway back to Leah's room, which stood catty-corner to Trish and Heather's, and shut the door quietly. Time to open the next can of Four Loko. I did the honors, diving underneath as many covers as I could pile on top of myself to muffle the sound as someone flipped the TV back on, turning up the lawyer show much louder than it needed to be. We kicked off our team-issued sneakers and hopped up on the beds, limbs strewn over each other, passing the can back and forth across the nightstand, basking in our pride. Instead of worrying about forgetting plays or what the coaches thought of us or accidentally elbowing each other in the face during practice, we simply enjoyed each other's company.

The can was almost gone and we were feeling pretty warm and glorious when there was a knock on the door.

My heart had never come to a halt quite so hard.

I grabbed the cans, bottle, and cups and shoved them under the bed. We turned the TV down. Sam got up and walked to the door, then peered through the peephole.

"It's Kaylee," she whispered. My heart started beating again as we began a whispered debate about whether to let her in on the secret. It would be kind of great to add another person to our little party of rebels—nearly half the team would be in on it this way—and we weren't sure we could hide it from her once she was in the room anyway.

Leah opened the door, checked the hallway, and hastily shooed Kaylee inside. Kaylee ambled in, gazing around at what was surely a snapshot of people looking exactly like they'd just gotten caught doing something wrong. Allie and I were badly feigning casualness on one bed. Sam sprawled on the other, choking back laughter. Kelsey was lying on the floor.

"What's up, guys?" Kaylee said, half-smiling the way confused people smile, taking us in. Unable to contain ourselves any longer, we burst out laughing.

"You cannot tell a soul," I said. I slowly reached under the bed and pulled out the open can of Four Loko. "Want some?"

Before long we were rip-roaring, cry-laughing, screw-everything drunk. If anyone knocked on the door now, I thought, there would be no playing it off. The television blared. Kelsey found a shower cap and wanted to know what it was—white girls!—and then jammed it onto her head. We danced an Irish jig. We bounced on the beds. We took pictures. In one of them Kelsey is wearing a surgical mask, and nobody has any idea where she got it.

It wasn't long before we decided we should leave the safety of the room and go exploring. Gathering at the top of the grassy knoll outside the room we thought was Coach Harris's, we luxuriated in the sweetness of our insubordination.

Somebody challenged Sam and Kelsey to take off their clothes and roll down the hill. The challenge went like this:

"You won't!"

We were a team of such fierce competitors that being told we couldn't or wouldn't do something was too much of an insult to bear. Most of us had fallen for this challenge at some point or another that season— whether it was to finish an impossible amount of food, make out with a particular person, or strip down to our underwear and roll drunkenly down the damp hill outside our head coach's hotel room the night we were eliminated from the conference tournament. We laughed so hard we had to sit down. Sam and Kelsey got dressed again, and we kept wandering.

We decided we wanted to find some boys. We knew there were still men's teams staying in our hotel. It was a huge complex and had hosted several men's and women's basketball teams from many colleges over the course of the tournament.

Giggling hysterically at our own creepiness, we tumbled past hotel room after hotel room, peering into each one. We came upon a pair of long sweatpants-clad legs through a window in a room on the ground floor. Two Western Carolina men's players were lying on their beds, watching TV. After spying on them for several minutes we conducted an extensive debate about whether to knock on their door. Sam and Kaylee, ever bold when it came to guys, knocked and, when the door opened, barged right in. I hung back, almost chickening out before piling inside behind everyone else.

The Western players, who were set to play our men's team for the Southern Conference Championship the next night, were thoroughly baffled by our sudden appearance in their room. But they listened patiently and with mild amusement as the six of us in our matching sweats and sneakers perched on the ends of their beds and in their desk chairs, introduced ourselves, and launched into a rapid-fire brag-fest about our evening's exploits.

By unspoken agreement my teammates and I understood we were ostensibly doing our men's team a favor by being here, keeping their opponents awake late at night—so we decided to stay and flirt a while. And anyway, one of them had beautiful eyes. We talked a lot of shit about the game the next day, telling them how good our men's team was and how we were supposed to have won, too.

Eventually, though, overcome with alcohol-induced drowsiness and general exhaustion, we started peeling off for bed. We all made it safely to our rooms.

When I was entering puberty my mom bought me a copy of the book *The Care and Keeping of You*, which contained a lot of helpful information about my increasingly confusing body. One of the questions in the book was, "Will anyone know when I'm on my period?"

The answer: "Not unless you tell them."

A slightly more grown-up version of that question went through my pounding head the next morning as, nursing my first hangover in five months, I walked as steadily as I could manage through the hotel dining room, past my teammates' families and our coaches, manager, athletic trainer, and assistant sports information director. It was, "Will anyone know I was drunk last night?"

The answer: "Not unless you tell them."

The Davidson men's team beat Western Carolina that night for the Southern Conference Championship. The game went into double overtime, and Davidson won by two, 93–91. Double overtime, my teammates and I giggled to each other, sure would be hard on boys who had been up half the night talking to girls. To this day we claim partial credit for that win, which sent our men to the first round of the 2012 NCAA Tournament, to my dream game.

Epilogue

"Last practice ever," Taylor murmured out the corner of her mouth as she jogged past me a few weeks later, holding out her palm for a low-five. Our eyes and hands met for just a second, one second in which the last five years flew through my mind like electricity. I thought of our first meeting in the Atlanta airport on the way to our recruiting visit, cheering for the men's team in the Elite Eight in Detroit, the four years of preseason parties and long practices and excruciating sprints and thick thighs and quick showers, of film sessions and Commons dinners and homework on the bus and empty, echoing arenas. Things between Taylor and me had been a little weird since I'd replaced her in the starting lineup. Olivia and Coop were gone from the team. But we all went back a long way.

We were in the gym at James Madison University (JMU) in Harrisonburg, Virginia, to play them the next day in the first round of the Women's National Invitation Tournament. Thanks to our regular-season championship, we had an automatic bid to the single-elimination WNIT, which was where they put all the decent teams that weren't quite good enough for the Big Dance. I had little interest in playing anymore.

Like Jenni had been when her career ended, I was ready to take back control of my own life—what I ate, what I wore, when I went to bed.

The coaches' attitudes indicated they didn't think we would win, either. If we lost this game, we were done for the season. If we won, we would advance in the tournament.

Certainly, none of us was going to throw the game on purpose. But I sensed, deep down, that our belief and our desire were damaged. We knew every muscle twitch, every movement in our teammates' body language. We knew who would hit free throws under pressure and who set the best screens and who always crashed the offensive boards and who committed dumb fouls when she was tired or frustrated. I could predict the outcome of a game simply based on the look in Leah's eyes or the bounce in Rory's step or the harshness of Alanna's voice. I could read every sweat droplet, every swiped tear, every fiber of my teammates' emotional and physical capacities, and I knew now that we were not going to win.

We'd had a practice the previous evening in our gym at home and then another one in Belk Arena that morning before driving a few hours north to Virginia. Coach Harris wanted to get in a full practice on JMU's court, so we had another one the same night, which would be followed by a shootaround the next morning, followed by the evening game. We would be lucky if we could stand up by then.

The last few weeks had been an awkward purgatory. We had never made it to any kind of postseason play in my career, so having two weeks of practice and no games between the Southern Conference Tournament and the WNIT was weird. Those of us who had broken dry season in Asheville continued to break it, showing up to practice so hungover that one day I reached down to grab a loose ball and almost toppled over from dizziness. It was mid-March, we were five and a half months into our season, we were exhausted and grouchy, and almost everyone had some kind of injury. Instead of focusing on rest and strategy and skill work, the coaches had us running full-court drills for hours. Nothing made sense anymore.

Leah and I were roommates in the hotel the night before the JMU game. On game day I woke a few minutes before the alarm. I stretched in bed and cringed, listening to my body in a series of long, rolling cracks, a symphony of soreness. I had grown dependent on regular doses of Tylenol PM that season because I was consistently in too much pain to sleep, but that day was a new low. Everything hurt, not just aches but intense, active pain.

"I feel like I got hit by a bus," I said groggily.

Leah was lying flat on her back, also awake, staring at the ceiling. "Me too," she said.

In that moment I knew for sure that the game might as well be over.

We did not even come close to winning. When the final buzzer sounded I did not look at the scoreboard. I did not cry. I wasn't happy, wasn't sad. I didn't feel anything at all. I walked to the huddle, put my fist in the air, mumbled "'Cats," and waved to our fans, one last time.

Taylor and I saw Erin, our own beloved senior, watching from the stands behind our bench. She was now in graduate school nearby. When we came out of the locker room we made a beeline to hug her.

"I love you, 'Cats," she said, squeezing us tightly. We had been there to hug her when her career ended, and she came back three years later to hug us. She understood.

I swaggered into our spring banquet defiantly drunk, annoyed, and belligerent. Taylor and I were presented with our jerseys in frames. When the banquet was over I yanked off my four-inch pumps and, barefoot, carried my framed jersey carefully down the hill to my apartment, where I put it on the floor in the hallway, slipped my heels back on, and kicked it until the glass shattered. Then I put on a sundress and sandals and went to the Third Eye Blind concert on campus with my roommates.

"At the college level, you gotta love it," Christina said to me years later. "To be able to do this, to grind like this, you have to love it. You have to be borderline crazy."

What happens when something you love deeply doesn't make you happy anymore?

Playing basketball in college made me both forget and deny that I loved it. I loved my teammates dearly, and they and my free ride to a bachelor's degree kept me on the team. But the pure love for the game I had felt as a teenager got lost in scouting reports, in thick playbooks, in punishment sprints, in silent and dusty bus rides and long games spent watching from the bench, wanting to play so badly I could physically feel the longing, a tingle in my legs, a weight in my chest. If I had let myself love my sport the way I used to, it might have hurt too much. I had to stop loving it so hard. So I did.

Four months later, I was in a school yard in Tanzania, a bumpy van ride from the northern city of Arusha. I had come to help teach English at an elementary school because I hadn't landed a job in the States. I left three months later with the knowledge that I wasn't the help these kids needed, that in fact I was part of the problem. They needed consistency and infrastructure. They didn't need clichés like me. They needed people who cared enough to stay.

But I had brought a few basketballs with me, bought them deflated at the $5 toy store near my parents' house and carried them across the Atlantic in a duffel bag, and as long as I was there figured I might as well teach these kids how to play. I missed my sport. No matter how far I went, I could not seem to stay away.

The second and third grade girls gravitated toward me the first time I brought a ball to school, clamoring to hold it.

"Guys, this is a basketball," I said.

"Basketball," they repeated.

"When you have the ball, bounce it with one hand, like this." I demonstrated, and little clouds of dirt puffed up.

"I am going to be the hoop." I circled my arms in front of me and touched my fingertips together. "When you're near the hoop, shoot it. Throw it in here, into my arms."

The girls nodded. I didn't speak Swahili and they didn't speak much English, so I was never sure if they were nodding because they actually understood or just to humor me, but we were about to find out. I made the hoop with my arms again. Agness picked up the ball.

"Okay, guys," I said. "Remember, when you have the ball, bounce it. When you're near the hoop, shoot it." But they were already off, Agness dribbling furiously in the dirt, one hand holding back her brown skirt, the other slamming the ball into the ground. Her control was astonishingly good.

I had never seen the girls so excited about a playground game before. Blinking in the dust, we played in the dirt road that ran past the school toward the river. Occasionally, we would have to step to the side as a *boda boda*, or motorcycle, chugged past. It was only a matter of minutes before someone bounced the ball on a stick or a rock or piece of broken glass and it popped and began to deflate, but that didn't faze anyone.

They picked up on the basics immediately. Agness was shoving people away with her butt and her free arm, but Zulfa, smart and calculating, found the right angle, swooped in and stole it, and ran away from the group as fast as she could.

"Zulfa, come back!" I hollered. "The hoop's over here, remember? And bounce the ball!"

Zulfa wheeled around and came flying back toward me, occasionally remembering to hammer the ball into the dirt, her toothy grin tossing joy all over her face, Agness and the rest hot at her heels. She wound up and heaved the ball at the hoop.

As anyone who has ever been a hoop will understand, when your face is the backboard you tend to hope for kids with a soft touch. Unfortunately, my students did not have that down quite yet. I leaned backward slightly and took this shot to the collarbone with a wince and tilted my arms so the ball fell through them. Zulfa let out a gleeful scream.

When a couple of the boys came moseying up to join the fun, the third grade girls shoved them away.

"No! This is for girls!" they shouted, scowling, clutching the ball tightly. "This ball is for the girls!"

Holding back laughter, I made an effort to include the boys, but it was too late—the girls had scared them off. Scrums for the ball seemed to be their favorite. Anytime it squirted free, seven or eight or nine little bodies piled on top of it, skirts be damned, limbs flailing. Seven-year-old Jonetha came up to me a few minutes later to show me her lip, which was bleeding in two places from a scuffle. I could have exploded with pride.

My teammates and I talked a lot in college about whether we would let our own kids play Division I basketball someday. A few years later, Lyss and Erin both had babies, and the question, hypothetical for so long, became a reality. Most of us, by that point, said yes, we would.

I started playing for fun again. College basketball had aged me in dog years, so my body complained more than it used to, but shooting hoops was my therapy. Those sunny, dust-filled afternoons in Tanzania reminded me how easy it could be to love this sport, how pure was the place in ourselves we played from. I learned how my love for the game had matured and toughened, weathered and worn and somehow hung in there, like a heart after a long, slow heartbreak. The love had seen pain and come back anyway. If you loved something, even if it hurt you sometimes, you found a way to do it, wherever and whenever and however you could.

A little more than two years after my return from Tanzania, I sat at my desk in my office in Washington DC and watched the blurry, halting ESPN3 live-stream of Davidson against Chattanooga in that year's Southern Conference Championship. With a minute and three seconds left in the game, Davidson down by twenty-five, senior Rory Stokes drove the right baseline and smoothly put in the layup that broke the Davidson all-time scoring record, set the year before by Alanna. The crowd exploded from the stands.

When Rory trotted, unsteady with exhaustion, to the sideline, she slapped Coach Harris's hand quickly without looking at her and headed straight for her best friend Sam's arms. It was their last game. I burst into tears at my desk as they slammed into each other, a raw, beautiful, bone-weary embrace, Rory collapsing a little into Sam's chest, knocking her backward a few steps. Sam cradled the back of Rory's sweaty head in one hand. Kelsey and Kaylee stood behind them, crying.

The coaches didn't matter. The losses didn't matter. The scoring record didn't even matter. That hug was all that mattered.

Almost exactly eight months later, on a perfect autumn day, Rory and David got married. Olivia, Taylor, Allie, Lindsay, and I sat in a row together during the ceremony. Rory walked slowly down the aisle with her dad, David gazing at her from the altar, delirious with love. As the bride passed us Olivia and I could spare her only a quick glance. We were busy, frantically scrambling to fix our Skype connection with Sam, who was in Mumbai on a prestigious research fellowship, studying the impact girls' sports have on communities around the world.

I got a bad concussion in a car accident a year after graduation, and Olivia helped me get an appointment with Dr. Collins and patiently talked me through the years of health problems that came with a head injury like that. I started to understand, firsthand, how much she had suffered as a result of her concussion. We apologized to each other for how we'd acted when we were young and dumb and hurting. We began to truly repair our friendship.

Nearly five years after I graduated, Davidson College dismissed Coach Harris from her job as head coach. Although Coach Katz had technically resigned, we strongly suspected the athletic administration had asked her to, which would make Harris's departure the second time in seven years that the Wildcat top brass had asked a Davidson women's basketball head coach to leave her position.

Mac became a physician assistant, just like she'd dreamed since her first ACL tear. Whitney became a PA, too. Olivia, Amber, and Allie got teaching jobs. Christina, Kelsey, Lindsay, and Ashley all went to medical school. Alanna and Marie played professionally in Europe. We began to understand the real-world value of our educations. Women's players at other Division I schools had made the same time commitment to basketball but gotten less out of their academic experiences. As Mac put it, "I would not have been at Davidson if it hadn't been for basketball. I would not have stayed at Davidson if it had not been for basketball." We had received an excellent college education, most of us for free, and we will always have those degrees.

My teammates bought houses, got married, paid taxes, had babies, got promotions; they went to graduate school at places like Harvard and Columbia and Tufts and Duke. On a visit to Nebraska I played in a pickup game in a church gym with Lyss's husband as she watched from the sidelines with their two-year-old daughter and five-week-old son.

"Go, Daddy!" Lyss's daughter cheered, in her tiny Davidson T-shirt. "Go, Otto!"

We will always have hoops.

I woke up the morning after my mother's funeral, four years, four months, and eleven days after my graduation from Davidson, and looked out my bedroom window to see Sam and Kelsey in the backyard of my childhood home, planting a young cherry-blossom tree on the hill.

The coaches and Terry had sent flowers to the funeral home. Alanna sent a card from Italy, where she was playing professionally, and Marie sent a box of chocolates from France, where she was doing the same. Mac and Jenni, who took such good care of me in college and took good care of me now, had come to town earlier that week to help our family out. They brought big cans of coffee and chocolate-covered almonds and cleaning supplies. They helped us scour the house. They drank red wine and chatted in the backyard with my mom's brother and sister. They concocted homemade decorations for the big party we'd organized to celebrate my mother's short, full life.

Kaylee drove six hours on a work night just to stand in line for another hour at the visitation and give me a hug. Olivia and Coop fed me bourbon and met my relatives and work friends and helped us transport dozens of flower arrangements from the funeral home to our house after the visitation. Kelsey had driven seven hours from medical school for the funeral ceremony, her car laden with shovels, gardening gloves, bags of dirt and fertilizer, and the tree, which she laid horizontally from the trunk all the way to the windshield. She and Sam treated it like a person, carrying it up to their hotel room and putting it on the balcony overnight so it could "get some air," which made me laugh.

I pulled on a sweatshirt, poured a cup of coffee, and padded out into the October morning. I watched as Sam and Kelsey, both wearing sneakers and streaked with dirt, squatted with perfect form, lifted the tree by the base, and gently placed it in the hole they had just dug.

"It's from the whole team," they explained as they wheedled dirt back into the hole. "It's an Okame cherry tree. It's supposed to bloom during your mom's birthday month."

I gazed at the tree. It was a skinny thing, not much taller than me, all spindly twigs and delicate leaves. But it was a gift from the closest thing I had to sisters, in memory of my mother. And it would grow. In March it would bloom.

They say you don't choose your family, and indeed, I did not choose these women.

But I choose them now, and I choose them forever.

ACKNOWLEDGMENTS

This book is a dream come true, but it was written at a time during which I needed a great deal of support. I received an overwhelming amount, and there are dozens of people who deserve more thanks than I could ever give them, but this is, at least, a start.

To my editors, Rob Taylor and Sara Springsteen, and the other wonderful folks at the University of Nebraska Press who helped make this real. To my copy editor, Annette Wenda. You have all been an absolute joy to work with. And special thanks to my whip-smart and endlessly patient literary agent, Laurie Abkemeier, who believed in the story first.

Thank you, Mom and Dad. I love you.

Thank you to my not-so-little brothers, Luke, Zachary, Jesse, and Casey, who have been supportive and enthusiastic throughout this process. You guys are budding feminist allies I am proud to know.

To the families of my Davidson teammates. It's a great day to be a Wildcat!

To Kirk and Mary Jeanne Weixel, for having read my writing since I was four years old, and especially Kirk, for still reading it now and dousing me with thoughtful edits and generous affirmation.

To Robert Strauss, for your guidance, friendship, connection making, and meticulous editing.

To the research goddess Jan Blodgett, a fount of information and resources about the history of Davidson College and sugar-supplying supporter of its women's basketball team.

To my team of feedback givers, who read chapters and drafts: Emily Baumgaertner, Shneeka Center, Meghan Dhaliwal, Rebecca Gibian, Katelin Kelly, Josephine LaBua, Jesse Ottaway, Luke Ottaway, and Evey Wilson.

To my brilliant colleagues at the Pulitzer Center, for teaching me how.

To the sparkling minds of FreeWord—peace, love & poetry, y'all.

To Professors Suzanne Churchill, Cynthia Lewis, Christine Marshall, and Alan Michael Parker in the Davidson College English Department, who gave thoughtful feedback to my angsty college writing (some of which eventually made it into this book). Thanks, too, to the countless other Davidsonians who graciously donated their time by granting interviews and sending information.

To the pioneers of Davidson women's basketball.

To Heidi Julavits, who told me this could be a book.

To the folks who spoke to me off the record, for your honesty.

To my high school and Amateur Athletic Union (AAU) coaches Joe Hurd, Anita Moore Jennings, Deanna Jubeck, Rick Genday, and Tom Olesky.

To Tom and Leslie Shinners and Connie Bewick, for everything. To the Schmits and the Obrochtas, for your energy and your love.

To the many friends who supported me through the difficult home stretch and let this vagabond writer sleep and work in their guest rooms and on their couches. I'd name you all, but that would take half a page.

To Ben Cushing, for being there at the beginning and the end.

To Flowe 101: Madison Benedict, Mary Marshall Meredith, and Hope Cain.

To my loves Evey Wilson, Lauren Hoy, Melissa Woods, Josephine LaBua, Emily Baumgaertner, Daniella Zalcman, Dominic Bracco. To Rachael Cerrotti, my GB.

To Rebecca Gibian, for your tireless, selfless friendship (and your fact-checking). To TommiAnn Tromm, my best friend since seventh grade; thank you for loving me so well. To my "sister" Meghan Dhaliwal—I love you to the moo.

To my teammates: The last line in the acknowledgments is typically reserved for lovers, but this one is for female friendship. I love you.

NOTES

1. THE BUBBLE

4 **thirty-two leagues, also called conferences**: "Women's College Basketball Teams, NCAA Division I," ESPN.com, http://www.espn.com/womens-college-basketball/teams.

5 **wanted to be a Division I basketball player**: "Legacy: SFU's 11 League Titles and NCAA Tournament Appearances Are Unmatched in the NEC," in Saint Francis University, *Red Flash 2016 Media Guide.*

6 **semifinals of the Southern Conference Tournament**: "Davidson in the SoCon Tournament," in McFarlin, *Davidson Women's Basketball Media Guide.*

6 **tenth total Southern Conference Championship**: Beeler, Gignac, and Kilgo, *2015–16 Davidson Men's Basketball Media Guide*, 47.

7 **LeBron James, wanting a better look**: Forde, "Even LeBron Has to Salute."

8 **Davidson graduate and writer Michael Kruse**: Kruse, "What It Means."

8 **received 332 email requests**: Biggers, "The Aftermath."

9 **"sleepy little town"**: Pitzer, "Davidson Wildcats."

11 **"Davidson was America's sweetheart"**: Biggers, "Good Times."

11 **four years after Yale and Princeton went coed**: Snowden, "The History of Women at Princeton University"; "Yale Will Admit Women in 1969"; Boss-Bicak, "25 Years of Coeducation."

11 **some male students were eager**: Paddock, "Davidson Trustees Approve Coeducation."

12 **that number was about two in five**: Women's Sports Foundation, "Get Your Game on, Girls!"

12 **"handful" of role models in the world**: Chastain, "The Best Play I Ever Made."

12 **Laurie Dunn, a freshman in that first class**: Laurie Dunn, personal communication, March 25, 2016.

13 **"players possessing statistics like 36-23-36"**: "Girls Now Playing Basketball."

14 **run the Davidson women's team alone**: Davidson College, E. H. Little Library Archives & Special Collections, *1975 Quips and Cranks*.

14 **including eight of their last nine**: "Women Have 8-3 Season."

14 **Holland had himself played for Driesell**: Bender, Kilgo, and Madden, *100th Anniversary Davidson Basketball Media Guide*, 66.

14 **Kay Yow's North Carolina State team**: Davidson College, E. H. Little Library Archives & Special Collections, *1975 Quips and Cranks*.

14 **Susan Roberts as a paid full-time coach**: Parker, "Coach Speaks Frankly."

15 **pitching in on her grandparents' farm**: Schmeidel, "High Heels on the Hard Court."

16 **guest-hosted it from their dorm room**: *The Davidson Show*, March 27, 2008.

2. I WANT YOU TO WANT ME

21 **Twenty-five percent of adolescent girls**: Kelley and Carchia, "Hey, Data, Data—Swing!"

21 **as many as fifteen full scholarships**: NCAA Membership Services Staff, *NCAA Division I Manual, 2008–09*, 185.

22 **the full-scholarship level**: "Women's Basketball: Estimated Probability of Competing in Women's College Basketball Athletics," NCAA.org, April 25, 2016, http://www.ncaa.org/about/resources/research /womens-basketball.

22 **the highest-paid player in the WNBA**: Payne, "Former U-Conn Star Maya Moore."

26 **the official wooing process**: "NCAA Recruiting Chart," NCAA.org, 2014, https://www.ncaa.org/sites/default/files/Division%20I %20Recruiting%20Overview%20Chart2014.pdf.

28 **UMass was still "extremely interested"**: Brent Ottaway, personal communication, May 21, 2007.

34 **head-coaching job at Penn State University**: Associated Press, "Penn State's Portland."

3. A NIGHT WITH THE 'CATS

40 **Davidson men's coach Lefty Driesell**: Davis, "Driesell Started Midnight Madness."

40 **"Being a student-athlete at Davidson"**: McNay, *Student-Athlete Handbook*.

41 **a minimum of 1.8 that year**: Katy McNay, personal communication, January 5, 2017.

51 **doubled as models for the brand's pantyhose**: Grundy and Shackelford, *Shattering the Glass*, 90.

51 **considered to be "manly" pursuits**: Grundy and Shackelford, *Shattering the Glass*, 117.

51 **"It is a lady's business"**: Gallico, "Letter to the Editor."

52 **"rough girls" and "nappy-headed hos."**: Faber, "CBS Fires Don Imus."

52 **founder of the sports website *Grantland***: Simmons, "This Is Who I Am . . ."

53 **Coach Katz told the *Davidson Journal***: "Women's Basketball Staff," 39.

54 **47 percent of Division I women's basketball players**: Lapchick et al., *2008 Racial and Gender Report Card*.

54 **at the time about 6 percent black**: Davidson College, Office of Planning and Institutional Research, *Davidson Factfile*, 2008–09.

57 **subtle weapon against programs**: Cyphers and Fagan, "Unhealthy Climate."

4. HEADING HOME

61 **about 5 percent of our injuries**: "Frequency, Distribution, and Rates of Select Injuries."

74 **similar things to his scholarship players**: Schnell, "UConn Walk-Ons."

5. WET SEASON

84 **any athlete hosting a recruit**: McNay, *Student-Athlete Handbook*.

6. KNOCKED OUT

101 **using an egg metaphor**: Conboy, "Football on the Brain."

112 **injury costs match or exceed $90,000**: "Student-Athlete Insurance Programs: Catastrophic Insurance Program," NCAA.org, http://www .ncaa.org/about/resources/insurance/student-athlete-insurance -programs.

116 **identity that she relates to her sport**: Grossbard et al., "Athletic Identity, Descriptive Norms, and Drinking."

7. SISTERHOOD OF THE TRAVELING SWEATPANTS

119 **thirteen full women's basketball scholarships**: Michele Savage, personal communication, January 5, 2016.

119 **that academic year cost $585,390**: Davidson College, Office of Planning and Institutional Research, *Davidson Factfile, 2009–10*.

127 **a McDonald's parking lot**: Slovin, "Five Funny Pat Summitt Stories."

127 **both women were born in the 1950s**: Pat Summitt biography, University of Tennessee website, http://www.utsports.com/coaches.aspx?rc =540&path=wbball.

127 **drove the team bus all night**: Smith, "Eyes of the Storm."

128 **a prison bus with defective brakes**: Grundy and Shackelford, *Shattering the Glass*, 139.

128 **"paid for [their] own gas and food"**: Grundy and Shackelford, *Shattering the Glass*, 139.

128 **"saving their precious basketball shoes for games"**: Grundy and Shackelford, *Shattering the Glass*, 50.

128 **was seen as an easy target**: Grundy and Shackelford, *Shattering the Glass*, 107.

128 **"less interested in the competitive aspects"**: "Pat Drake Is Women's First PE Teacher."

8. A POSTGAME SURPRISE

133 **nearly twice the size of Davidson**: "About Boone, NC," Town of Boone website, http://www.townofboone.net.

137 **eight of the last nine games**: "Wildcats Fall 71–62 on the Road to Mountaineers," DavidsonWildcats.com, January 23, 2010, http:// davidsonwildcats.com/news/2010/1/23/WBB_0123101012.aspx.

142 **After one loss at Ole Miss**: Slovin, "Five Funny Pat Summitt Stories."

142 **"the half you didn't play last night"**: Smith, "Eyes of the Storm."

142 **five weeks with her 1989–90 team**: Smith, "Eyes of the Storm."

147 **NCAA violation to hold a practice after a game**: Michelle Hosick, personal communication, January 25, 2017.

147 **allowed to require twenty hours**: "Defining Countable Athletically Related Activities," NCAA.org, May 13, 2009.

147 **"countable athletically related activities"**: "Countable Hours," University of Notre Dame Athletics Compliance Office, November 4, 2010, http://www3.nd.edu/~ncaacomp/countable_hours.shtml.

9. A TEAM IN TRANSITION

156 **"right move for her and the program"**: Associated Press, "Watts Resigns."

157 **their National Letters of Intent**: Vince Gmerek (NCAA), personal communication, January 6, 2017.

159 **increased publicity and money**: Grundy and Shackelford, *Shattering the Glass*, 181.

159 **down from 90 percent in 1972**: Barrett, "There Are Fewer Women Coaches in College Basketball."

161 **All-American at Northwestern**: "Davidson Names Michele Savage Women's Basketball Coach," DavidsonWildcats.com, May 28, 2010, http://www.davidsonwildcats.com/news/2010/5/28/WBB_0528102043.aspx?path=wbball.

161 **8 percent of Division I athletic directors**: Lapchick, Hoff, and Kaiser, *2010 Racial and Gender Report Card*.

161 **two women in high-level positions**: Davidson athletic administration staff directory, DavidsonWildcats.com, http://davidsonwildcats.com/staff.aspx.

10. OUR BODIES, EVERYONE'S BUSINESS

173 **no other black head coaches**: Gignac and Kilgo, *Davidson Wildcats 2010–2011 Media Guide*, 144–47.

173 **4 African American full-time professors**: Davidson College, Office of Planning and Institutional Research, *Davidson Factfile, 2010–2011*.

173 **slightly outnumbered black players**: "Sport Sponsorship, Participation and Demographics Search," 2010–11, Division I, Southern Conference, Basketball, NCAA.org, http://web1.ncaa.org/rgdSearch/exec/saSearch.

173 **11 percent of Division I**: Lapchick, Hoff, and Kaiser, *2010 Racial and Gender Report Card*.

181 **"vaginas that can speak to each other"**: Dominique Christina, "The Period Poem," YouTube.

11. STUDENTS OR ATHLETES?

188 **false-positive rate**: Keating, "Concussion Test May Not Be Panacea."

190 **concussions were "on the rise"**: Burton, "Youth Concussions on the Rise since 2010."

201 **blow-off "paper classes"**: "Timeline of Events in the UNC Scandal."

12. FTP

214 **"You peer at a bench"**: Powell, "A Long Hardwood Journey."

13. THE POPULARITY CONTEST

232 **we would have thousands of fans, too**: Beeler, Bender, Gignac, and Kilgo, *Davidson 2016–17 Media Guide*.

232 **fourteen thousand fans a game**: "2012 NCAA Women's Basketball Attendance," NCAA.org, http://fs.ncaa.org/Docs/stats/w_basketball _RB/reports/Attend/12att.pdf.

233 **the first WNBA game in 1997**: "WNBA History/Timeline," WNBA.com, http://www.wnba.com/archive/wnba/about_us/wnba_history_timeline _2012_04_30.html.

234 **Hundreds of thousands of women**: "NCAA Participation Rates Going Up."

234 **iPads and TVs and gift cards**: Elavia, "Kale."

238 **an offense that breathes**: Branch, "Carril Is Yoda to Notion of Perpetual Motion."

14. THE DREAM

243 **Southern Conference Coach of the Year**: "Women's Basketball All-Conference Honors Announced."

EPILOGUE

270 **Davidson all-time scoring record**: Davidson women's basketball box score versus Chattanooga, DavidsonWildcats.com, March 10, 2014, http://www.davidsonwildcats.com/boxscore.aspx?id=3449&path =wbball.

BIBLIOGRAPHY

Associated Press. "Penn State's Portland Makes 'Difficult' Decision to
Quit." ESPN.com, March 25, 2007.
———. "Watts Resigns after Nine Seasons." ESPN.com, March 29, 2010.
Barrett, M. C. "There Are Fewer Women Coaches in College Basketball Now
than There Were a Decade Ago." FiveThirtyEight.com, January 19, 2016.
Beeler, Joey, Marc Gignac, and John Kilgo. *2015–16 Davidson Men's Basket-
ball Media Guide*. Davidson NC: Davidson College, 2015–16.
Beeler, Joey, Rick Bender, Marc Gignac, and John Kilgo. *Davidson 2016–17
Media Guide*. Davidson NC: Davidson College, 2016.
Bender, Rick, John Kilgo, and Erica Madden. *100th Anniversary Davidson
Basketball Media Guide*. Davidson NC: Davidson College, 2015–16.
Biggers, Lauren. "The Aftermath." *The View from Press Row* (Davidson ath-
letics blog), March 23, 2008.
———. "Good Times." *The View from Press Row* (Davidson athletics blog),
March 30, 2008.
Boss-Bicak, Shira. "25 Years of Coeducation." *Columbia College Today* (July–
August 2009).
Branch, John. "Carril Is Yoda to Notion of Perpetual Motion." *New York
Times*, March 30, 2007.

Burton, Tyler. "Youth Concussions on the Rise since 2010, Peaking in Fall." CNN.com, October 11, 2016.

Chastain, Brandi. "The Best Play I Ever Made." *Players' Tribune*, August 17, 2016.

Conboy, Sean. "Football on the Brain." *Pittsburgh Magazine*, August 23, 2011.

Cyphers, Luke, and Kate Fagan. "Unhealthy Climate." *ESPN: The Magazine*, February 7, 2011.

Davidson College, E. H. Little Library Archives & Special Collections. *1975 Quips and Cranks* 77 (1975).

Davidson College, Office of Planning and Institutional Research. *Davidson Factfile, 2008–09*. Davidson NC: Davidson College, December 2008.

———. *Davidson Factfile, 2009–2010*. Davidson NC: Davidson College, December 2009.

———. *Davidson Factfile, 2010–2011*. Davidson NC: Davidson College, December 2010.

Davis, Seth. "How Maryland Coach Lefty Driesell Started Midnight Madness with a Midnight Run in 1971." *Sports Illustrated*, October 15, 2014.

Elavia, Serena. "Kale: What It Takes to Get Students to a Women's Basketball Game." *Atlantic*, April 6, 2015.

Faber, Judy. "CBS Fires Don Imus over Racial Slur." CBSNews.com, April 12, 2007.

Forde, Pat. "Even LeBron Has to Salute the Brilliance of Curry, Davidson." ESPN.com, March 28, 2008.

"Frequency, Distribution, and Rates of Select Injuries (Ankle Ligament Sprains, Anterior Cruciate Ligament Injuries, and Concussions) for Games and Practices Combined for 15 Sports, 1988–1989 to 2003–2004." *Journal of Athletic Training* (April–June 2007).

Gallico, Paul. "Letter to the Editor: Women in Sports Should Look Beautiful." *Free Press*, August 6, 1936.

Gignac, Marc, and John Kilgo. *Davidson Wildcats 2010–2011 Media Guide*. Davidson NC: Davidson College, 2010–11.

"Girls Now Playing Basketball." *Davidson Update* (January 1974): 20.

Grossbard, Joel R., Irene M. Geisner, Nadine R. Mastroleo, Jason R. Kilmer, Rob Turrisi, and Mary E. Larimer. "Athletic Identity, Descriptive Norms, and Drinking among Athletes Transitioning to College." *PubMed* (2008). doi:10.1016/j.addbeh.2008.11.011.

Grundy, Pamela, and Susan Shackelford. *Shattering the Glass: The Remarkable History of Women's Basketball*. New York: New Press, 2005.

Keating, Peter. "Concussion Test May Not Be Panacea." ESPN: *The Magazine*, August 26, 2012.

Kelley, Bruce, and Carl Carchia. "Hey, Data, Data—Swing!" ESPN.com, July 11, 2013.

Kruse, Michael. "What It Means." *Charlotte Magazine*, March 25, 2008.

Lapchick, Richard, Brian Hoff, and Christopher Kaiser. *The 2010 Racial and Gender Report Card: College Sport*. Orlando: Institute for Diversity and Ethics in Sport at the University of Central Florida, March 3, 2011.

Lapchick, Richard, Colleen Lerner, Eric Little, and Ray Mathew. *The 2008 Racial and Gender Report Card: College Sport*. Orlando: Institute for Diversity and Ethics in Sport at the University of Central Florida, February 19, 2009.

McFarlin, Gavin. *Davidson Women's Basketball Media Guide*. Davidson NC: Davidson College, 2015–16.

McNay, Katy. *Student-Athlete Handbook, 2009–2010*. Davidson NC: Davidson College, 2009–10.

NCAA Membership Services Staff. *NCAA Division I Manual*. Indianapolis: NCAA, July 2008.

"NCAA Participation Rates Going Up." NCAA.com, November 2, 2011.

Paddock, Polly. "Davidson Trustees Approve Coeducation." *Charlotte Observer*, May 6, 1972.

Parker, Emil. "Coach Speaks Frankly, Carries Hockey Stick." *Davidson Update* (September 1976).

"Pat Drake Is Women's First PE Teacher." *Davidson Update* (October 1974): 11.

Payne, Marissa. "Former U-Conn Star Maya Moore Laments the Current State of the WNBA." *Washington Post*, May 6, 2015.

Pitzer, Matt. "Davidson Wildcats." *Deadspin*, March 16, 2008.

Powell, Michael. "A Long Hardwood Journey." *New York Times*, July 16, 2015, https://www.nytimes.com/2015/07/19/sports/a-long-hardwood-journey.html?mcubz=2&_r=0.

Saint Francis University. *Red Flash 2016 Media Guide*. Loretto PA: Saint Francis University, 2015–16.

Schmeidel, Stacey. "High Heels on the Hard Court." *Davidson Journal* (2009): 27.

Schnell, Lindsay. "UConn Walk-Ons Describe What It's Like to Walk on with a Dynasty." *Sports Illustrated*, April 5, 2016.

Simmons, Bill. "This Is Who I Am . . ." ESPN.com (2005).

Slovin, Matt. "Five Funny Pat Summitt Stories from Charity Event." *Tennesseean*, July 11, 2015.

Smith, Gary. "Eyes of the Storm." *Sports Illustrated*, March 2, 1998.

Snowden, Vanessa. "The History of Women at Princeton University." Princeton University Library Gender and Sexuality Studies Resources. http://libguides.princeton.edu/gender.

"Timeline of Events in the UNC Scandal." *Charlotte News & Observer*, December 19, 2012.

"Women Have 8-3 Season." *Davidson Update* (March 1974).

"Women's Basketball All-Conference Honors Announced." SoConSports.com, February 29, 2012.

"The Women's Basketball Staff: Coaching Is Teaching." *Davidson Journal* (2003).

Women's Sports Foundation. "Get Your Game on, Girls! Celebrating the 40th Anniversary of Title IX." Press release, June 23, 2011.

"Yale Will Admit Women in 1969; May Have Coeducational Housing." *Harvard Crimson*, November 15, 1968.